THE STRUGGLE FOR
THE GREAT BARRIER REEF

THE
STRUGGLE FOR THE
GREAT BARRIER
REEF

✳

Patricia Clare

WALKER AND COMPANY · New York

First published in the United States of America in 1971 by the Walker Publishing Company, Inc.

Library of Congress Catalog Card Number: 77-159515

ISBN: 0-8027-0352-6

Printed in Great Britain

Contents

⚜

Illustrations

✻

Acknowledgments

❋

To my friends, Leone Harford and Bryce Fraser, go my grateful thanks for their unfailing helpfulness while I was working on this book.

I should also like to record my indebtedness to the many people – scientists, conservationists, concerned citizens – who helped me by supplying information about the Great Barrier Reef or related matters. I would mention especially: At the University of Queensland: Dr Robert Endean, Dr Patricia Mather, Professor Gordon McKay, Professor James Thomson, Mr Howard Choat. On Heron Island: Mr Peter Woodhead and Dr Robert Bustard. The Chief Inspector of Fisheries (Queensland), Mr Geoffrey Harrison; Fisheries Research Biologist Mr Ernest M. Grant; and marine biologist Mr Robert Pearson. Mr Leon Henry, Chief Sewage Engineer, Department of Local Government (Queensland); Dr D. W. Connell and Mr E. J. Hegerl of the Queensland Littoral Society, Dr Donald McMichael, Mr Pat Parry, Mr Harry Scholer, the late Mr Lloyd Morgan, Lieutenant-Commander T. F. Roberts (R.A.N. retd). Mrs Yvonne Webb Jay.

Government departments and other bodies which furnished information included Queensland's Department of Primary Industries and Department of Aboriginal and Island Affairs; Cairns District Canegrowers' Executive; the Oceanarium, Cairns; Australian Gulf Oil Co, The Petroleum Information Bureau, Sydney.

My sincere thanks also go to the P & O shipping company for assisting in my return from England to Australia.

Newspapers and other sources consulted on Reef and conservation issues included *The Courier-Mail*, Brisbane, *The Australian*, *The Sydney Morning Herald*, *Time* magazine, *Science*, The Australian Broadcasting Commission, and publications of the Queensland Littoral Society and the Wildlife Preservation Society of Queensland.

Books consulted included *Australian Seashores* by William J. Dakin, assisted by Isobel Bennett and Elizabeth Pope; *Australian Shells* by Joyce

7

ACKNOWLEDGMENTS

Allan; the *Australian Encyclopaedia*; *Birds of the South-West Coral Sea* by K. A. Hindwood, K. Keith and D. L. Serventy; *Cannibal Cargoes* by Hector Holthouse; *Great Barrier Reef* by William J. Dakin.

ILLUSTRATIONS

For their permission to use copyright photographs, the publishers are grateful to Keith Gillett for numbers 2, 3, 4, 6, 7, 8, 9, 10, 14, 15; to John Harding for numbers 1, 5, 12; to Ron Taylor Film Production; for number 11; and to Ken Wilder for number 13.

CHAPTER I

Prologue

✳

IN the sea gardens of the Great Barrier Reef, under the blue transparencies of the south-west Pacific, the flowers are flesh. They are animals. Underwater, in the shape of daisy or cactus-dahlia, they bloom on banks, in grottoes, in shallow valleys and down the sides of cliffs. They are the main reason these reefs are literally alive with colour; they are, in fact, the reason for the reefs, since they built them. Taking calcium from the sea, these animals, the coral polyps, convert it into limestone. They fashion an external limestone skeleton, a petrified lace cup in which they live. The cups, with their occupants, are usually joined together in colonies which take on a variety of shapes but most often those suggesting bushes or boulders. Covered with flowerlike polyps, these shapes combine to make the underwater landscapes of the reef. When the polyps die their skeleton cups become a part of the reef, a bequest to the limestone base on which a new generation builds. Working in this way for perhaps a million years, the polyps have created a world – a world of flowering cliffs rising through translucent blues, of forests and arcades and grottoes sheltering enamel-bright fish, of tentacle-trees streaming like willows on the water. The fantastic reef-forms built by the polyps make up a structure which is not only the largest ever created by any species including man: it is also quite possibly the most beautiful.

There is great variety in the structure. Sometimes the animals have built upwards from the sea floor; sometimes they have attached themselves to a partly submerged mountain and built their gardens out around it; sometimes reefs have turned into islands. The Great Barrier Reef is therefore a name for much more than a chain of reefs extending for about twelve hundred miles down the edge of the north-eastern Australian continental shelf – it also covers hundreds of reefs and islands, certain of them still uncharted, between these outer ramparts and the Australian coast. As the width of the continental shelf supporting the corals varies between about sixteen and two hundred miles, so, too, does the width of the Reef area vary. An island in this area might be the top of a seagirt mountain, coral fringed and echoing shapes in the mainland ranges from which the ocean has separated it; or it might be a true coral island – an accumulation, basically, of sand and coral debris piled up on a reef by the action of sea and wind. All the islands seem to float in a composition of blue on blue on blue – an azure sky holding its colour against the gold blaze of the sun, a sea running blue-green over the shallower reefs, and then over deeper reefs and sandy bottoms and submarine falls of cliff turning sapphire and cobalt and deep purple-blue. Beneath these shades there are yet others, the transparent blues of the world of the flowering animals.

This world is unique. The creatures which share it with the corals make up a marine fauna richer, more various, stranger than that found anywhere else. The American marine scientist, Dr J. F. Grassle, has said, "If we did not know of the Reef and it were suddenly discovered today, it would be like discovering an area from the age of dinosaurs. Not only does the Reef have many species found nowhere else; it is the most varied, the most complex and perhaps the most productive biological system in the world." And again, "There are two kinds of human experience which enable man to partially understand his position in nature. One is looking up at the stars and I think the other is swimming out over the Reef."

In the first days of the nineteen-seventies it seemed that this Reef, unique creation of a million years, could die before the decade ended. In an era everywhere witnessing the end of the natural world, it faced the possibility of extinction.

Until Captain Cook sailed through the Great Barrier Reef in 1770, the area was isolated from civilization and virtually exempt from human exploitation. Small bands of Aborigines lived on the mountain-islands and visited the reefs and cays, but their taste for fish and turtle and dugong affected comparatively few animals. When the Aborigines were supplanted by the heirs of Captain Cook, the Great Barrier Reef was still as they had found it aeons earlier – the home of hundreds of species of coral and fish and bird, the playground of the dolphin, a safe summer place for the shearwater flying down from Siberia and the whale swimming up from Antarctica.

Within relatively few years of the Aborigines' passing it seemed that the Reef, too, was doomed. By the late nineteen-sixties – approaching the second centenary of Cook's voyage of discovery – it was apparent that the search by industrial civilization for more and more resources was moving in on the Reef. Of the various developments arising from this, it would not be easy to say which posed the gravest threat of destruction to the area and its animals.

One nomination would have to be the search for oil, with its seismic underwater blasting and its threat of pollution. By the end of the nineteen-sixties, drilling permits covered eighty percent, or about 70,000 square miles, of the Great Barrier Reef. In Queensland, the Australian State concerned with administering the Reef, the parliamentary Opposition had expressed dissatisfaction that a major interest in one of the companies with a permit to explore for oil was held by the State's Premier. A suggestion had come from the State Mining Engineer of Queensland that Heron Island, one of the Reef's loveliest islands, should be used as a testing ground for a theory that escaping oil would do little harm to corals. Drums of oil, he had suggested, could be emptied on Heron's untroubled waters and the results analysed. Alarmed conservationists reasoned that a State Mining Engineer would be unlikely to make such a seemingly fantastic proposal unless he knew of marine scientists whom he could expect to agree with him; and they wondered who these men could be. In the attitudes of certain scientists towards plans to exploit the Reef it was already possible to see a rather disturbing reasonableness. Listening to them on the subject of changes to come to the Reef could be somewhat like listening to an atomic scientist playing down fears of a human genetic disaster on the ground that two heads are better than one. There seemed to be an excess of optimism. But there were other scientists who saw oil exploitation as threatening tragedy for the Reef, and this split in scientific attitudes carried through to a number of issues – for instance, to the mining of mineral sands, and to the moves to take the lime secreted by the polyps and feed it to the canefields on the nearby Queensland coast. This area to which Cook had led the white man now supported one of the world's largest sugar industries, and it had farms hungry for lime. There were millions of tons of handily located limestone in the Reef – a fact which had also caught the imagination of the cement industry.

The opening up of coast and Reef had introduced other hazards. By the nineteen-sixties, no marine animal, from the seahorse and firefish to the dugong and dolphin, was safe from net or line. No colony of corals, no shell, no bright little fish suitable for an aquarium, was safe from collectors. Everything living in the waters of the Reef faced the possibility of a polluted environment. DDT, noted for the way it persists in soil and in rivers and seas, was being used along with other persistent insecticides on the cane farms of the coast. Sewage and industrial wastes were pouring out from the towns. Along the booming coast there was a growing need to expand shipping, and this need was coming up against the well-named Barrier Reef. Shallow, coral-strewn waterways blocked any plan to use the gigantic vessels which were beginning to be built in the nineteen-sixties, and from this viewpoint it was possible to see the Reef as an impediment to the export and import trade, and especially to the traffic in Queensland's immensely valuable minerals.

In September 1967, the Australian parliament listened to a member outlining a suggestion that nuclear explosions might be used to clear Australia's waterways, including the inner route of the Great Barrier Reef. The idea might sound impossible, fantastic, yet over several years there were signs that some Australians were in earnest about using nuclear power to shape their continent's future. In 1969, for example, Australia invited the United States to collaborate in detonating five hydrogen bombs at Cape Keraudren, on the north-western coast, to excavate a harbour for exporting the iron ore deposits. The plan had been advocated by the American physicist, Dr Edward Teller, sometimes known by the rather uncomfortable-sounding title of Father of the H-Bomb. There were world protests, and biologists spoke of the threat to marine life not only in local waters but, with nuclear contamination spreading through the food chain, to life thousands of miles from the explosion. The harbour plan was dropped, ostensibly on economic grounds, but really, some observers suggested, because of an impasse with the United States over Australia's refusal at that time to sign the nuclear non-proliferation treaty. The incident did nothing to lessen Australia's interest in nuclear blasting, and if ever it became possible to clear a way through the Great Barrier Reef there would certainly be some people in favour of clearing it.

As it was, there were reports that Dr Teller had suggested nuclear explosives for the deepening of Torres Strait, just inside Reef waters off the northern tip of Queensland. That was at the beginning of 1967. In September of the same year the Australian federal parliament was addressed by one of its members on the need to consider plans for the deepening of Torres Strait and some other passages in the Great Barrier Reef, possibly with nuclear devices. It could be necessary, he said, to blow a hole in the Reef. The member (C. W. Bridges-Maxwell, of Robertson, New South Wales) referred to the mineral riches of the almost unsettled northern and north-western areas of the continent and to the necessity of getting them out by sea. They had to be delivered to centres in, among other places, the United States and Japan, as well as to the south and east of Australia. In many cases the best route was through the Torres Strait, but this was so shallow that no ship larger than 50,000 tons deadweight could use it. Bulk carriers of one hundred thousand and two hundred thousand tons were now being developed, and if other countries employed them, Australia would have to compete. Bridges-Maxwell made reference to the silica which had to be brought out from Cape Flattery, on the northern coast inside the Reef, and to the bauxite – the raw material of aluminium – shipped from Weipa, on the north-western Queensland coast, to a number of processing points, including Gladstone, the coastal industrial centre on the southern waters of the Reef. The Weipa deposit is one of the world's largest. From it, Comalco was supplying more than one third of Japan's bauxite requirements, as well as markets in Europe and the United States. Comalco, Bridges-Maxwell said, was one of the companies interested in the plan for deepening a shipping passage; another interested company was B.H.P., which had expectations of ore sales to the United States. He also referred to the possibility of an oil discovery, and urged members to consider that minerals were of immense importance to Australia's future.

A little more than a year later, in October 1968, Bridges-Maxwell asked in parliament if there had been progress in the study of the deepening project, and received the reply that there had been inter-departmental discussion. The subject of nuclear engineering subsided. In 1969, though, there was Cape Keraudren and the hydrogen-bomb harbour project to suggest that nuclear clearance of its waterways might yet become one of the hazards of the Reef's future. Meanwhile, present hazards included the medium-sized tankers which were making their way among its corals with their cargoes of oil. In waters rated among the world's most dangerous, each was a potential *Torrey Canyon* disaster, a possible wreck which could spread death and pollution through mile after mile of the Reef.

In the later nineteen-sixties, people began to realize that they were no longer sighting whales in Reef waters. Once, thousands of humpbacks had swum north each year out of the Antarctic winter. Melville, in his roll-call of the cetaceans in *Moby Dick*, said of the humpback, "He is the most gamesome and lighthearted of all the whales, making more gay foam and white water generally than any other of them". He also sang. He belonged to that species which, recorded in the northern hemisphere by scientists of the Rockefeller and Columbia Universities, delivered himself of long and complex songs like those of a tremendous bird. Making his way through the Reef, then, through the blue sea of corals, the humpback sang and made gay foam. Even into the early nineteen-sixties people on the islands watched for the whales. Beyond the green-streaked blue of some reef, there would be time's most tremendous animal, idling with its young, or flinging itself upward, leaping like that smaller member of its family, the dolphin, and crashing down again with the sort of splash – the unbelievable, thumping white splash – that can only be made when a creature vastly larger than two elephants attempts to leap like a dolphin. It was an absurd and joyful sight. But the whales were hunted in the Antarctic by the factory ships sent down by nations of the northern hemisphere, and hunted again by Australia as they travelled along its coast. By the end of the nineteen-sixties the waters of the Reef were undisturbed by Melville's gamesome and light-hearted leviathan.

At the same time another threat to the Reef was developing – the population explosion of one of its own animals, *Acanthaster planci*. These starfish – popularly called crown-of-thorns because of their covering of thorn-like spines – could grow to a span of twenty inches and produce as many as seventeen arms. Once, the crown-of-thorns had been unexceptionable members of the Reef community. Certainly they had fed on coral polyps, but there hadn't been enough of them for that to matter. And then, inexplicably, they began to multiply, until there were hordes of them eating their way through the gardens of the Reef. Later, they were noticed on other reefs around the Pacific – reefs where previously they had been rare – and soon it was realized that there were infestations at such widely-spaced points as Guam and Fiji, Borneo and Majuro. In the opinion of Dr Robert Endean, an Australian marine biologist, no other threat to the existence of the Great Barrier Reef could compare in urgency with that of the polyp-eating starfish. After all, he argued, unless the population explosion of the crown-of-thorns could be stopped, and the animal forced back into its normal role, there would be no Reef left for anything else to spoil. Dr Endean was in charge of the crown-of-thorns research project. He was also chairman of the Great Barrier Reef Committee, an international association which concerned itself with the Reef's future. The crown-of-thorns plague, Endean believed, had been released by human interference with the ecological system of the Reef. An enemy which had helped control the crown-of-thorns population by preying on it had somehow been wiped out, and so the starfish had been able to multiply unchecked. The vanished enemy, Endean surmised, had been the animal which lived in a shell up to eighteen inches long – *Charonia tritonis*, the giant triton. This animal had survived the many centuries of the Reef's isolation, when an occasional Aboriginal had collected it – usually because he wanted to make a hole in the handsome brownish shell and use it as a ceremonial trumpet – but it had been decimated in the new era of the tourist trade, when it had been collected for the thousands of visitors who liked the look of a shell on the mantelpiece. It had been this mass transfer from reef to souvenir shelf which, Endean thought, had permitted the uncontrolled population rise of the crown-of-thorns, and this belief was behind certain of the experiments he had planned for his research project.

The story of that project, and of the difficulties it encountered, seems a good one with which to begin an account of the many threats which, at the beginning of the nineteen-seventies, shadowed the future of the Great Barrier Reef. It makes a point relevant to all of them – that when the natural balances of the Reef are upset, the finding of a way to control the result could occupy an army of scientists for a lifetime, and then might not be found.

CHAPTER 2

On the Reef:
Scientists versus Starfish

❋

THE crown-of-thorns research party had assembled on a charter boat in Cairns, the Barrier Reef port on the tropical north-eastern coast of Australia. I called a taxi at my Cairns hotel at about six-thirty in the morning. The scientists and divers were leaving early for the reefs around Green Island, and because I was gathering material about the Reef and its chances of survival I was going along to watch them work. In the early quiet the taxi drove through streets flowering with white frangipani, pink cassias, scarlet poincianas. Already the air was warm. Big-verandahed old weatherboard houses with accommodation signs made a stand between shadeless new glass and aluminium motels. Arresting names slipped by – The Lido, Bermuda, Tropicana, Tropic Moon – and a lot of palm trees. Then we were in the waterfront district which, without carrying any sign, is widely known through the South Pacific by the name it acquired during a wild past – the Barbary Coast. Its old hotels are left-overs from the time when Cairns was a port for the pearling luggers, and for seamen who might spend a month in the pubs while their ships took on a cargo of sugar. Now that the plastics industry manufactures the pearl buttons once made from the trochus shell – a main income-earner for the luggers – and mechanical loading turns a ship around in a day, the Barbary Coast is quieter than it used to be. As we drove past the Barrier Reef Hotel, strings of coloured paper under its wide first-floor verandah streamed against a sign which read, "Barrier Reef Lounge – Never a Dull Moment". Cairns is a town which says it has no colour bar, and that the Barrier Reef is the hotel where the Aborigines drink.

Over from the hotel was the wharf. The taxi set me down and I walked out towards the charter boat, *Kuranda*, lying white against grey water and a far silhouette of hazed olive-green hills. George Clarke, the boat's owner and captain, waved to me and I went on board. Divers' air cylinders, like small torpedoes, were stacked on the deck.

Down in the galley, washing up, was a tall man with a moustache. This was Geoffrey Harrison, executive member of the Great Barrier Reef Committee, and its deputy chairman. He was also Queensland's Chief Inspector of Fisheries, and as such the boss of the young marine biologist, Robert Pearson, who was handing him plates to wash. Pearson, twenty-five, had been doing the field work on the crown-of-thorns project for Dr Endean, who hadn't come to Cairns. The report of the work to be done on this trip would be sent to him at the University of Queensland. In the cabin, the three police divers, up from Brisbane to help Pearson gather underwater clues on the latest activities of the crown-of-thorns, were sitting over the last of breakfast. One of them – Senior Constable Bob Telfer, a migrant Scot – was saying that his boy at school had decided to learn Japanese. He had been impressed by the expansion of Japan and its interest in this coast. What the boy said was, why learn European languages? He saw his future here, where obviously Japanese was the language you were going to need.

"Just in case of stinger attack," George Clarke interrupted, "you know, just in case – the methylated spirits is down by the shower."

"Stingers?" said the Scot, who hadn't dived on the Reef before. "That's right," said Sergeant Ivan Adams, who had. He and Senior Constable Pat Sheahan, the third diver, began to joke about the box jellyfish, which looks like a gelatine box with tentacles and has a sting that can kill. This jellyfish is more feared than the shark. Telfer listened to the jokes, smiling dubiously. His skin was noticeably softer and fairer than that of the other two, who had an Australian sun-cured look. "Methylated spirits – for the box jelly, it's the only known thing," Clarke assured them, going out. "If you're stung, pour metho on."

It was nearly half past seven when *Kuranda* started out for the Reef. The mountains were misty-dark beyond the town's flat strip of palms and white verandahs, of new glass cubes and hitching-post facades. We drew away from the cargo ship with *Sulu Sea* on its rusty grey bow, and passed the wharves where the big-game fishing boats tied up each night. The wharves were empty, which meant the hunters must be out already trying to get their hooks into a thousand-pound marlin. There was a scatter of prawn trawlers, a lot of shallow water, and then we were through the wide arms of the bay and travelling smoothly for Green Island. The sky was heat-haze grey, and the breeze was hot.

Back on the coast, spirals of smoke were going up in front of brown bald cones of hills. "Did you see that cane fire this morning?" Sheahan called, going by with a black rubber wetsuit on his arm. "Smoke hung there like an atom bomb." I said I hadn't, but I'd noticed the fires the night before. For miles, the sky had been red over the canefields, which were being burned to prepare them for cutting. Along this coast that looks out towards the limestone of the reefs the fire signals of the cane industry seem to go up all the time.

Harrison was on deck unpacking equipment and checking it off against a list. Dr Endean was responsible for working out the research programme and analysing the results, he explained, but he was responsible for funds and staff and for seeing the job was done. He stood there surrounded by yellow aqualungs, coils of wire, towels. Near him was a high box, padlocked and with a chalked-on notice, "Caution – air under pressure". As he opened another crate he said to Ivan Adams, "Just shallow work this morning, I think."

"Good," the sergeant said. "Give the boys an idea." He had deepset eyes with the look of having been permanently narrowed by the sun, and his hair was clipped all over to within a fraction of an inch of the scalp.

Harrison saw Clarke and called to him, "Think we can tow that dredge?" He was referring to a trap for starfish – a steel frame with a mesh net in it which Dr Endean wanted dragged along the sea bottom between reefs. The aim was to pick up any crown-of-thorns starfish which might be migrating from reef to reef.

"First lump of coral we hit," Clarke said doubtfully, "we could lose it."

Harrison said he thought then it would be best to use a buoy. If coral snapped the line the buoy would mark the dredge's position and a diver could go down and release it. Clarke said right, and he'd keep the echo sounder on if the bottom looked like getting rough.

The echo sounder was on when I went in to the wheelhouse a little later. Clarke talked to me with one eye on the grey surface of the water and one on the sounder's screen, where a profile was being drawn of the contours of the sea bed passing under the boat. In these waters, he said, you hadn't much chance without a sounder to show the pattern of the bottom, and even then... *Kuranda* had a draft of only six feet, but it could still strike one of the reef formations that could suddenly come up ahead of you almost to the surface of the water. As well as watching the sounder you had to watch the sea for reef shadows, or for danger signals such as white water breaking on a high formation. On this expedition the sounder would come in handy for finding coral at certain depths. "They might ask me to pick up a piece of reef in, say, twenty fathoms of water, and then one in five fathoms," Clarke said, "and with the sounder I can do that."

When I asked him what other sort of charter jobs he'd been doing lately he replied instantly, "Mining parties," and started to laugh. "Mining parties," he repeated. "They hear on the grapevine that some other outfit has found a sample of something or other, and they want to rush off immediately and look for themselves." The big thing now for the Cairns charter boats, he said, were these geologists who were always looking for someone to take them out prospecting. He laughed again, but slowly, his eye on the sounder screen. He was a solid, genial man who had earned some money in real estate down in Sydney and then retreated to this coast to run a charter boat. One trip recently, he said, he'd towed a twenty-foot speedboat from Cairns to the Fly River in New Guinea and back, and carried special fuel for the jet helicopter that hovered over the expedition. While his boat waited at anchor, the prospectors used the speedboat and helicopter to explore the coast and islands. Gradually sample hunks of rock and bags of sand began to weigh down *Kuranda*, but whether they presaged more big mineral discoveries Clarke didn't know. "A mining party doesn't tell you a thing," he said. "Suppose they do make a find, they still make you steam around a couple more days so you never can tell where they made it. Then they say right, let's turn around and go back, and you don't know whether they've found anything, or, if they have, where it could be." All through that trip, he said, he kept sighting other mining parties. Those gold rushes in the old days up here – they were nothing, he reckoned, compared with this new minerals rush.

We could see Green Island now, a dark platter of trees resting on grey water. There was nothing to suggest the characteristic blue seascape of the Reef. The sky was sultry grey and so was the water. Robert Pearson, the marine biologist, came in, looking bulky in his diver's black wetsuit coat over swim trunks. He had straight dark hair and freckles. He had come to talk to Clarke about where they should put down the anchor. The first dives of the day were to be made on areas of coral which he had marked with underwater stakes the previous year, and now he had the job of relocating them. The coral in the marked areas had been eaten out by the crown-of-thorns starfish and one of the objectives of this expedition was to find out whether there had been any new coral growth. Pearson had to judge the location of the stakes by taking marks from Green Island and the mainland, about eighteen miles away. When he told Clarke he thought the dinghy could start out from about where we now were, Clarke said right, he'd look for a bomby and drop the pick. With the echo sounder he picked up the shape of a bomby – a huge boulder of coral growing up towards the surface – and the reef anchor, a four-pronged grappling hook made to catch in coral, went down into it. Then Pearson and the three police divers climbed into the dinghy and started off to look for the staked-out corals.

By this November of 1968 Pearson had been working on the crown-of-thorns research project for a little more than two years. His association with it dated back to an interview with Dr Endean at the University of Queensland, where Endean was reader in zoology and Pearson had worked on aspects of the stingray for his M.Sc. Endean had told him about the Reef surveys which were being planned to examine the crown-of-thorns problem. Pearson was an obvious choice for such underwater field work. He had gone to school near a southern Australian beach, had learned to dive there, and was now one of the new breed of marine biologists – one of those scientists who, using face mask and snorkel, or drawing on air from an aqualung, could work in the water almost as easily as in a laboratory. Earlier generations had also worked in the sea, of course, but they had been handicapped by having to explore in diving bells, or submarines, or in cumbersome diving suits at the end of an air hose. Pearson belonged to a generation given the freedom of the seas by snorkel and scuba. When Endean asked him if he would like to go north and have a look at the starfish damage around Green Island, he accepted with enthusiasm.

Pearson's first view of the crown-of-thorns plague was by courtesy of a diver employed by the Green Island tourist interests. This diver's job was chiefly to protect a patch of coral for tourists to view through glass-bottomed boats. He couldn't dismember the crown-of-thorns on the reef because it was suspected that, as in some other species, a piece of this starfish could grow into a new whole. Therefore he spiked the animals, loaded them in a boat and took them ashore to die of exposure. Sometimes he spiked as many as 370 in a day, yet when he returned there was always a new crop of thorns on the coral. Where the starfish had eaten the polyps the colour had vanished and a mucus-like substance streamed from the skeleton. To show Pearson the crown-of-thorns at work this diver took him out in a dinghy from Green Island. He then invited him to drop over the side, swim along the surface and look down on the ruined gardens.

"I saw all these bugs twined in amongst the coral – I just couldn't believe it," Pearson said, still sounding incredulous as, more than two years later, he told me the history of his work on the crown-of-thorns. "There might be a hundred starfish on a patch of staghorn coral – a patch, say, four feet high and ten feet in diameter. You couldn't tell exactly how many there were because you couldn't count them. They'd be intertwined with the branches and with each other. They looked like an enormous cactus." The starfish were multi-armed, and it wasn't easy to tell where, say, a fifteen-armed animal ended and a seventeen-armed specimen began. Later, with his own diver-assistant, Kem Cason, Pearson made a survey of other reefs to check on infestation. He worked out a way of counting the intertwined starfish by counting the central discs in the thorny tangles and ignoring the arms. By this method he once counted thirty-seven starfish in a square yard. During the survey, the scenes he looked down on through the crystal water continued to strike him as fantastic – "just thousands and thousands of these starfish, the bottom in some places completely covered with them." Yet at Low Isles, to the north, there were suddenly no starfish at all. Commenting on the first of many mysteries with which the investigation was to confront him, Pearson said, "That still amazes me. I can't figure out why there were no starfish there. Low Isles is surrounded on the seaward side by a number of infested reefs, and yet it's not infested itself. This may be important. But I haven't had time to investigate it fully."

Time to investigate – this was always in short supply on the crown-of-thorns programme. The starfish were eating their way through the reef, and the demand, especially from the tourist interests, was for a way of stopping them. Yet to find a way of altering one aspect of the animal's behaviour, scientists had to know a good deal about the rest, and they knew practically nothing. The dossier on the crown-of-thorns was almost a blank. The animal was staging a population explosion, yes – but where did it spawn? What happened to its eggs?

Where did its larvae develop? What preyed on it in its earliest stages of life? For questions like these, inevitably asked by anyone hoping to control an animal's breeding rate, there were no adequate answers. And then there was the point that not only was the population explosion being staged by a relatively unstudied animal, but in relatively unstudied waters. Scientists working around the Great Barrier Reef could draw on nothing comparable with the information available about northern oceans and their inhabitants. Unlike the benign south seas, the northern oceans forced the people who fished them to battle for their food. These people kept records, and later made them the basis of scientific investigation. Around the south-west Pacific much of the work had still to be done. Oddly, though, one of the few tenets on which a scientist might have placed his bet was that a population explosion wouldn't happen on a coral reef. A reef, he'd have said, is a stable environment. In the tropics there are none of the extremes which make life so hazardous for the animals of the colder seas. There are variations of temperature, but only between warm and warmer. The reef gives shelter and refuge. It also provides, with its crannies and ledges and holes and corridors, a great variety of habitat occupied by a great variety of animals living in a complex, stable inter-relationship. There is no parallel here for the immense hauls of one species taken, say, from the north Atlantic. A haul around the Barrier Reef would consist of an astonishing variety of fish, but only a few representatives of each variety. Using the part of the reef each needs, animals and plants exist together in a tight organization which leaves no opportunity for one species to expand, dominate, get out of line. The complexity and diversity of the life makes for stability. Population explosions don't happen.

To explain the one that did, and to find a way of suppressing it – these were the objectives of the crown-of-thorns research project. "There was almost nothing known – we had to go off in all directions," Pearson said, looking back on that period when, under Endean's direction, he set out to find solutions to the multiple mysteries of the crown-of-thorns plague. Before he could even get around to those, though, another problem had to be solved: a way had to be found to tag the crown-of-thorns, so that animals being used in experiments could be distinguished from others crawling on the reefs.

The first tagging idea was to slip tiny rubber bands over the spines on the upper surface of the animals. "But the old starfish was a bit smarter than that," Pearson reported respectfully. "He'd just drop off any spines that had bands on them." Then there was the silver-wire idea. The wire was passed through one of the arms of the starfish and tied in a loop to hold a plastic tag. Within a week or so the tissue had parted and the wire had slipped out. Another attempt at tagging, this time with non-injurious dyes, encountered problems with the variable body-colour of the animal itself. Under its thorns, or spines, the starfish has a reddish tinge when its red-brown respiratory palps protrude through the skin, but when these palps retract – which they do, for instance, if a shadow passes over the animal – the actual skin colour is exposed. This might be grey-green or grey-brown, though it might also be whitish, or yellow. "This tremendous colour variation didn't help with dye," Pearson said. "You'd choose, say, a blue dye and inject it. Well, it might show up on some of the starfish, but on others it wouldn't. I've recently read of another method, though, which I wasn't aware of at that time. This is to place the whole animal in a bucket and leave it there for, say, ten minutes to absorb dye. Later, to identify an animal marked like this, you'd turn it over and examine the paler areas, such as its tube feet. With blue dye, these should be stained pale blue." If ever he had the time, Pearson said, he'd like to try out this method of soaking the starfish in dye. But there was also the question of how long a dye would last. "The skin of humans just keeps flaking off," he said. "You get some stain on your hand, it soon wears away. In the case of the starfish, too, the tissue may slough off and the dye not be evident. The dye would need to be retained by the starfish for at least three months, and preferably a year." It could therefore take a year for a scientist to make sure that if he used a dye it would last through a year-long experiment.

Crown-of-thorns starfish are difficult animals to work with because they must be fed on corals. To keep them supplied, experiments are best done near or even right on a coral reef. For an experiment in tagging starfish by removing certain of their many arms, Pearson worked on a reef with animals kept in cages under the water. There are many stories of starfish growing new limbs to replace those they have lost, and Pearson needed to check on these. Would his experimental starfish be recognizable in several months' time from the fact that they lacked the arms he had removed – or would the arms have grown again? For that matter, would a part of the crown-of-thorns become a whole animal, as happened with other species of starfish?

And then, if the arms grew again, how fast would they grow? Would the animals, by regrowing their arms, become indistinguishable too quickly from other starfish on the reef?

The starfish being used in this experiment were caged underwater – that is, they were being maintained in an environment in which other starfish all around them flourished – so the experiment should have worked splendidly. Instead, it didn't work at all. The caged starfish died, disintegrated, in some cases actually vanished. Arriving to make a check, Pearson would find they just weren't there. It was a while before he found out the reason, which was that an underwater surge from which the animals couldn't escape was smashing them against the sides of the cages. Eventually he worked out a way of keeping starfish alive in the cages by providing them with the sort of coral formations in which they would normally wedge themselves on the reef. He never did get time, though, to repeat the experiment of the regenerating arms.

Another tagging idea he tested gave rather more hopeful results. He marked starfish by cutting away some of their spines. After a month all but one of the animals had been battered to death by the underwater surge; on the one survivor, though, the spines had grown very little, and the starfish was still recognizable as having been tagged. Unfortunately, starfish which Pearson had never handled kept turning up on the reef with broken spines. Spine breakages, it appeared, were a hazard of starfish life. It became apparent that if Pearson were to distinguish starfish marked by him from those marked by the exigencies of life on the reef he would have to cut off the spines to a carefully selected pattern. Other questions he would have to settle related to the rate of regrowth of the spines. They would eventually grow again much as human fingernails and hair regrow – but at what rate? Comparatively quickly in the first months, perhaps, and slower thereafter? Or – how? The questions had to stand over. Two years would scarcely have been too long for the tagging experiments alone, but Pearson had to proceed with other aspects of the work.

When he began to investigate the reproductive cycle of the crown-of-thorns, he found that the early stages in the life of this animal which was crawling in its thousands all over the reefs were a mystery. The crown-of-thorns appeared on the reefs in the form of a young starfish, about half an inch in diameter, secreted amongst the coral and already feeding on it. Of its development through the egg stage and the larval stage, and of the enemies which, presumably, still preyed on it, there were no observations, and it was to prove remarkably hard to make any. During his entire study of the population explosion, only once did Pearson manage to see the crown-of-thorns spawning, and he succeeded then only because he kept records from which he was able to forecast the probable spawning period. The records were of changes in the size of the animals and their gonads. Since both grow heavier as the spawning season approaches, and lighter after spawning, it was possible to predict from a graph of such changes when another spawning might occur. There could be no certainty about the prediction until the records had been kept for a number of years, but for once Pearson was lucky; acting on work carried out the previous year, he was able to make one observation of the initial stage of the population explosion, a crown-of-thorns starfish releasing eggs. He had found that the gonads of both sexes developed about April and built up gradually until December, when they were fully mature. The spawning season, he calculated, would begin about mid-December. Still, it was early in January before he witnessed the spawning. Working on Arlington Reef, he was struck by something odd about the way large numbers of the crown-of-thorns were sitting flat on top of staghorn coral, the tips of their arms curled upwards. If the animals had been feeding, the arms would have been pressed to the coral. Pearson remarked on this peculiarity to his diver-assistant, who was then John Bloomfield, before swimming back to the boat to collect some gear. This few minutes' absence cost him the sight of male starfish releasing sperm from the gonad ducts in the upcurled arms. "When I got back," Pearson recalled, "there was this huge milky cloud in the water, and John was raving on about having seen a lot of males spawning." Pearson's first thought was to look around for the females which should have been releasing eggs into the fertilizing milky cloud. He couldn't see any. After a search he found just one female, sitting about fifteen feet from the males, with tiny eggs streaming out from the gonad ducts in its arms. Several green-blue damsel fish were there too, eating the eggs as they were released.

This solitary female represented the first and the last time Pearson was able to observe a spawning, and in a way the experience added to the mystery surrounding the birth of the crown-of-thorns. Pearson knew, for instance, that with some other types of starfish the spawning of the male stimulated the spawning of the female – yet on Arlington

Reef this hadn't happened. A lot of males had spawned, but only one female had released its eggs to be fertilized. Since in the crown-of-thorns species the sexes exist in a one-to-one ratio – where there are ten males, by all the rules there should be ten females – on Arlington Reef that day there must have been numbers of females not releasing their eggs. Which, as Pearson said, was ridiculous. "I mean, it'd be useless – wouldn't it? – if they just spawned whenever they felt like it. They wouldn't get too many fertilized eggs that way. And if the female spawned first and the male spawned next day – well, it'd be absurd." It was clearly no way to run a population explosion.

Then there was the question of what happened to the eggs that reached the milky cloud and were fertilized. "Presumably they're carried around in the current for some time," Pearson said. "But whether it's a few days or a few weeks. . . ." He shook his head. "They would develop into larvae and then these would settle on the bottom. But where exactly? The first knowledge we have of them is as young ones hidden in the coral, feeding on it." To help fill in this biographical gap between the egg and the coral-consumer Pearson tried to rear some crown-of-thorns starfish of his own. He mixed eggs from mature females and sperm from mature males; but although the method had worked well with other species of starfish, the creature which swarmed all over the reefs refused to emerge in his laboratory. Worse, the short duration of the breeding season made it impossible to restage the experiment; it would be another year before there would again be mature crown-of-thorns to provide the materials for further work. The experiment had to be allowed to lapse – and this foredoomed another of Pearson's investigations, into the animal's larval stage. In a net with meshes small enough to stop a pin slipping through he had collected samples of plankton, his hope being that amongst the young animals and plants there would be crown-of-thorns larvae. Examining these hauls back in the laboratory he found they contained very few larvae of any starfish species. He had probably been unlucky in missing a concentration of the larvae floating somewhere near his net, but it scarcely mattered; the refusal of the crown-of-thorns to develop from eggs in his laboratory meant he had no check sample of its larva – nothing against which to compare any other specimen suspected of being larval crown-of-thorns.

As a coral eater, the starfish was more amenable to assessment. It had to eat, and while it ate, Pearson measured. Even so, it wasn't precisely easy to find the answer to the question, "If thousands of starfish are eating the Great Barrier Reef, how much does each starfish eat?" The assessment was made from starfish caged on the reef. "We placed sprigs of coral in the cages and sketched them," Pearson said. "Next day we'd measure the areas that had been killed and put these in the sketch so we wouldn't confuse them with the following day's feeding scars. We kept starfish going like this for about a month and then we calculated how much they had consumed per day. It worked out at something like twenty square inches a day of coral." To feed on the coral, the crown-of-thorns reduced the polyps to a sort of soup, then absorbed them through the wall of its remarkable stomach. This stomach went out after its food. As the starfish descended on the polyps they retracted into their cups, but this scarcely helped them because the starfish everted the stomach through its mouth, placed it over the coral and released digestive juices. These seeped in around the polyps and broke down tissue. The starfish then absorbed the nourishing soup through its stomach wall.

Crown-of-thorns research could not only be baffling, it could be physically exhausting, especially when there were experiments going on in two places at once, as at the laboratory at Cairns Oceanarium and in cages on the reef. To commute between Cairns and the reef three days a week, Pearson had a hired speedboat and driver. The speedboat was eighteen feet long, with a hundred-horsepower motor. Compared with the performance of the speedboat in a rough sea – and the sea off Cairns was often rough – an old car on a rocky road would be a wonderfully smooth ride. The speedboat would leap off a wave and smash down, leap and smash down – each time, it seemed, on to concrete. Pearson was never able to relax long enough even to think about being seasick. "You had to hang on with both hands. If you let go for a second and the boat hit a wave at an odd angle you could easily break a leg. John Bloomfield was thrown out one day. Boat hit a wave and he somersaulted straight out. Unpleasant. By the time you got back to Cairns at night you had a headache and all the salt spray would be sort of eating into your flesh – or felt like it – and you weren't very pleased to have to start unloading your boat and maybe attending to starfish you'd brought back."

The going was smoother during the trip north to look for giant tritons. This journey in a charter boat was part of an effort to collect evidence on the effectiveness of this large variety of triton as a control on the crown-of-thorns population – on the extent, that is, to which the triton preyed on the starfish. If this turned out to be significant, then perhaps more of the tritons might be imported to combat the crown-of-thorns plague. "The idea was to obtain a large number of tritons," Pearson said, "place them on reefs infested with the starfish and see what happened." If they ate large numbers of crown-of-thorns, then the problem of controlling the plague might be close to solution. But it was a case of first catch your tritons, and the trip lasting several weeks and extending north from Cairns to within about fifty miles of Princess Charlotte Bay yielded only eighteen specimens. Certainly the dives were restricted to depths of about thirty feet – air supplies for aqualungs were difficult to organize on this lonely northern stretch of the Reef — but that should not have affected the chances of finding a large number of tritons if they had been there to find. Using snorkels, Pearson and Bloomfield swam along the surface looking down through the light blue water, diving occasionally to thrust a hand into a cave or crevice. About a third of the tritons were found lying fully exposed on the bottom. In all, though, there were only eighteen, and one of the questions arising from the trip was, why?

In a way, the poor result of the search seemed to support Dr Endean's theory that the tritons had been cleaned out by the shell trade. A few years back in this area the trade had been supplied by Torres Islanders employed to collect trochus shell. The trochus browsed on algae in the same sort of environment as the triton, and the islanders would pick up tritons, too, to sell on the local market. But there was another possible interpretation of the extraordinary shortage of tritons revealed by Pearson's search, and that was that they did not flourish in these waters, and never had. There were local people who maintained that the Torres Islanders, and other collectors, had never taken many tritons here, for the reason that there had never been many to take. There had certainly never been enough, they insisted, to act as a control on the population of the crown-of-thorns.

The eighteen tritons caught by Pearson and Bloomfield were kept on board the charter boat in buckets. When an animal voided material from its last meal Pearson was able to tell whether it had been feeding on the crown-of-thorns. Some had been, but others had been feeding on its relatives, the blue star and the pincushion star. Those which had made a meal of the crown-of-thorns voided parts of it as evidence, and these parts included the spines which, capable of inflicting a poisoned wound, might have been expected to deter any animal from dining off their owner. They deterred the human handler, since they could even pierce leather gloves to inflict a wound. Pearson had given up wearing gloves after realizing that they prevented him from feeling anything before a spike drove right into his hand. Bare hands, retaining their sensitivity and quickness, were safer, he had come to believe. The triton seemed to have no worries at all about the spines. It was a large snail-like animal, one of the molluscs whose very name means soft, yet it simply ate its way through the formidable spines. It disposed of an animal which few predators would have been capable of tackling, and there was in this fact something, perhaps, to suggest that the triton had had a long and special relationship with the crown-of-thorns.

Pearson took his eighteen tritons back to Arlington Reef. With small plastic tags cemented to the shells, they were released. The plan was to return each day to plot their movements – but these movements, like so much else connected with the crown-of-thorns project, turned out to be exasperating. "Some of the tritons were able to move considerable distances overnight," Pearson said. "They just wandered about every-where. We gave the experiment up after a while because it was getting too difficult to find the damn things. There were crown-of-thorns in the vicinity but you couldn't determine if a triton had been feeding on them unless you found one of the starfish caught up in the triton shell – or unless the triton had voided ossicles and spines right where it was located. If it had moved on after feeding, and then voided these things, and then moved on again – well, you couldn't be sure what had happened."

He built an underwater cage for the tritons. It was forty feet by forty feet by three feet high, was made of wire and iron stakes, and was located in an area of considerable coral growth. The coral was to provide meals for the crown-of-thorns which he put in the enclosure, and the crown-of-thorns were to provide meals for the tritons. Over a period of three months he returned every other day to check on the starfishes' fate. In some cases, he found, the tritons had eaten the whole animal, voiding the spines and ossicles within a day or so. At other times the triton ate some of the internal organs, leaving the rest of the animal. Over three months, the tritons averaged about one crown-of-thorns each per week.

One starfish each per week. Would that rate of feeding ever have made the triton an effective control on the crown-of-thorns? Pearson said this was something I should take up with Dr Endean when I saw him.

Another phase of Pearson's work was to try to find out what preyed on the juvenile crown-of-thorns. "In February and March of 1968," Pearson recalled, "we spent a lot of time searching around for the juveniles we expected would appear in the coral as they had the previous year. We finally came across a large number of them and we collected one hundred and fifty in a couple of days." The juveniles were placed in aquaria along with animals which might reasonably be suspected of preying on them – crabs, for example, and live spider shells, stroms, bailer and helmet shells, trigger fish. "Nothing that we placed in the tank," he reported, "fed on those juvenile starfish."

That was his last experiment before he went south to work in Brisbane and report to Endean and Harrison. When he left the north he left behind the stakes which he had placed under the sea in 1967 on test regeneration areas. These were the areas of coral which had been eaten out by the crown-of-thorns starfish and which now, towards the end of 1968, he had again come north to examine.

Had the areas regenerated? I wondered about it as the little boat bringing Pearson and the three police divers puttered back to *Kuranda*. As they came in close, Geoffrey Harrison, the Chief Inspector of Fisheries, leaned down to ask how things had gone. Pearson shook his head. The Scotsman Telfer swung up on to the deck and I asked him how he had enjoyed his first look at the reef. Had he seen any good coral? He grimaced. Dead, he said.

Pearson had found the stakes by taking marks from the island and the mainland and then, as he swam along face down, searching back through his memories of the configuration of the sea bottom. With the areas located he examined them as he continued to swim along the surface, looking down. Sometimes he would dive for a closer look or to measure specimens he thought showed signs of new growth. He wrote his notes underwater, using an ordinary lead pencil and a plastic slate which had been roughened with steel wool. The police divers also went down to look at the corals and help gather the specimens they were now showing Harrison.

Some of these specimens had a dark coating of algae, of the sort which invaded a coral skeleton after the crown-of-thorns had eaten out the polyps. The exact effect of this algae on the chances of regeneration was another of the mysteries set up for the scientists by the crown-of-thorns plague. One theory had it that the algae would block regeneration, for reasons which had to do with the earliest stages in the life of a coral polyp. An adult polyp, unable to move out of its limestone cup, releases sperm. Much of this is lost in the sea, but some will drift into another polyp waiting to be fertilized. Eventually the young – the larva – measuring perhaps a sixteenth of an inch, floats away from the parent to find its own place in the marine world. Having settled, say, on a piece of limestone, it proceeds to grow the tentacles it needs for feeding – petal-like tentacles which sting tiny animals and help them down into the centre or mouth of the polyp-flower, which happens to be carnivorous. With its food problems attended to, the polyp now begins to found its own colony – which is to say its flesh begins to bud, the bud grows into another polyp, and the process continues, with each new polyp secreting a limestone cup, until from one larva there is a colony of perhaps twenty-five thousand small, flower-like carnivores.

But there would be no colony, and in fact no future at all for the coral larva (or so one theory had it) if the larva settled on a limestone skeleton already coated with the sort of algae which appears after an attack by the crown-of-thorns. This algae would attract herbivorous fish and molluscs and these, grazing on the skeleton, would accidentally eat the larva. That was one theory. Another held that exactly the opposite could happen – that the herbivorous fish would scrape off the algae and expose clean skeleton, thus ensuring for any coral larva which elected to settle there a good start in life. The larva by its process of budding would eventually take over the whole site from the algae. Multiplying these events, you had entire areas of coral restored to life after being practically wiped out by the crown-of-thorns. This was certainly the more cheerful view of the prospects awaiting any coral larvae wandering the local currents, but the coral specimens which the divers had brought up from the regeneration areas unfortunately lent it little support. There was some new growth, but nothing impressive, and altogether it looked as if the larvae might be finding life amongst the algae a distinct battle. As Pearson began to gather in the specimens to photograph them for his records I asked him if the new growth was significant. Did these bits of living coral on dead branches mean that, after all, the area was regenerating? Pearson answered that that was another question I should put to Dr Endean after he had studied the results of this expedition (when I did put it to Dr Endean, he answered that he thought it could be twenty-five years before the area recovered).

George Clarke, the skipper of *Kuranda*, called out, "See the giant clam down there?" and I went to the side of the boat. The grey was clearing both from the sky and the water, and looking straight down you could see through blueness to the sandy bottom. Lying there was a specimen of the clam that is the largest bivalve ever known. The great white shell alone might have weighed five hundred pounds. The colours of the animal inside were difficult to make out without a glass observation box, but it seemed to be the variety marked in blues and greens. This animal had one of the sea's most fearsome legends. It killed divers, so the story went, by clamping shut on a foot and holding on while the captive drowned. The legend was widely circulated, and I had last seen it reported on an exhibit card in an English museum, though without conviction. It had always puzzled me, because the clam lived on the plankton it drew in and surely would have no interest in trapping a diver to make a meal of him. Of course, it might close up out of nervousness. Eventually the matter was illuminated for me by a fisheries research biologist in Brisbane, a man who struck me as having encyclopaedic knowledge and a passion for adding to it. He had personally tested the legend of the giant clam. Was there a doubt whether the clam would shut on a foot? Well, then, present it with a foot. Having presented it with his own, he was able to report that the clam did indeed close, and smartly – within one-third to one-half of a second. It was a bruising experience. After about fifty seconds the clam's muscle relaxed and it was possible to withdraw the foot, though only if you acted quickly, before the muscle tightened up again. It all depended on having your wits about you. After fifty long seconds underwater, struggling to disengage from what appeared to be an enraged oyster of nightmare proportions, it seemed to me you might not have them immediately to hand. You might not even be quite conscious. The government biologist was fully conscious. He had been willing to risk his foot in the jaws of a giant clam but only on a reef where he could keep his head above water. I felt the experiment suggested that many divers must in fact have drowned in the giant shell and been held there until the clam felt it safe to open up and get

1. Crown-of-thorns starfish (upper side)

2. Crown-of-thorns starfish (lower side)

3. Islands of Whitsunday Area from the air

4. Trees and beach – Heron Island

rid of the intruder, but the biologist didn't think so. A diver in those waters would surely take a knife with him, he argued; if caught, he would only have to insert the knife in the shell and hack at the clam's muscle to make it relax. But as for the diver who put his foot down in these waters without looking – well, obviously he found it hard to believe in such a character, and regarded him as belonging in poor fiction. Just how would it be possible, he demanded, *not* to see a clam that was both huge and brilliantly coloured? My answer was equivocal. Perhaps because I had a writer's vested interest in legends I managed to see in his experiment at least some evidence for the fearsomeness of the giant clam. It still seemed to me that this specimen lying down there beside *Kuranda* would be a pretty nasty hazard for any colour-blind halfwit without a knife who put his foot in it. Looking down, I wondered about the age of the animal inhabiting such an immense shell. How old would a clam that size be? I'd checked on that once, too, and the answer had been fascinating: perhaps ten years, perhaps several hundred. As with other Reef animals, more research was needed. There were interesting questions to be answered about the algae that grew in its tissues. Some scientists believed the clam was a farmer, growing these little algal plants to supplement its diet of plankton. To support the idea, algal cells had been discovered in the clam's digestive system.

There was something else about the giant clam: it was one of the main reasons for the cops-and-robbers game now being played fairly regularly around the Barrier Reef by Australians and Chinese. Sighting of a Taiwan Chinese fishing vessel would bring Australians rushing out from the coast to protect the clams which they regarded as their own. The Chinese were accused of cutting out the muscle – the only part of the clam they considered edible – and leaving the rest. In this liking for clam muscles the Chinese were no different from generations of Pacific peoples. But sail- and canoe-power had carried very few of these earlier Pacific gourmets as far as the Great Barrier Reef, and those who did come were not the emissaries of huge populations in search of food. Today, motor-driven vessels were bringing reef-raiders from thousands of miles away – for fish as well as for clams – and they were all foraging on behalf of large and inexorably expanding populations. The Reef had never known such an invasion. Human predators – the shell collectors and tourists as much as the commercial fishermen and clam hunters – were outside its experience, outside its whole system of life; it had never had reason to evolve defences against them. Thus the human population explosion threatened to be as serious for the Reef as the explosion of the crown-of-thorns – more serious, probably, since the evidence was that the starfish imbalance was simply one effect of the new human presence in the area. As for the results of the clam-hunters' actions, these could only be guessed at at this stage. They might turn out to be negligible, or they might turn out to be as grave as those currently being ascribed to the disappearance of the giant triton (eventually the decision would be that they were grave – that the killing of the clams, feeders on the plankton which contained the eggs and larvae of the crown-of-thorns, could be contributing to the spread of the starfish). The evidence was that the Chinese were killing as many clams as they could find. Certainly great numbers of the clams were being slaughtered, and all through the north there were reports of gaping shells in which the brilliant flesh had been left to putrefy. Protecting the clams was difficult. Ships could move at night in these waters only in the shipping lanes, and this was not where the pirates dropped anchor. They sheltered out in the coral patches, incompletely charted areas which were no place even in daylight for a chase sequence. On the sort of grey, calm day which hid the reefs ahead of a boat in opaque water, the chase was practically over. Even when it was on, the visitors had the advantage, because they always knew what their pursuers' next move would be. They picked up the wireless messages passing between the big-game boats and prawn trawlers and fishing launches which were the unofficial guardians of these waters. When one of the little Australian boats reported seeing a strange ship in a certain area, the message was picked up by the intruder, which proceeded to vanish.

Sometimes, though, it stayed, because in fact the question of the right of the Chinese, or anybody else, to take the clams was part of a larger question, "Who owns the Great Barrier Reef?" The answer to that was involved – so involved that even when the clam-raiders had been apprehended they had often been able to argue their way out of formal charges. The position was that the Australian State of Queensland owned all the islands, and claimed territorial waters for three miles around each island. Any piece of reef which dried at low tide was regarded as an island, and as having three miles of Queensland's territorial waters around it. Thus it could happen that within this three miles of territorial water there would be a dry piece of reef from which another three miles of water could be measured. And within that further three miles there could be yet another area of dry reef, so that yet another three miles. . . . The process was known as reef-hopping, and no one was sure how it would stand up under the international law which governed such matters. The whole thing was complicated even further by the fact that the Commonwealth of Australia had claimed a twelve-mile limit for fishing rights around its territories, and this twelve-mile limit, adding nine miles to Queensland's three around the islands, theoretically extended Australia's rights even further through the reef. Confronted by Australians armed with such legalisms, intruders made rather a habit of replying that perhaps indeed they were within these so-complicated limits, but the truth was that the clam meat which happened to be on board their vessel had come from somewhere else entirely, a place indubitably beyond Australia's jurisdiction. To this the Australians hadn't much reply, because to make a charge stick they had actually to witness the clams being taken inside their waters.

Currently they were working to remove these frustrations. They had a plan to claim the giant clams and certain other creatures living on their continental shelf. Australia had already claimed the oil resources of the shelf, and now, at the end of 1968, was preparing to establish other rights under international law to sessile organisms – to creatures, that is, which sit on the sea bottom or move only in contact with it. Again the position as to national rights was either complicated or not especially clear. Molluscs such as tritons could be claimed, and so could live corals (dead corals, meaning lime skeletons, were being claimed separately and, rather unsettlingly, as minerals). A non-swimming crab could probably be claimed, but a swimming crab would retain its international status. So would fish, except when swimming within the twelve-mile limits – and thus there didn't seem to be a great deal Australia could do about the Russians, say, when they appeared in a very large research-and-fishing vessel, inside the Reef but outside the limits. Still, the new claims did mean that Australia would at last be able to do something about those eminently sessile organisms, the giant clams, anchored to the bottom in their huge shells. In future, it would be illegal for any unauthorised vessel to have clam meat on board in Australian waters, regardless of arguments as to where the meat had been taken.

There was one rather unexpected result from this planned extension of the Australian Commonwealth's claims to its continental shelf and that was the effect it was having on a friendly State – the State of Queensland. For some months now the Queensland State government had made no reply to Dr Endean's appeals for backing to extend his research on the crown-of-thorns plague. This, it was suspected, was because it was pondering an important question: just who *owned* the plague? Undoubtedly Queensland owned Green Island and certain other reefs that had been eaten out; but while the Commonwealth was making all these other claims, oughtn't it to consider claiming some part of the starfish which were crawling around its continental shelf, starting off their own population explosions outside Queensland's jurisdiction? Shouldn't the Commonwealth, in short, come across with some money to combat the crown-of-thorns?

From the other side of *Kuranda* there was a laughing shout. I walked around to investigate and found Harrison looking down at two of the divers who had just gone over the side for a pre-lunch swim. They had yellow aqualungs on their backs, and they were moving out into water of a blueness I had never seen before. It was a dark blue, going on for ink, but underlit and made brilliant by reflections coming up from the pale sandy bottom. The divers with their aqualungs were moving through the blue like yellow-backed fish. Overhead, the grey had rolled away from a big patch of sky, revealing cloudless azure. Later, as the divers surfaced and came towards the boat, George Clarke came out and called jovially, "Come on, come on now – lunch!"

The meal was spread out on the cabin table. There were hot pies, mashed potatoes, a bottle of tomato sauce, piles of cut bread, mugs of tea – a reminder of the Englishness of these Australian tropics, where in heat and humidity, in wet season and dry, people dine on hot roasts and lunch on hot pies. The divers ate their pies standing up, dripping water on the deck. During their explorations they had picked up a couple of shells, and Harrison brought them to the table to show them to me. Both were beautiful. One was an egg cowrie, a shell somewhat larger than a hen egg and made, it seemed, from heavy and lustrous white china. Underneath, you could see a section of the mantle, very black inside the polished white. Tourists liked this shell, and in that they resembled the Pacific peoples who had always valued it as anything from a fertility symbol to a fishing-net weight. The other shell was a cone, a member of a notable family of poisoners. This one was a cloth-of-gold or textile cone, patterned in rich orange-brown on white. The animal inside the four-inch shell could launch a poisoned harpoon which would kill an octopus. It wouldn't kill a fish, though; and an octopus could dine with impunity off another cone, the geographer, which could kill a man. The oddities of cone venoms were another of the subjects being investigated by Dr Endean down in Brisbane, and this specimen of the textile cone was being taken back to him. One of Endean's arguments for preserving the Reef was that its marine life would almost certainly turn out to be a source of therapeutic drugs. Just as the land's toxic substances such as curare and atropine had been shown to have a use in medicine, so marine toxins, he believed, would also turn out to have medical uses, among others as antibiotics and anti-cancer agents. Almost before he could test his theories, though, the animals which he believed would yield such substances were disappearing from the reefs. The venomous cones were of particular interest to him, but their attractive appearance made them of particular interest to the shell trade, too, and some species were already impossible to find on reefs accessible to collectors. And so the fine cloth-of-gold cone rested only briefly beside the tomato sauce on the cabin table; it was then picked up with care and returned to a bucket of seawater to preserve it for experiments in Dr Endean's laboratory.

After lunch, as the boat moved on to another anchorage off Green Island, there was an extra seriousness about preparations for the dives, which were to be much deeper than those of the morning. With Pearson, the police divers were going down to check on reports by private observers that the crown-of-thorns had been seen eating corals at deeper levels than anybody had suspected – at eighty and a hundred feet. If that turned out to be true, then dealing with the starfish would be even more difficult than had been anticipated. It meant that at those depths the animal would be out of range of observers equipped only with snorkel and goggles – out of range, that is, of most of the amateur divers along the coast who had been thought of as a reserve army that might be thrown into action against the crown-of-thorns. To track the movements of starfish at a depth, say, of a hundred feet would require skilled divers with aqualungs and an air supply. The problem of transporting the amount of air needed for a protracted job on these lonely reefs would require an elaborate and expensive solution. Since the starfish couldn't be dismembered in the depths where they were found, for fear of the parts regenerating and several starfish appearing where there had been one, each animal would have to be brought up the eighty or a hundred feet to a boat and taken ashore to die. The man hunting the animals in these conditions would have to be a skilled diver. A miscalculation in the rate at which he should ascend from such depths could result in an agonizing attack of the bends. Since there were no decompression chambers in which to treat him in the Reef area – none, in fact, for hundreds of miles to the south – he would not have a large chance of survival.

These were the risks which also faced the men on board *Kuranda*, and so the preparations for the afternoon's deep dives were now being made with some care. Still, as Sheahan murmured, if Ivan Adams said you'd be all right, then you'd be all right. Sergeant Adams, being the sort of man who wore an underwater watch under water, had a Rolex strapped on his wrist beside the depth gauge. He was going down on the first dive with Robert Pearson. They would begin the dive in shallow water, going straight to the bottom at thirty feet, and would then swim down the reef slope into the deep water. Adams would be holding a rope going up to the dinghy, which would move slowly along on an agreed course ("you've got no sense of direction under-water," Adams said. "The rope gives direction – and of course the tow does help."). Pearson would follow Adams, taking his direction from him, his hands free for note-making on the plastic slate.

Pearson was about to hand a diver's lead weight into the dinghy when somebody called, "Hey, is that a box jelly?" The weight stayed in Pearson's hands. In silence everybody peered down into the water and examined the soft glass shadow that might be a killer. It was a jellyfish all right, but – "Not a box jelly," Harrison said, and Pearson handed on the lead weight. It weighed about three pounds, and was one of those he intended wearing on his belt to speed his descent.

After Pearson and the divers had gone, I sat on deck and talked to Harrison. In the story of the Great Barrier Reef, he was one of the scientists with a dual role – both Chief Inspector of Fisheries for Queensland, and executive member of the Great Barrier Reef Committee. This committee had a membership which, both in Australia and overseas, included a number of distinguished marine scientists.

Harrison was a tall, gentle-mannered, field-and-stream sort of

Englishman with a moustache and a tweedy look which survived even the cotton shirt and shorts and rag hat he was wearing on *Kuranda*. Sitting out on deck, we talked mainly about his work in Africa. He had been in Ghana for thirteen years from 1949, first as a fisheries officer and then as Director of Fisheries. Ghana, located in the tsetse fly belt and unable to breed cattle, had been short of protein foods, and its aim had been to make up for this by developing fishing. Harrison became involved with a programme to stock dams in farming areas with freshwater fish and to set up schools to teach the villagers how to catch them. The fishermen of Ghana were already, in Harrison's view, the best in Africa, but they needed modern equipment. Harrison helped set up boatyards which built over two hundred and fifty motor fishing vessels, and something like fifteen hundred canoes were fitted with outboard motors. The fishermen went to school to learn how to handle the new equipment. There was also experiment in the processing of fishmeal, and in the canning of the most plentiful of the local fish, the sardinella. Because the season for this fish lasted only about four months, Harrison worked at combining it with a pineapple-canning programme to take up another four or five months of the year. He designed some of the machines which eventually processed the pineapple. One of his problems in Ghana was with Mediterranean fishermen, mainly French and Spanish, who, having fished out their own waters, were working their way down the African coast. They used a small-mesh net which killed everything that tangled with it, and they aimed not only to take fish from the grounds off Ghana but to cash in on the Ghanaian home market by selling their fish ashore. Eventually life was made suitably difficult for them by Ghana's refusal to allow them to land their catch. For much of the time Harrison found it easy to work with the Ghanaians, whom he recalled as a peaceable and light-hearted people. Their public servants were well trained and honest, he thought, but unfortunately he could not feel as warmly about the politicians who, during the regime of Kwame Nkrumah, began to interfere in his department. Eventually it was their interference, plus a wish to get away from Ghana's trying climate, which influenced Harrison to take the Queensland fisheries appointment based on sub-tropical Brisbane.

Now, nearly six years later, the job he held must have been subject to as many pressures as the one he had left. In addition to politicians there were conservationists interesting themselves in the administration of coastal waters. Instead of the Spanish and French off Ghana there were the Russians and Japanese off Queensland – and the Japanese, at least, were Australia's valued trading friends and not to be offended lightly. Fishing for tuna, they were using lines that were each between forty and fifty miles long, supported by buoys and with baited hooks at intervals along the line. From reports on the effects of this long-line device in other waters, conservationists knew that a lot of fish besides tuna got themselves hooked on it. In Japan, the marlin and sailfish which rose to the long-line baits were regarded as reasonably good eating, but all around the Pacific there were enraged sporting fishermen who had come to regard such animals as fair game for themselves. Now, with Australia's agreement, the Japanese were beginning to lay the long lines off islands in the Coral Sea and inside the twelve-mile limit starting at the outer edge of the Great Barrier Reef – in an area, in short, where there were plenty of game fish, including black marlin weighing more than a thousand pounds. Then there were the Russians, who appeared every so often just outside the limits. They had huge refrigerated factory ships built to work on the Russian technique of cleaning up all the fish in one area and then moving on to the next. The theory was that life in the sea was virtually inextinguishable and that stocks would build again in a few years' time (when the Russians would be back). This might be true of other seas – though again it might not – but conservationists were fearful of the results of intensive fishing in the special and little-studied conditions of life in Reef waters. Australia's counter to the foreign fishermen had been to take evasive action not unlike that taken by Ghana against its Mediterranean visitors; it was denying the use of its ports to foreign fishing vessels. Still, the Russians and Japanese were by way of being Great Powers of the fishing industry, and their interest in the waters close to Australia, including the waters of the Great Barrier Reef, would be a continuing one. In short, the job Harrison had taken in Queensland was not exactly carefree. Still, if he was feeling the pressures he wasn't showing it. As Chief Inspector of Fisheries he was a pleasant, helpful but politically circumspect public servant.

When Pearson and the divers returned from their deep exploration of the reef it was with news of more frustration in the task of working out the life style of the crown-of-thorns. They had seen dead coral in the depths and they suspected it had been killed by the crown-of-thorns, but they couldn't prove it because they hadn't been able to find a single specimen of the starfish. Pearson went into the cabin with his underwater plastic slate and sat writing up notes from it, frowning all the time.

Later the divers went down again beside *Kuranda*, sinking under their yellow aqualungs into the late afternoon's darkening blue sea. When they came up one of the trophies they brought with them was a sponge. Pat Sheahan stood holding the yellow-brown-green blob which was throwing off sheets of a mucus-like substance. "Smells," Sheahan said. It was an unlovely creature, but possibly a useful one. It too might have a future in medicine, possibly as a source of antibiotics. The sponge went back over the side. A fish lying on the deck wasn't so lucky. It was a beautiful animal, shiny grey with yellow spots. While its tail beat the deck, Harrison and Pearson discussed whether it should be thrown back or kept as a specimen. In the end it went into the ice box as a specimen. Looking at the box afterwards Pearson said, "I get emotional about fish. I just don't like to see them killed." He remarked that he didn't use a spear now, except to take a fish for eating, or in self-defence. "I used to indulge in a bit of spear fishing, but after a while I just sickened. One time I helped spear this great mound of fish. We couldn't eat them and we just had to go and bury them. I don't like killing things for no reason at all. I mean, fish – they can't sort of communicate with humans. Fish don't lie on the deck and make shrieking noises the way, say, monkeys would." As he moved off, looking moody, he said, "I don't like what they do to whales, either."

Kuranda now was approaching the jetty at Green Island, where I was going ashore. The boat was to stay at the jetty overnight, and next morning Harrison and Pearson and the divers were to leave for other reefs, where they were to repeat today's search for evidence on the activities of the crown-of-thorns in deep water. And they would again trail the dredge which today had remained empty of starfish.

Where *were* the starfish, the thousands of them that had eaten out Green Island's reefs? Had they travelled on to new coral gardens?

Were they in fact the starfish which were appearing in other sections of the Barrier Reef? Or were the starfish on other reefs locally bred? Or even migrants from some other area entirely? This was the sort of question still being asked more than two years after the beginning of the crown-of-thorns programme.

CHAPTER 3

On Tourism's Special Island

✷

Kuranda drew in to Green Island. I had visited the island for the first time ten years before, when it had seemed impossible for any place to be lovelier than the cool little jungle rimmed by hot white beach and domed and encircled in blue. Accommodation for visitors had been in simple cabins, and the island's sounds had been the slap of water on the reefs, the wind flinging about in the trees, and a conference of birds. A few weeks ago I had made another visit to the island, and found it changed into a sort of seagirt motel. The new atmosphere had announced itself as the tourist ferry idled to a stop at the jetty, and people rose to get off and found they couldn't, because nobody was putting down the gangways. The passengers were a captive audience for the man in striped shorts waiting on the jetty with a loud-hailer. The man raised the big grey trumpet and began to shout. Much of what he said blew away, but we caught phrases, exhortations, tributes to Green Island and the entertainments that had been arranged for us. "The attractions –" he shouted. "The wonders of –" but the breeze plucked at his words and tossed them out over the water. The rest of the message came in wind-blown fragments: "– Luncheon arrangements. Beautiful fish. Glass bottom. Nowhere else in the world. Underwater observatory. Also remind you. Colour slides, photographic requirements. Flash bulbs and. World famous wonder. Thank you." They were letting us off now, but still he hadn't finished with us. As we stepped on to the jetty he handed out leaflets about island entertainments headed AMAZING – ENCHANTING – UNIQUE.

Some of the visitors stopped to investigate the glass-bottomed boats waiting near the jetty; others turned off into the souvenir shop over the underwater observatory; the rest of us continued on through the white glare of the jetty's concrete towards the sand and greenery of the island. Over to the left, two boats set up a sudden speedboat roar and began to race. Below, under its shallow covering of water, the reef looked brown and dead. From the island, broken fences ran out over the sand into the water; these were groynes, installed apparently to control a threat of erosion which must long ago have been forgotten, since the wood had been allowed to rot away. Between the posts, which leant in many directions, much of the planking had disappeared. The groynes looked as desolate as the forgotten fences of a dustbowl – or they would have looked that way if it hadn't been for the irresistible glitter and blueness of the water, and the white sand, and the tossing green plumes of the palm trees. Now the jetty crossed the beach, leading us out of the glare into the green darkness of the trees. It was at this point that we encountered the music of Hawaiian guitars, piped through the palms, vibrating through the shade, yearning nasally over us as we turned again to read the notice which welcomed us to Green Island:

ANY PERSON FOUND CAMPING OR DISPOSING OF RUBBISH
ON THE ESPLANADE SHALL BE LIABLE TO PROSECUTION.
PENALTY NOT EXCEEDING $100. BY ORDER....

The shady area on to which the jetty had delivered us had the look of a well-trampled fairground featuring a multi-coloured exhibition building, the Coral Cay Hotel. There were picnic tables, and these too were multi-coloured. One group of visitors rested a food basket on a tabletop painted red, grey and yellow, and subsided on the red forms alongside it. Another group wandered off towards a seat painted yellow and red and blue. A palm with ripening coconuts on it grew out of the concrete path, and there was a wishing well with a grass-hut roof. When the guitars stopped a voice began to broadcast instructions which again blurred in the breeze. There was something about making your arrangements at the kiosk, and something about glass-bottomed boats and marineland. People began to scatter through the island or to queue at counters. I walked along by the hotel, past the liver-brick wall with yellow louvres and grey amplifier, past the red-floored verandah and the black-and-white tiled columns, and turned in by the cement patio where the chairs had aluminium frames, and seats and backs in yellow and green and red. There was a large upright soft-drinks dispenser bearing the message that things go better with Coke, and there was a display stand of souvenir corals, their greens and pinks and mauves and yellows gleaming through cellophane to create an impression of indigestible confectionery. They were not really corals, of course, but the painted skeletons of corals. There was no suggestion here of their beauty in life, when animals like flowers had bloomed on this gift-wrapped lime. Naturally enough the polyps had died when they were removed from the sea, and what was left was the skeleton they had lived in, the petrified cups arranged in shapes which suggested trees or branches or little boulders. Such skeletons would have their own considerable beauty as patterns in white lime, but no beauty at all when, as now, the patterns had been smothered under a coating of thick colour. People crowding around to buy these souvenirs of the Great Barrier Reef would be taking home proof that the famous coral looked like violently coloured cement. The display stand showed only a small part of the dead coral on sale; there was more behind a counter which extended for yards along the opposite wall. This counter also offered such items as plastic leis, toy koalas, sun hats and shells – shells made into ashtrays, earrings, necklaces, bracelets, sailing ships and ornaments which combined them with such items as black children smiling watermelon-slice smiles. At the end of the counter a few feet were given over to serving refreshments, and there I joined the queue. Ahead of me, a woman with an American voice asked her companion, "Is it what you expected?" There was a rather long pause, and then they both began to laugh, but tiredly. I drank a cup of tea, and as the juke box released a reverberating Beatles' announcement that they wanted to hold your hand I decided to return for a ride in a glass-bottomed boat.

Walking back along the jetty I could see visitors already beginning to wade out from the beach on to the reef flat. When the tide went lower, this accessible part of the reef would be covered with fossickers, turning over stones, poking their sticks at the interesting creatures underneath, even, every so often, picking one up for a closer look. Green Island had something of the order of 80,000 visitors every year, and the life of its reef flat had barely survived the enthusiasm of so many people to examine it. Walking on a reef meant walking on living organisms. It was rather as if the admirers of a terrestrial garden were to trample over the beds to get closer to the flowers, and then pulled up the plants to have a look at the roots. Some of the damage to this inner part of the reef would have come from the crown-of-thorns, but much more, according to the old hands, had come from the tourists innocently exploring it. And sadly few of these tourists would have much enjoyed the experience.

A walk across a reef flat can no doubt be a fascinating exercise for a marine scientist, knowledgeable about its complex and often very small organisms, but for the layman there is little that normally would not be more easily seen, and in a more spectacular form, from a glass-bottomed boat. The boat floats over the deeper water where the corals grow best and the fish congregate. The boat, too, has certain advantages of safety. Anyone who walks over a reef takes a number of risks. One is that he will crash through a thin roof of coral into the hole underneath and suffer cuts that are peculiarly resistant to healing. Coral cuts may itch and suppurate for weeks. Another risk is that he will encounter a stingray which, lying in the sand not interfering with anybody, will flick its barbed tail at the foot which disturbs it. From this wound, too, he may take a long time to recover.

And then if he is really unlucky, dead unlucky, he will step on the stonefish. How many of these lethal fish there are along the Great Barrier Reef is the subject of a good many arguments. These are necessarily inconclusive, because you can't count fish you can't see, and few people can see a stonefish even when they're told they are looking at one. I belong in this category. I have stared at three lumps of rock and sand and shellgrit, knowing one to be a stonefish, and have been unable to pick out the fish until it moved. Then I was able to make out the little eyes sunk behind the hair of weed, the frog mouth, the pitted, amorphous flesh. It was the sort of countenance an inspired make-up artist might achieve for a horror movie, and then voluntarily censor. When the fish changed its position and froze again I was again unable to separate it from the surrounding rocks. Small fish and crabs have much the same difficulty in discerning the camouflage, with the result that moving in too close they end up as a meal for the living stone. In this matter of spotting a stonefish the Aborigines are cleverer than either fish or white people. They have tribal ceremonies which pass on ancient warnings about the stonefish and the need to watch out for it. There are many stories of an Aboriginal unmasking a stonefish where a white man saw only rock. Aborigines maintain that stonefish are common on the reefs, so perhaps they are. At any moment a tourist fossicking amongst unmoving stones may be closer than he imagines to the thirteen venomous spines which this fish raises against anything threatening its blissfully inert way of life. If the fossicker has been warned against such hazards and happens to take them seriously, he will wear heavy boots (sandshoes are no protection against stonefish spines) and these boots will increase the damage he does by walking on the reef.

Near the jetty a glass-bottomed boat was filling up with passengers. I climbed in with perhaps twenty other people. We sat under an awning which, as well as protecting us from the sun, cut out the reflections of our heads as we leaned over the glass in the middle of the boat. Staring downwards, we floated out over water of palest blue with waves of sunlight in it. There was no coral yet, only sand. The clarity of the sea created an impression of shallowness, so that a creature like a huge black sausage lying in water perhaps thirty feet deep seemed to be only a fathom or so below the glass. On the sand nearby was another immense sausage, this one speckled and about a foot long. Both were varieties of beche-de-mer. In the eighteen-seventies Green Island had been a centre for fishermen exporting beche-de-mer to the East, where it was rated a delicacy. But the enterprise ran into staff trouble. As a labour force the Aborigines who collected the beche-de-mer and helped cure it were unpredictable; they burned two schooners, and before the venture lapsed had killed off at least seven whites. Under the glass-bottomed boat, the beche-de-mer disappeared. We were floating now above a clump of anemones with mauve and brown tentacles. And now we were over coral – but it was coral covered in a brown fuzz of algae. More coral, but this time grey and dead, lying in pieces on the bottom like a felled forest. We were drifting over the area which a diver had been employed to protect against the crown-of-thorns. Well, he had had some success, because here was a patch of blue staghorn. A forest of staghorn, its deep, soft blue appearing through the lighter blue of the sea, is one of the loveliest sights of the Reef. We caught something of this beauty as we looked down at the small area of staghorn which had survived the crown-of-thorns. But it passed too soon, and again under the glass there was devastation, a coral graveyard in which the broken skeletons lay on the bottom like heaps of bones. Then there was some more staghorn, green this time, its colour in the clear water seeming to have a springlike delicacy. Its beauty only increased the feeling of loss, the impression that we were floating over the memory of a coral garden. As we climbed back out of the boat on to the jetty, a man echoed the American women's disappointment – "It's not what I expected." Another said, "If that's their coral, then it's not worth bothering with the underwater observatory."

Yet it was. When I walked down the steps into the observatory, sunk in the water like a stationary submarine, I came on a view of reef life I would never forget. Beyond the portholes the pale blue sunlit water was in motion, and in the wide arc of its surge dozens of fish were swinging slowly backwards and forwards, each on its own invisible pendulum. No bird could have been more gorgeously marked than these animals, which must have ranked among the most beautiful in creation. They drifted slowly across the blue water, and then they drifted back, all facing in to the observatory as if to examine the creatures on show inside it. Floating out there in the surge were the shining blues and greens of the parrot fish, and the striped chiffon wings of butterfly cod. There were fish with iridescent spots, and lengthwise stripes, and around-the-body bands. There were black tails on silver fish, silver fish with yellow tails, bright pink fish, fish with lipsticked yellow mouths, small all-blue fish, striped yellow-and-brown fish with neon-blue eyes – all lazing there and swinging in this slow, wide surge. There was a great tranquillity which I had glimpsed before in these underwater scenes. Big fish ate little fish, without the option, but the mercilessness of the system was no more obtrusive here than on the land. This, too, was a beautiful world; the fish, too, could forget their predicament. Illuminated from above, the blue world of the sea looked as innocent and good as that sky on which Botticelli's angels danced. Relaxed in the ocean's rhythms, the fish seemed enchanted.

Below them, the poisonous tentacles of the giant anemones were tossing in the same protracted rhythms, and so were the tentacles of the small, daisylike coral polyps. Some corals feed only at night, but in these daisies – which were mauve or brown and about half an inch across – the petal-tentacles were moving, as if searching out the tiny planktonic animals which were their prey. The anemones and the corals were basically the same animal, except that the anemones did not deposit a lime cup in which to live; in both, the tentacles stung and paralysed the animals they caught. The specimens outside this observatory were part of what was virtually an artificial reef. The builders of the observatory had brought their exhibits from reefs for miles around and arranged them close to the portholes. Then they had stood guard over the corals during the onslaught of the crown-of-thorns. In Cairns I had met one of the observatory's builders, Vince Vlasoff, and he had described a night-and-day vigil to save this

5. Spanish dancer

6. Anemone fish – Great Barrier Reef

7. Heron Island

8. Common reef clam

collection. At night, his helpers had had to dive by torchlight to pick off the starfish.

Even so, a suggestion of the fate of the surrounding area had penetrated to the observatory's reef. A brownish fuzz coated some of the corals further back from the windows, and in places out there it looked as if someone had smothered a garden in sawdust. Nevertheless the view through the pale blue water remained one of astonishing beauty. Again and again the eyes came back to the tossing anemones, the animals whose name, from the Greek, means "daughter of the wind". They stood on fleshy trunks, and the long tentacles with which they were crowned were in some cases brown with purple tips and in others fawn with white tips. When the tentacles drooped around the trunks the animals turned into underwater willows. When the tentacles streamed out like hair in the wind the anemones were dancers, flinging their hair forward, then swinging it slowly to the side, then tossing it back, then flinging it forward again. This eurhythmic movement of the tentacles on the trunks of flesh was languorous, sinuous, with a suggestion about it not simply of hair but of serpent hair: Medusa dancing. Swimming in and out of the lethal tentacles, or floating just above them as they tossed, were the small bright anemone fish which were the exception to the rule that a fish within reach of these tentacles died. The anemone fish – one was orange with a black-outlined white stripe, another red with a blue stripe – were immune from attack by the anemones for no reason anybody could be sure of. One speculation was that they were tolerated because the fish-eating anemone valued them as bait, their presence being an encouragement to other fish to swim to their deaths in its tentacles. The advantage for the anemone fish in this arrangement, or so it was surmised, was that behind the tentacles it was safe from its enemies. Apparently each fish had immunity only from its own particular anemone and not from anemones in general. A fish knew its own anemone, and the evidence was that an anemone knew its own fish. If a fish blundered into the wrong anemone it was stung by the tentacles and presented to the mouth around which they were arranged. Nestling in its own anemone, though, the bright little anemone fish could look as contented as a lapdog.

Not far away, a velvety, purplish-black fish appeared to be seeking much the same sort of accord with a giant clam. The huge shell lay fully open to reveal a valley of mauve flesh with pinkish-white striations down the middle of it, and a siphon raised like a volcano cone opening and closing. The clam was probably feeding, taking in water, retaining microscopic plankton as food and expelling the residue. As the fish swam along just above the mantle of mauve flesh spread out over the shell, the mantle began to rise. The fish darted away. Did it sense a threat that the clam would shut? And would the clam in fact shut on such an intruder? Apparently not, because now the fish was back and swimming through the clam canyon. Nearby, another fish of the same species hovered over another open clam. No other type of fish seemed to attempt the swim.

When I climbed back out of this world of giant clams and tossing anemones and swinging fish it was to find myself once more amongst dead corals and empty shells. The way to the jetty led through a shop with a large display of souvenirs and especially of shells, each the memento of an animal removed from its place in the ecology of the reefs. Nobody could be quite sure about the ultimate results of this removal, but there were scientists who were pessimistic about it. Dr Endean ranked shell collecting as second only to the crown-of-thorns among the immediate threats to the Reef's survival. Shell collecting was banned in three small areas along the Reef – at Heron Island, Wistari Reef and here at Green Island – but the increasing scarcity of shells even in these areas seemed to indicate that it was little use banning the collection of shells while it remained legal to sell them. "Ban the whole trade? They couldn't," a government official had assured me. "Too many people are getting something out of it." Making coral and shell souvenirs was a cottage industry not only on the islands but on the coast running for hundreds of miles alongside them. Even as far south as Brisbane, miles below the point where the Reef ended, Barrier Reef shells were on sale by the bucketful. The fact that some of the shells being offered in the souvenir shops were said to have come from other parts of the Pacific was no comfort to people worrying about the future of the Great Barrier Reef, because there was a growing feeling that the Pacific reefs were all part of an inter-related system to which the Barrier Reef also belonged. Damage done to one reef might affect all the others.

One discovery supporting this suspicion was that the larvae of coral and some other species travelled back and forth across the Atlantic: might not this happen in the Pacific, too? The possible interconnection of the Pacific reefs had also been emphasized lately by the fact that the crown-of-thorns had begun to appear in overlarge numbers in other parts of the Pacific – at Fiji, for instance, and the Western Solomons and Guam. As the bell tolled in the Pacific, it began to seem that no island was an island, entire of itself; it was a part of the main. The alarm was to grow in the next few months, and by the middle of 1969 the United States Department of the Interior was to become concerned for the U.S. trust territories in the Pacific. One of the fears was that as the crown-of-thorns ate the polyps and the corals died, the edible fish which were part of a living coral reef would disappear, leaving the islanders without their chief protein food. The Department was reported to be organizing a crash programme of research into the crown-of-thorns. In this spreading crisis, Dr Endean continued to feel that his giant triton hypothesis was a useful one, arguing that the handsome shell of the starfish's enemy had been collected on these other affected reefs, too, by the tens of thousands. Certainly, shell collection was a lucrative business all around the Pacific, and whether or not it was directly responsible for the crown-of-thorns plague, there seemed to be plenty of grounds for banning it. The results of removing so many animals from their place in the reef system could not as yet be proved, but they could scarcely be good. The only brake on the trade in Australia had been applied after it had been realized that the giant triton was a predator on the crown-of-thorns. Then it had been declared illegal to collect the tritons. But the shops still sold them, presumably drawing on old stocks, and the main effect of protection seemed to be to give scarcity value to any shells that were left. I had inquired after a specimen on sale in Cairns and had been quoted eight dollars for it (later there were reports of thirty-five dollars as the going price for a giant triton). In front of this shop there was a "Shells Wanted" notice which amounted to an invitation to the public to gather shells and bring them in for sale.

The Barrier Reef's corals did have a degree of protection, in that only a licensed operator could legally collect them, and then only from an area defined in a lease. It might seem a reasonable enough policy, this of allowing coral to be taken from very limited areas in a vast chain of reefs, but as a coastal official had explained to me, the policy just couldn't be policed. "You might spot something that makes you suspicious," he said, "but you've got less than no chance of doing anything about it. You can go in to the shop and ask them where they got their coral, and they'll produce receipts for the purchase of that coral from a licensed source. But the question is, where did the licensed source get it? From a lease area? Not necessarily. They can take it from anywhere that's convenient, and then pass it off as having come from a lease. Say a man's on his way to his lease when he sees coral he knows will bring a good price. There's no one around to watch him, and there's no way anyone can tell afterwards where the coral came from. Does he leave that coral where it is? Or does he take it? Well, let's say if he's a fine, upright, old-fashioned gentleman he leaves it where it is."

In the shop over Green Island's underwater observatory coral was being sold in the usual cellophane-wrapped sprays and ornaments, but it was also being sold in a new and spectacular combination, with a bailer shell and electric globe as a TV lamp. The light glowed in the big, pinkish-fawn shell, and the painted coral skeleton added extra touches of colour. This bailer shell had once been collected by the Aborigines to bail out their canoes and store water. Now, fitted up as a lamp, it was on sale for between eleven dollars fifty and twelve dollars.

I walked back over the jetty to the island and then strolled along in the sunlight of the beach. Out on the edge of the reef, where the ocean ran up against the island's underwater wall of coral, a thin line of white spray divided the turquoise and mauve of the reef shallows from the blue of the deep water. Under my feet was the sharp pale sand containing fragments of coral. Coral was the basis of this whole island, which was a true cay – not a partly submerged mountain with a fringe of reef, but something that had developed on the reef itself as the coral debris built up on it, and the tides and winds and birds deposited plantlife. Amongst the broken coral pieces littering the beach I saw something that looked like a mushroom cap made of white stone. It was a perfect disc about four inches across, one side of it fluted with radiating ridges suggesting the underside of a mushroom. It was the skeleton of a *Fungia* or mushroom coral – a large polyp remarkable for the fact that instead of joining with other polyps to form a colony, it lives alone. At first it is attached to a stalk, and the structure which is to turn into the mushroom-like disc is a cup at the top of the stalk. Gradually this cup widens and flattens and then, with the polyp inside it, breaks off and drifts to a new location. The stalk it leaves behind proceeds to grow another cup which follows the same pattern of development. *Fungia*, with its many tentacles extended from its ridges, can be mistaken for an anemone. It illustrates a point not very clear in a number of other polyps, which is that the coral and the anemone are much the same animal. It is not particularly easy to see the resemblance between a polyp measuring, say, half an inch across, and having a daisy-like ring of small tentacles, and an anemone the size perhaps of a small plate, its long tentacles extended to give it something like the look of a cactus-dahlia. It is this cactus-dahlia look which, with its tentacles extended to cover its fluted base, the large mushroom polyp approximates. On occasion, an anemone will change its location, perhaps inching its way along on a basal disc, or floating off its rock and resettling. On this point, too, there is some resemblance in *Fungia*, with its ability to drift and slide and take up a new position – an ability not shared by polyps anchored in their colonies. It could have been no part of a mushroom polyp's plan of action, though, to end up on this beach and die of exposure, so the skeleton I was looking at must either have been washed in by a rough sea or dropped by a collector. It was in any event a most attractive form, displaying in its bleached and fluted disc a beauty unhinted at in the painted coral souvenirs.

As I walked along the sand I was aware of the exhilarating breeze, and then I was aware of the breeze dropping, and from somewhere along the edge of the beach, or perhaps from out in the blue-diamond glitter of the water, a rising smell of sewage. It carried a reminder of one of the difficulties of accommodating a mass human invasion of the Reef. An island such as this lacked even the fresh water required for an adequate septic tank system. On this little platter of coral and sand, approximately a mile in circumference, there now arrived each weekday a boatload of about two hundred and eighty visitors, with two boatloads on Sundays. In addition, seventy-five guests, plus staff, were accommodated at the hotel. All fresh water had to be brought from the mainland and was delivered each day by the tourist ferry. This meant that sea water had to be used in the septic system, though salinity inhibited the growth of the bacteria needed to reduce sewage to innocuous substances. Around Green Island, it seemed likely that inadequately treated wastes, piped out into the deeper water but carried back on the tide, were contributing to the difficulties being encountered by the local marine life.

The whole question of pollution of Reef waters was one more complex subject awaiting a research team. Exactly what was arriving from the coast in the way of sewage, insecticides and agricultural fertilisers was not known. In the wet season, though, the question tended to be dramatized by the arrival of the waterlilies. After the rains, trails of pink and white and mauve lilies from the swollen coastal rivers drifted out over the sea, regularly arriving at Green Island and other reefs. They came from green glass rivers which flowed past walls of wild hibiscus and shiny black-green jungle and, where the country had been cleared, past cane farms. These farms were users of persistent pesticides such as DDT. The quality which made DDT such a danger to wildlife – its failure to decompose and disappear – was what gave it its value to the sugar industry. As the cane grew the fields turned into small jungles, extremely hard to penetrate with sprays. What was needed was a pesticide which would last while the crop developed, and this was DDT. The torrents of the wet season scoured the sugar fields, flowed off into the rivers and sent them rushing out towards the reefs. The waterlilies made the distance. The question was, what else did? And even if pollutants did not carry as far as the reefs, but subsided nearer the coast, they could still affect Reef life. On the principle that big fish eat little fish and are in turn eaten, the DDT absorbed by small fish near an agricultural coastline could travel thousands of miles, transferred from predator to predator. It had even reached the Antarctic, where it had been found in animals such as penguins and seals. It did not seem unlikely, then, that it could reach out from the Queensland coast to the farthest ramparts of the Great Barrier Reef, and beyond.

In the complex whodunit which was the crown-of-thorns mystery, DDT was one of the suspects. There was a suggestion that it may have wiped out something which, say, had preyed on the starfish's eggs or larvae. The effects of DDT could escape notice for some time, since it did not necessarily produce big fish kills, but might simply lead to sterility. Eventually the failure to reproduce, which had been observed in fish affected by DDT in other areas, would just as certainly wipe out a species as a direct kill, and would thus wipe out a population control over the animals on which that type of fish had preyed. Much the same indirect extermination might result from the presence of sewage or agricultural fertilisers in the sea. At first their nutrients might seem positively good for the water, encouraging growths of algae capable of feeding more animals than ever before. But naturally these animals would have to be of a type able to feed on the new algae; animals seeking other food which would no longer grow would disappear, with unknown consequences. When Professor L. C. Birch, head of the School of Biological Sciences at the University of Sydney, suggested that pollution should be looked at as a possible cause of the crown-of-thorns plague, he mentioned the wastes which entered Reef waters via rivers polluted by the sugar mills and other industries. He also mentioned the proliferation of sea urchins near sewer outlets on the U.S. Pacific coast. The first sign of trouble there had been the disappearance of giant kelp beds, originally blamed directly on the presence of the sewage. Then a study revealed that the kelp beds were being destroyed by sea urchins, and that it was these which were being affected by the sewage. They were thriving, multiplying. And the sea urchin, as Professor Birch pointed out, belonged to the same echinoderm family as the crown-of-thorns starfish.

The smell of sewage decided me to turn in off the beach. Ahead of me, the white shadow of a heron slipped into a low palm. My feet sank in leaves aged to pale yellows and dry browns. The sky was green, clouded over with leaves and palm fronds, and from it vines dropped in thin verticals to the leaf-covered ground. At points around the shadowed greenness there were glowing panels of light, gothic spaces framing the sun. There was the uh-*hmm*, uh-*hmm* of pigeons. And then there were people calling, and a transistor radio's sung shouts for love. Unseen, the visitors passed beyond a screen of palms. A blue-and-black butterfly rose and swooped off in another direction, and I followed it. The ground began to have a littered look. There was a scatter of broken-off branches, so dry they must have fallen some while ago. The paradisial atmosphere into which I had first stepped faded. Now the forest seemed as if invaders had passed through it, leaving behind a trail of broken branches, a dump of old iron, empty bottles. When I turned outwards to the beach again I came on the groynes, the gap-tooth fences spreading their rotting wood and leaning verticals in crazy barricades against the sea. Lying between them, compounding the dustbowl look, were long-fallen trees, their roots and branches clawing out of the sand.

There was another Green Island, and I decided to retreat to it. It existed in the memory of Noel Monkman, who first landed on the uninhabited cay in 1929, and now lived just out of juke-box range of its Coral Cay Hotel. For much of the intervening four decades he had worked along the Great Barrier Reef. He had given up a career as a musician to pioneer the underwater photography of the Reef. Some of his sequences had been used in Hollywood's film of *The Sea Around Us*. He had also become the author of popular books about the Reef and his own life; a specialist in the use of the microscope; and a photographer of microscopic marine organisms. On evidence drawn from observations with the microscope he had evolved yet another theory about the cause of the crown-of-thorns plague, a phenomenon which, he insisted, had nothing to do with the disappearance of the giant triton. In particular he had engaged public attention lately as a conservationist, emerging as the northern sentinel of the forces opposed to the exploitation of the Reef. I had seen one of the warnings Monkman had passed down the coast – a letter to other conservationists about the oil drilling going on in the Capricorn Channel near the Swain Reefs. In this letter Monkman had urged his view that the public was unaware of the Reef's danger, and of the fact that there could be an accidental oil spillage which could ruin a series o reefs.

It would seem fair to say at this point that if Australians in general were unaware of the oil companies' activities, it was not because the oil companies had misinformed them. Rather it was because for a long time it simply did not occur to people to think the unthinkable, that their government was allowing an oil search along the Great Barrier Reef; and when they did come to think that, they put their questions to politicians and government authorities, and received from them answers requiring a degree of skilled interpretation. For example, more than twelve months after the drillings in the vicinity of the Swain Reefs the Deputy Premier of Queensland could say, "I am pledged to protect at all times the wonders of the Barrier Reef ... I will not be a party to any drilling either on or close to the Reef that could endanger its preservation." Anybody interpreting this statement would need to know that the important words were the last five, and to be aware that in the government's view such drilling would *not* endanger the Reef's preservation. The government held to this view even after the Santa Barbara catastrophe, off California, when escaping oil spilled out over four hundred square miles of sea, fouling beaches, killing sea birds, and exterminating marine life in depth, from surface swimmers to the bottom dwellers buried under sinking, emulsified oil. The Queensland government remained certain that such destruction could never spread through the miraculous gardens of the Great Barrier Reef because the local explorers had undertaken to be careful. The explorers themselves seemed to take a rather more reserved view of the risks. An official of the Australian subsidiary of the giant U.S. corporation, Gulf Oil, emphasized to me that his company took every conceivable precaution against an accident, but added that he was puzzled by a demand in the Queensland parliament for an assurance that there would absolutely never be a blowout in Reef waters. How could anyone give such an undertaking? "You cannot guarantee that," he said, "any more than an airline can guarantee that a plane will never fall. It's one of the risks."

The confusion reached its height before the state elections of May, 1969, when the Leader of the Opposition (John W. Houston) alleged that the Queensland Premier (Johannes Bjelke-Petersen) had made a fortune out of dealings in oil shares, and had acquired half a million shares in a company controlling Exoil No Liability, one of the firms preparing to operate in Reef waters. Since the Premier had taken office, the Opposition leader said, Exoil had applied for a valuable offshore oil-drilling authority. He believed the Premier's shareholding would make it impossible for him and his cabinet to make an impartial decision on such a matter. In reply, the Premier did not deny an interest in oil, although he did deny there was anything improper in it. He spoke of himself as a pioneer of Australia's oil search. He saw no reason, he said, to sell his Exoil shares; being merely a shareholder and not a director, he did not influence the company's affairs, and as Premier he did not deal with applications for offshore leases. As the election campaign proceeded, the question of who held oil rights in Reef waters was obscured by rhetoric. It was often said that there had been no drilling on the Reef, a statement which rather went around the fact that there had been drilling *in the waters of* the Reef (by Gulf Oil, for example) and that there could be no graver threat to the life of the reefs than pollution of the waters which circulated around and over them. It was even said that there were no oil leases at all along the Reef, a statement which seemed to mean that by the government's definition a lease was something issued after oil had been discovered, and oil had not yet been discovered. It was being searched for by companies holding either an Authority to Prospect, or a Petroleum Exploration Permit (Offshore) – terms used at different periods for much the same thing, permission to search for oil. Defenders of these permits sometimes argued that they conferred no right on the companies holding them to extract any oil they might discover (which could only mean that the explorers were spending fortunes looking for oil they had no expectation of acquiring). Yet when the Opposition said that if it were returned to power it would withdraw every lease, or permit, or authority to drill or explore along the Barrier Reef, the government dismissed the possibility of such an action. Queensland was pictured as involved in a sort of breach-of-promise case; repudiation, it was said, would mean the State government could be sued for millions of dollars' compensation. The government was returned to power (in what a number of political commentators regarded as a gerrymander, the Opposition winning more votes but fourteen fewer seats) and proceeded to interpret its victory as a mandate for its policy on the Great Barrier Reef. It was announced that later in 1969, Japex, the Australian subsidiary of Japan Petroleum Exploration Company, would drill in Reef waters. The government's statements that the Reef was in absolutely no danger continued, and in general the public found the arguments very hard to follow.

Certain of the scientists, though, had been for some time reasonably well informed about oil exploration. For example, in its trips over the waters of the Great Barrier Reef, Gulf Oil's survey plane on occasion carried Peter Woodhead, the Scientific Director of the Heron Island Research Station (operated by the Great Barrier Reef Committee). The Scientific Director was interested in tracing the currents in the southern section of the Great Barrier Reef, and the oil executives were also interested in the currents, mainly because they wanted to know where any escaping oil would be likely to end up. Gulf Oil paid for the manufacture of plastic drifters (the journey made by each drifter through the sea would provide information about the patterns of the currents) and then its plane dropped them over fourteen thousand square miles of Reef waters. Each drifter carried a numbered tag asking the finder to return it, with the place and date found, to Australian Gulf Oil: reward, fifty cents. The company looked after the clerical

work and the reward-paying, while the Scientific Director concen-
trated on analysing the results. The oil interests also gave help to
W. G. H. Maxwell, of the University of Sydney's Geology Department,
in preparing his important *Atlas of the Great Barrier Reef*.* The atlas,
which appeared early in 1969, included in its acknowledgments a
note that "from 1965 extremely generous support has been received
from the American Petroleum Institute, and the Petroleum Research
Fund of the American Chemical Society". As one oil man said to me,
"We're interested in any kind of research on currents, sea bottoms,
coral reefs, because they're all part of processes that have gone on in
the geological past". Some of the biologists were distrustful of the
geologists, suspecting that they regarded the living coral primarily as
something standing between them and the most exciting geological
possibilities. Even the biologists, though, could look with a kind of
fascination at the work of the oil explorers. When Gulf Oil drilled, it
brought up materials from great depths – materials which were
indicative of the pre-history of the Reef and which the scientists could
obtain in no other way. Full reports on the results of the drillings were
lodged with the University of Queensland. The word for scientist
derives from the Latin *scire*, to know. The oil explorers catered for the
need to know.

On the outside of all this, the conservationists as late as 1968 were
struggling to piece together bits of news about operations on the Reef.
Their main difficulty was in working out just what was taking place
where in the huge areas of reef and ocean covered by the oil search.
One official counter to their expressions of alarm was that any
companies which might be at work were only exploring. Surely, the
conservationists reasoned, the explorers couldn't be certain they had
found oil unless they drilled, and once they drilled they had brought
the Great Barrier Reef to the edge of an oil-spillage disaster. And then
there was the preliminary survey work. Few people realized that prior
to the Gulf Oil drillings in the Capricorn Channel there had been a
survey of a type which, in other parts of the world, had been blamed
for damage to marine life. Even the Queensland State Mining
Engineer, I. W. Morley, an advocate of oil exploration, said that the
explosives used in such surveys killed marine life and should perhaps
be banned. However, his observation came long after completion of
the Capricorn Channel-Swain Reefs survey, with its four months of

* Elsevier Publishing Company, Amsterdam, London and New York.

daylight-to-dark blasting and its aim of one explosion every ten minutes. The survey was an operation of the type in which technicians deduce the possibility of oil being present under the sea by using a method related to the measuring of earthquake shocks with a seismograph. They create a series of small earthquakes on or near the surface of the water, either with dynamite or electric spark explosions. The shock waves travel down through the seabed and are reflected back by the various layers in the rocks. From the time it takes for the sound waves to travel down and reflect back the scientists can map the configuration of under sea rocks. If this map indicates a structure which is likely to contain oil, then the next step is to drill. This was the type of survey which took place before the two wells were drilled in this southern area of the Great Barrier Reef. During preliminary air surveys Gulf Oil had to make its own charts of the Swain Reefs, a maze of coral and sandbanks best known in the past to the gannets and terns and frigate birds, and to the migrants which each year fly down thousands of miles out of the northern winter.

During the four months the ships worked on the seismic survey – beginning at first light and ending at dusk – the waters of the Great Barrier Reef constantly exploded into the high fountains which marked a marine disturbance. Both electric spark and dynamite charges were used (sometimes as much as thirty pounds of dynamite at a time) and the results compared. The aim was to explode a charge every ten minutes. It was only after this procedure had been completed that the drilling began. As the drills probed for oil, the risk was not primarily that it would escape but that it would be found at all. An oil discovery would almost certainly transform a marine fastness into a tanker base, a place of man-made Meccano-set islands, an outpost of that empire of fuels and petrochemicals which had already changed the earth and was now moving into the sea. If oil were to be discovered at one point, other exploratory wells would be drilled. The results would help the technicians decide the quantity of oil and gas down below, and the number of wells needed to drain the reservoir. That number, which might be ten, say, or might be fifteen, would then be drilled. The slight but real threat of an oil escape would then be multiplied by ten, or fifteen. The oil might be taken from the wells to tanks on platforms, and from there sent ashore through an underwater pipeline. But in an area far from shore – and the Swain Reefs are more than a hundred miles from the mainland – the oil would probably be stored in a huge tanker permanently anchored near the wells and connected to them. This would act as a mother ship, feeding smaller tankers which would deliver the oil to various Australian ports. Each tanker would multiply the risk already existing, the risk that oil ships making deliveries to Queensland ports would be wrecked in Reef waters, full of hard-to-chart coral formations and subject to cyclones.

After the drilling of the wells near the Swain Reefs it was around twelve months before the public heard about some other risks inherent in the operation. The message came in a letter to Brisbane's *Sunday Truth* from Louis Salzman, an engineer who had worked on the Swain Reefs drillings and had then gone on to Santa Barbara. Salzman had heard that the Queensland State Mining Engineer, I. W. Morley, had stated that the Santa Barbara oil leakage had not affected marine life, and he felt impelled to warn Australians about the destruction he had witnessed. "As the Santa Barbara area deteriorates, marine life dies, and birds struggle for life," he wrote, "I keep thinking that the same thing could have happened while we were working on the *E. W. Thornton*." (This was the drilling rig used by Australian Gulf Oil near the Swains. Drilling began in November, 1967 and finished in March, 1968. In other words, despite the assurances that every possible care would be taken, drilling took place within that November–April period which is the most dangerous time of the year on the Reef, the cyclone season.) "Time after time," Salzman wrote, "bad weather caused breakdowns that would have caused oil spills if we had struck oil. . . . As it was, thousands of gallons of drilling mud were released into the water, and all kinds of scrap was dropped overboard during the drilling operation." He sent along the clipping of a Santa Barbara editorial which said, "The people of Santa Barbara have learned one thing: bland assurances are not enough to keep an oil catastrophe from happening". As it turned out, the drilling near the Swains did not yield oil. The company was not discouraged, though, and planned more surveys. It would be ready to drill again, perhaps, in 1970. Back in 1968, when news of the drillings came to Monkman on Green Island, he sent his warnings south, to the conservationists whose campaign against the oil operations was then gathering force. Meanwhile his own campaign for the Reef continued. He was well known in Australia, not only for his books and films but as a personality, and his ability to generate public emotion on behalf of the Reef had become a factor to be included in any calculation of its chances of survival.

It was Monkman's wife, Kitty, who saw me as I walked in off the tourist track in the direction of their timber house. Smiling, her bobbed grey hair bouncing like a schoolgirl's, she raced through the tree-shadows and hugged me. Then she said in that strong, warm voice which ought to have belonged to someone far more substantial-looking – she couldn't have been five feet high – "Noel hasn't been well again. He mustn't get tired. If he wants to talk too much, stop him." I stared down at her, and then we both began to laugh, in recognition of the unlikelihood of anybody being able to stop her husband talking if he felt like talking. Monkman was known the length of the Reef and beyond for his talk. He was by way of being the raconteur of the Reef. Smothering her mirth Kitty said, "But really, we must do what we can," and walking towards the house with her I agreed. I had heard that Monkman's heart condition was serious enough to stop him diving, and from previous meetings with him and knowledge of his love of being under the sea I knew that this must mean it was serious indeed. Kitty, on the other hand, looked fine. There was something in the way this small, brisk woman stood guard over Monkman which suggested a strong and loving daughter managing a temperamental father, and so it was rather easy to forget that she was in fact four years older than her husband, who was seventy-two.

As we walked into the small front room with the louvred windows Monkman rose, his big body seeming to fill up any space left over by the upright piano. He greeted me, looked out through the door at the crowded island, and then turned his back on it. Sitting down again he said, "I am really an Elizabethan." It did not seem an unlikely statement. He looked Elizabethan, with his domed forehead, his aggressively pointed white beard, his flourish of white moustache and his quiet and melancholy eyes. As the voices came to us of people going by on the tourist path, he said, "It was the perfect coral island. Coconut palms, reef, birds. And nothing else."

"And the corals –" Kitty said. Together, then, they began to conjure up for me the Green Island reef – the brown, denuded reef on which the visitors were at this moment fossicking – as it had been almost forty years ago, when they had first seen it in 1929. At low tide, they said, the corals had stood up out of the water, the way they still do in the travel posters. In the reef flat there had been little pools full of corals and fish, and you would find you had been standing over one pool for an hour, unmoving. "Further out," Monkman said, "there was an immense area of blue staghorn coral. I could never pass it without diving down to get closer to it. But that's gone now, because the crown-of-thorns went for it. And of course the other corals have gone because so many people have walked on them, and smashed them, and taken pieces away.

"To preserve anything at all," he said, "you have to fight so many people. I've been an honorary fisheries inspector for twenty-five years – I'm also a flora and fauna protector – and I've found that everyone who comes here thinks they're entitled to take something away. '*One little piece of coral*,' they'll say – over and over again you'll hear it – '*just one little piece. I only want this one little piece* to take home and show the family.' I say to them, 'First of all it will be dead long before you get home. You'll only arrive with the skeleton. And also,' I say, 'there are tens of thousands of tourists come to this reef every year. That means tens of thousands of people take one little piece. Just look at the reef that's left. Besides, you're stealing. You're a thief. It doesn't belong to you, it –' "

"Now Noel," Kitty said.

"– it doesn't belong to any living person. It doesn't belong to our unborn children. None of us own it. We're only privileged to see it. *Not* to take it away, *not* to sell it. We're caretakers, and that's all.

"And then," he said, refusing to catch Kitty's eye, "there was that bastard with the whole boatload of coral. That was in the days before we had the telephone here. I sent a wireless message to the mainland: 'Nab this fellow when he comes in, he's got a load of coral'. But when he got there he had none. Next time I saw him he laughed at me. 'You didn't get me,' he said. 'No,' I said, 'what happened?' He said, 'I listened in and picked up the message. I got rid of the stuff before I got there'. Well, that fellow is still on the job. He has a big trawler now – then he had only a small one. Now he trawls for shells. Trawls between the reefs on the sandy bottom, where a great many of the shells are. He brings up everything that's down there. And he makes a lot of money. The only thing to do," Monkman said, "is put an absolute stop to the sale of all shells and all coral. The shops could be given three months to sell their stocks, and then – finish. After that, a very, very heavy fine for anybody caught dealing in these things. Because look, I'll give you an example of what happens. There is a unique shell on Heron called the Heron Island Volute. You've heard of it?" I had. Another name for it was the Beautiful Volute. Which was a strange name, since all the volutes are beautiful. The whole family is celebrated. For the design of their markings, for their colour and polish, its members have been called the nobles among shells. Yet even in this company the small Heron Island volute, with its cream and pink and black markings, shines out. It is a Beautiful Volute. "That volute," Monkman said, "is a very easy shell to collect. Or it was – it's almost extinct now. As the tide starts to wash in, the volute comes up out of the sand and lies there, just waiting to be picked up. I tried once to protect it. There was a fishing boat at Heron Island that I'd been told came there regularly to collect the volutes – though Heron is one of the few places where people aren't supposed to take shells. The boat belonged to a fishing family, two young men in their early twenties plus Mother. Well, I found the deck of their boat covered with these volutes. While I was talking to the sons, Mother came back with two sugarbags full of the shells. I said to her, 'You know, these shells are unique, and the reef has been almost stripped of them. If you go on like this, there'll be no Heron Island Volutes left'. And you know what she replied? 'That'll be good. We've got big stocks at home, and if there were none left we could push up the price to ten times what we're getting now.' At that I just gathered up the shells and said they were going back on the reef. I told them I was an honorary fisheries inspector and I was reporting them. But –" he shrugged – "the fine wasn't much, and people like that just regarded it as part of their expenses. The Heron Island Volutes were practically wiped out.

"And then once we were down south on an island about fifty miles out from the mainland. I said, 'My God, Kitty, somebody's been here collecting coral. Huge patches of this reef that were good last time we were here are gone'. Soon afterwards I caught sight of some boilers, and got the faint smell from them – they'd been used for boiling coral. That's what these people do, they boil the coral in weak caustic soda to get the animal out, and then they rinse it in the sea and put the skeleton in the sun to bleach. An uninhabited island like this one was an ideal place to work. Fifty miles out from the mainland, who's to see them? I heard afterwards who this man was, and he was making a fortune. He was taking packing cases full of coral from lonely reefs. But you'd never get evidence. And anyway he was a nice fellow, like so many of them, and I wouldn't have liked to have had to put him in. But that's why I say," Monkman said vehemently, "that they've got to stop this trade altogether, so there's nowhere to *sell* their damned coral and shells."

Kitty was frowning. Obviously she didn't much care for the emotional exertion involved in this sort of reminiscence. So I asked Noel how it had felt, in the days when still so few people had ventured undersea, to explore a coral reef. Monkman began to smile. The anger had passed, but now there was another sort of emotion. "My God, the beauty," he said. He looked as if he were seeing the beauty again. "You were underwater, so you couldn't shout for joy. But you wanted to, at the wonder of it. That *gorgeous* blue world! The first time for me, though, wasn't here – it was in Tahiti, when I was on my way back from the First World War. That was where I was given my first underwater goggles, carved out of coconut shells by the Tahitians. I had been swimming under the sea since I was five – I was born in New Zealand, and a Maori boy taught me – but I'd only had that dim vision you always get when you try to keep your eyes open undersea. Then the Tahitians gave me these goggles they'd made from coconuts. They'd put glass in them, and you tied them on and they enclosed the eyes. That was the first time I really *saw* underwater. It was an ecstasy – I can't describe the joy. I knew it was where I belonged."

Nevertheless between this recognition and his arrival on the Great Barrier Reef there was for Monkman almost a decade of doing other things. Back in New Zealand he worked as a theatre musician, and later he did the same sort of job in Australia. During Pavlova's visit to Melbourne he played the cello in the cello-and-harp accompaniment to her dance of the dying swan. "She floated. Floated," he said. His eyes had the same expression as when they had looked back on Tahiti. "You think of all the beauty in your life, all the beauty," he said, "and so little of it you can hold."

"Oh Noel," Kitty said, "you've held on to a great deal." She smiled to soften the no-nonsense tone with which she was striving to guard his heart against its own emotions.

Monkman was talking now about the bad times when he had had to play the pops of the late twenties in the movie theatres. He had even had to sing (his tone inferred he still didn't quite believe this himself).

He never knew the words, and he had managed such items as the Pagan Love Song by singing them through a megaphone with the words pasted on it. "Almost put me on the grog," he said. But he was saved by the revival of a childhood interest in the microscope, and by his wife's encouragement to extend the interest. He began to photograph the world his microscope revealed, and a Sydney newspaper wrote up his work. It was the beginning of a switch both to the microscope and the camera as a means of livelihood. Soon afterwards he and Kitty came to the Great Barrier Reef to make films. There was a good deal that was experimental in this early undersea work. Monkman had a diving helmet made which he called the Ned Kelly, because it was shaped like the head armour worn by the Australian bushranger. It was a cube of galvanized iron with a windowpane in front, a flat top, and an air hose connected to the side of it. It worked, as Monkman said, on "Kitty-power". "We had one of those old-fashioned motor-car pumps that used to screw on to running boards – two cylinders with a handle – and you rocked it backwards and forwards to pump up a tyre. Kitty used to sit up there in the dinghy pumping. As the air got short down below I'd know her arms were giving out." Kitty was the mate every diver must have. She never dived herself. As well as pumping, she watched for sharks. She had a stick with a leather flap on it and if she saw a fin she would flap on the water. "The signal down below was almost as if somebody had touched you," Monkman said. Forewarned he would round on the shark, which always went off without attacking.

"I've never used a speargun in my life," he said, "and I've done a lot of talking to spear-fishermen to get them to leave their guns and take cameras down instead. I've had a good deal of success, too. After all, what justifies the feeling that because you've crossed into another world you're entitled to start killing the inhabitants? Down there, you're a privileged visitor. Some of these fellows, of course, aren't interested in anything but hunting. Often they're showing off. Or there's a girl somewhere and it's a case of 'Me Tarzan – me *underwater* Tarzan – me Tarzan bring Jane big fish'." He didn't say "bah!" but he looked as if he had.

The early cameras with which he had gone armed underwater had to be hand-cranked, a process involving much the same effort to overcome water resistance as swimming. He put in a lot of practice to acquire the rhythm of turning the handle so that a steady twenty-four frames a second went through the camera, no matter what in the way of a shark or a giant groper might be swimming into the picture. "It had to be automatic," he said. "You just had to be able to turn at twenty-four frames a second without looking at a dial." For steadiness, the camera rested on a tripod. Later on, with a camera which didn't have to be cranked, and an aqualung, he gained mobility. He mounted the camera on wooden wings, so that he got a steady picture as he piloted the camera through the water like a plane. Flippered feet kicking, he could make the camera dive and circle and bank to get the views he needed of his subjects. Gradually his films won recognition, and some of his sequences were bought for other people's films, such as Hollywood's "The Sea Around Us".

In search of material he and Kitty travelled all over the Reef. On North West Island, in the southern part of the Reef, he found a horrific sequence which he could never bring himself to photograph in any detail. Frequently he had to put down his camera to rescue his subjects, newly hatched turtles. "Those little turtles would pour out of the sand, a hundred or so of them, and struggle down towards the sea. But first there would be the crabs waiting to tear them to pieces. You'd see a crab get hold of a baby turtle by the neck and tail and hold it like a guitar – reminded you of a pop singer – as it ran away down the beach with it. Then the gulls would swoop and grab the turtles just as they were racing into the water. And the ones that actually got out into the water – well, the fish were waiting for those. Every sort of reef fish, waiting for a feed. After all that. It was just too much for me. There was a tub there, so I used to put the little turtles in it and take them right out to the end of the reef, beyond the gulls and crabs and fish, and empty them out into the deep water. Gave them a chance." Apologetic, he added, "It was wrong, of course. It was interfering with the balance of nature, and so forth. But I couldn't take it. The turtles were so helpless. I've seen bitter tragedies in the sea, but somehow that was the one I couldn't stand." Rising, he said, "I'm going to get us a drink." Kitty was sitting near the piano and as he went by he said, "Play us something."

"Every night here once," Kitty told me, "I used to play dinner music. But now we watch TV." Sitting down at the piano she said, "Perhaps Brahms – ? Yes," and began to play. She was the daughter of a Russian father and a Polish mother, and her name was not really Kitty but Getela. Before her marriage to Monkman and the Reef she had been a professional pianist. Something of all this was now asserted in the firm and passionate music with which she filled the small room on Green Island. Coming back with the drinks, Monkman listened. In a few months' time – after 29 May, 1969, to be exact – he would no longer be alive, and his expression now was that of a man turning over the thought that he hadn't much left of life. When the music ended he murmured wonderingly, "All that beauty, eh?" Then, shaking his head, as if to rid himself of this melancholy, he began to remember the beauty which had opened to him under the microscope, and his joy the first time he had seen the magnificent structures in very small marine organisms. The feeling with which he recalled the experience reminded me again that he was, in a way, the embodiment of all that the anti-conservationists deplored, of that emotion they were always warning against. The future of the Reef, they urged, should be discussed without emotion, and in this they set an example. Monkman, on the other hand, would keep bringing in feeling, would keep indulging this uninhibited sense of the marvellous and trying to plant it in other people. Looking back now on the world revealed to him by the microscope and his first explorations of it he found himself surprised, stopped, by the force of his emotion. ("Still," he said, recovering, "Elizabethan man wasn't ashamed to feel. Was he?") The microscope's fascination for him had scarcely been less than that of the sea. In studying and photographing microscopic marine organisms, he had brought his two worlds together.

It was from his microscope that he had obtained the evidence for his own theory about the cause of the crown-of-thorns plague. His suspect was the sardine – or rather, the millions of sardines which, he believed, had once acted as a control on the starfish by eating great quantities of its eggs. There had never been enough of the giant tritons to act as a control, he believed. Under the microscope, eggs which he had found in the gut of local sardines had been revealed as identical with the eggs of the crown-of-thorns starfish, and this was the basis of his theory. The population explosion, he argued, derived from the fact that large numbers of sardines had been netted, and that shoals of them had been driven away from Green Island by the noise of the piledriver used to build the jetty. In the absence of the sardines, the eggs they would have eaten survived to form the basis of the plague now spreading through the Reef, and perhaps beyond it. Each female starfish produced between twelve and twenty-four million eggs; without the sardines to dispose of them, untold numbers of eggs could have escaped in one season. Monkman had explained this theory by letter to the government authorities down in Brisbane, and in reply, he said, had been told that it was felt he could not have any proof that the eggs in the sardine gut were crown-of-thorns eggs rather than one of the many other types from which they would be virtually indistinguishable. After reporting this opinion Monkman stroked his pointed beard rather rapidly and laughed. He had no university degree to back his theories, but on the other hand his work with the microscope had made him a Fellow of the Royal Microscopical Society. The microscope, he maintained, was an instrument which many scientists regarded as a glorified magnifying glass, whereas it was an instrument to be learned as one learned the cello, through practice, practice, practice. Monkman had no doubt of his ability to tell crown-of-thorns' eggs when he saw them.

"So I got in touch with the then fisheries inspector in Cairns," he said, "and asked him to come over and look at the evidence. When he got here I said, 'Right. Here's a scalpel, and here's your crown-of-thorns starfish. Cut it open down here and you'll find its eggs'. He did that. 'Now,' I said, 'go and get some sardines – there's a small shoal back out there.' So he went and collected some sardines. I said, 'Good, now pick up one of the sardines, cut it, and inside the gut you'll find some eggs mixed up with the other plankton it has eaten.' " When the fisheries inspector had done that and had found the eggs, Monkman asked him to examine them for himself under the microscope along with the eggs extracted from the crown-of-thorns. "He found that the two lots of eggs were identical," Monkman said. "He said to me, 'The guts of these fish are packed with the eggs of the crown-of-thorns'. 'Yes,' I said, 'and so will you now inform your people down in Brisbane?' Well, he wrote. But nothing happened."

If sardines and another small fish, the hardyhead, were the main natural control on the crown-of-thorns population, as Monkman was convinced they were, then the next step would be to stop the practice of netting them. Although the marine life around Green Island was protected by law, the exact meaning of this protection was hazy. Visitors wanting to catch the beautiful reef fish were not thwarted. The fish were said to be protected, yet fishing was permitted by handline (with not more than two hooks) and by rod and line. The speargun was outlawed, but the use of nets was permitted to make hauls of bait. It was not only tourists who netted the sardines; it was also the commercial fishermen, Monkman asserted, and the commercial fishermen not only took bait for their own needs but to sell by the bucketful on the coast. Monkman launched a campaign against the netting which included statements to the press and letters to government departments ("I'm a nuisance," he told me joyfully. "I'm an absolute pest.") Eventually, he said, a high bureaucrat up from Brisbane came and talked to him. "This man said, 'Look, Mr Monkman, you're causing a great deal of trouble'. I said to him, 'Your department is causing a great deal of trouble – the Reef is being destroyed'. He said, 'You want a ban on all netting of sardines, and that's impossible. Now look, to start with, the professional fishermen would be sore as a boil. They get their bait here quick and easy. And they and their wives, and their children, and their friends, they all have votes. And then there are the amateur fishermen – and you know how many of those there are. Now that there are all these speedboats around, they can get over here in an hour and net their bait and be on their way. And they've got votes, too, and so have their families. Look at all those votes, will you, Mr Monkman, and then think: you've got one'. Well," said Monkman, "so much for the sardines."

Beyond the louvres the light was softer. Now that the afternoon boat had left for Cairns there was a quietness, and you could hear the throaty purring of the pigeons. Monkman began to talk about the Reef, digging into the lore he had gathered over almost forty years. Take the hermit crabs, he said. Fascinating. Once he had seen a fight between two hermit crabs go on for three days. These crabs have tender abdomens which they protect by taking up residence in a univalve mollusc shell. Since the shell doesn't grow with them, they have to keep finding a new and larger shell, and sometimes they have to fight for it. In this three-day fight the attacker tried every possible way of digging out the resident crab, including pulling off its claws, but the crab in possession stayed on, its delicate abdomen safely encased in the shell. Eventually the attacker, having failed to beat it, joined it – it climbed into the shell and rammed the other down to the bottom. These same crabs, Monkman said, wear a small anemone on the shell, and when they change shells they take the anemone with them. "I've seen them do that," he said. "Very delicately, with their claws, they transfer the anemone to the new shell." And then there were the ghost crabs which –

Somebody passing called, "Hi, Noel," and Monkman said, "Oh Chuck, come on in". The man who came in was in his thirties, spare, dark-haired, his skin a polished tan. This was Chuck Jackson, Monkman said. He worked as crew on a charter boat. Jackson said he was a bit tired at the moment, and laughed apologetically as he put his hand over a yawn. Nearly everybody you met here was on holiday, he said, and it was easy to get caught up. He had been working along the Great Barrier Reef for the past seven years. He came from the Hebrides, and had lived in Canada, Iraq and Brazil. Like so many people who had at last found these islands, he had been willing to take any sort of job just to stay here. He had worked as a diver, a handyman, a cook. Now he was a hand on a charter boat, going away for a couple of weeks at a time with big-game fishermen or prospecting parties. The next trip would be with a group of geologists wanting to explore the north. It was a fine life. Still, for people who had to earn a living the Reef was not an unflawed paradise. There was the risk of the alcoholism that got so many of the men who worked on the islands and handed their wages back over the bar. Among these men there was a fair percentage of loners, individualists, wanderers with wives and children or divorces somewhere years behind them in another place. Here they lived in an almost continuous party atmosphere. His own greatest enjoyment was probably when the charter boat went on a trip through the lonelier parts of the Reef – this was a marvellous experience. In Canada he had studied marine biology, though without completing a degree, and he was constantly fascinated to find himself so close to Reef life.

"Do you ever see any whales?" I asked. It was a question I had fallen into the habit of asking along the Reef, and I went on asking it despite the fact that the answer was always predictably the same: haven't seen a whale in years. I think I had developed a superstitious feeling about whales; in my mind they had come to stand for the Reef itself and its chances of survival. Something in me insisted that if the whales could be wiped out then so could anything else. I kept feeling there was some sort of parallel between the consortium of nations which had crossed the world to hunt down the whales, and the current presence in the Reef area of the international technicians and businessmen who were all so willing to help in developing its resources.

"Yes, I saw a whale," Jackson said. "Only last season. Down east of Mackay. A humpback. It had a calf with it."

My delight and sudden optimism must have been visible, because he added, "But the sharks got the calf."

A whole school of sharks had attacked, he said. The big whale had sent three or four of them hurtling through the air, but there were perhaps twenty more. Once, the calf would have been protected by other adult whales in the big group with which this pair would have been travelling. Now there were no groups left to travel with – the calf and its mother were on their own. When the sharks closed in, there was just one whale to beat them off the calf which represented the future, and it failed.

Prompted by nothing, apparently, Kitty Monkman said, "You know, when we first came to Green Island there were such beautiful shells just lying on the beach. You'd go for a walk and see them everywhere. But you don't see them now."

"That's right," Noel Monkman said. "You don't see them any more."

That had been my last visit to Green Island, a few weeks before. Now, having said goodbye to the scientists and divers on *Kuranda*, I was again standing on the Green Island jetty. The daily tourist launch had already left for Cairns, and the jetty was almost deserted. In the late sunlight, walking over the concrete above the purple and turquoise dapple of the reef shallows, I began to realize, with pleasure gradually supplanting disbelief, that I was encountering some of the island's old tranquillity. Down on the reef, parrot fish were browsing, their brilliant blues and greens flowing under the water. Nearer the island, a large bird hunched on a groyne post unfolded into a long-necked heron. Trailing stick legs it rose and in wide white-feathered curves of wing floated on blue, and drifted, and then dropped slowly down a diagonal into the green feathers of a palm. Where the jetty reached the sand I began to listen for the Hawaiian guitars. There were none. The power boats which on my last visit had rip-roared around the island now were silent, pointing up to the shining edge of the beach. In the quiet evening, it seemed I had arrived at that place which all tourists search for, the place unspoiled by tourists. I was unwilling to leave the scene, and so I strolled back along the jetty to have another look at the parrot fish. Scientists were turning up some fascinating material about these fish. The shining blue-green specimens below the jetty would all have been males, but the odds were that they had begun their lives as drab females. In collections of parrot fish made around Heron Island no young male had ever been found, and this contributed to the belief that some of the females underwent a sex change. It was even possible that all parrot fish ended their lives gloriously as males. The fish had an odd influence on the structure of the reefs. They had beak-like mouths and extra teeth in the throat to grind up the fragments of coral they took in while hunting for the algae which was their food. The teeth reduced the hard fragments to a dust, which passed through the body and was excreted. Since the fish were numerous, they were responsible for a substantial redistribution of sediment on the reefs. Below me, several of the fish stopped grazing and began to move out over the reef, flowing together under the water like a segment of drowned rainbow. They were probably moving towards the deep water at the edge of the reef, where great numbers of parrot fish would congregate at sundown and then retire to their roosting sites in crevices and on ledges. They would not move again until dawn, when they would emerge for another day of grazing over the corals. As the fish streamed on towards the edge of the reef, I turned back towards the island and the Coral Cay Hotel.

It was late in the season, and the hotel was not crowded. Many of the tables in the dining room were vacant, and I sat at one looking out on tall, wind-bent palms framing the blue-dark brilliance of the sea, and a flurry of white gulls, screaming. In the evening the guests scattered to watch television, or to drink on high stools in the muted light of the bar, or to play the juke box. I went early to my room in one of the multi-coloured wings of the hotel. It was a comfortable room except that it had louvres to let the breeze in and no mesh to keep the insects out. One set of louvres had been built to stay permanently open, an oddity which seemed to be widely appreciated by the island's insects. They streamed in to get at the light, and large beetle-like creatures made disconcerting bashing noises as they hit against the glass. Eventually, to make some notes, I went to bed and sat up writing under a tent of mosquito netting. Next day I called again on the Monkmans, and they took me for a walk through the island. Monkman talked a great deal about his hopes of a conservationist victory in the battle for the Reef. Kitty looked very small as she hurried beside him, he strolling along with his head up, chin out, the white pointed beard travelling just a little ahead of the rest of him and some invisible extension of it, it seemed, parting a way for us among the visitors.

I said goodbye to the Monkmans, and then I took the ferry back to the mainland. It arrived in the late afternoon. The sunset clouds above the purple ranges of the coast were rimmed with white gold as we sailed down the bay towards Cairns, home port of the tourist excursion, the sugar ship, the big-game boat.

CHAPTER 4

Outer Barrier Big-game Hunt

❋

THE black marlin which swam along the outer edge of the Great Barrier Reef were bigger, Cairns people said, than black marlin anywhere else in the world. The ones that got away weighed over two thousand pounds; the ones that were caught weighed over one thousand. The giant billfish often surfaced in the local dream of Cairns as an international resort. It was the fish which could bring the sporting rich, who would spend money on charter boats by day and hotels and restaurants by night. Already the dream had substance. By 1968 American sportsmen in particular were beginning to appear in Cairns, chartering big-game boats for twenty and thirty days at a time at ninety dollars a day. And this was not really surprising, according to Michael Leahy, the tall, thin, bookish-looking solicitor who was President of the Cairns Game Fishing Club. In big-game fishing, Leahy said, Cairns was now "the hotspot of the world". More black marlin were being caught here than anywhere else.

"I suppose the thing that put Cairns on the map," Leahy told me, "was the thousand-and-sixty-four-pound black marlin caught in 1966 on an eighty-pound breaking-strain line. It was a world record, and it received a great deal of publicity both in Australia and overseas. I think it brought people here. Of course, the other thing that has brought people here is the fact that game fishing in other parts of the world is so lousy." It was lousy, he said, because of the great number of boats which for years now had been competing for game fish around the Bahamas, Florida, Mexico, Hawaii. Three years ago a man he knew, a skilled angler, had gone to Hawaii and fished for forty days straight and never even had a strike. That couldn't happen at Cairns. Someone coming to Cairns and taking a boat out for a week would be bound to get a marlin. These waters hadn't begun to be fished out. There was also a policy here of encouraging the angler to let a fish go free, unless it was the first marlin the angler had caught or was a record. Unfortunately, a number of fish died in battle with the angler.

The marlin which ran and jumped and tail-walked on the water – putting on that fighting display which so thrilled the spectator – was feeling the hook it had swallowed and was trying to get rid of it. "Sometimes it will throw its stomach right out," Leahy said, "and this will kill it." But there was also the fish which could fight for more than seven hours and not tire. One boat hooked a fish which two experienced anglers estimated to weigh about two thousand five hundred pounds. It was on a one-hundred-and-thirty-pound breaking-strain line. "It just towed them around," Leahy said. "A couple of hours after it was hooked they went through a school of dolphins and it started chasing the dolphins. A tremendous fish. After seven and a half hours it was still fighting fresh. Eventually it just broke off."

It would be wrong to think, Leahy intimated, that just anybody could arrive in Cairns and expect to hire a big-game boat. No skipper was anxious to take on the novice who hadn't a hope of catching a fish to enhance his boat's record. The skippers weren't in the business just for the money. They were devoted fishermen. Still, after a talent for fishing, money was probably the most useful thing the aspiring angler could have. "It's the wealthy man's sport," Leahy said. "The people in it, you wouldn't even call them middle class. They'd be above middle class, because basically you've got to have plenty of money to go game fishing." People he could think of who fished out of Cairns did not include any representatives of the arts or the professions, apart from law; they were business people. This sport really had no place for the visitor who couldn't afford to charter a boat and hoped merely to buy a place on one of the four-passenger boats for, say, a quarter of the hire. Even if there were a spare place on board, these people had no need of the twenty or twenty-five dollars which would add a stranger to their party for the day. If in addition the stranger was a woman and didn't even fish, just wanted to watch, the chances of her being able to buy a place on a boat, the President assured me, were markedly slight.

I was grateful, then, to Allan Collis, skipper of *Marlan*, for putting it to three of his clients that I would make an unobtrusive fourth on one of their excursions, and so arranging for me to make a big-game fishing trip along the Outer Barrier Reef.

Marlan left Cairns at a quarter to seven on a fresh blue morning, heading north by Upolo Cay, a little mound of sand rising out of a sea of pale and brilliant turquoise. The slight, twenty-seven-year-old skipper, Allan Collis, stood high above the deck on the flying bridge, under the white plastic hood which made the boat look rather like a seagoing sulky. At each side of the boat a white outrigger – a painted bamboo pole about thirty feet long – extended out above the water, trailing baits for fish which were intended in their turn as baits for the black marlin. Occasionally there would be a cry of "strike", the boat would almost stop, and someone would leap for the rod and bring in a fish. It would be handed to the boatman to prepare for the marlin lines, and the anglers – three Australian car dealers from the south – would go back to soaking up the sun. This was their third day out on *Marlan.* On the first day one of them had caught a black marlin which had weighed in at over eleven hundred pounds. On one-hundred-and-thirty-pound tackle that wasn't a record. All the same, the skipper pointed out, there probably wouldn't have been thirty marlin that size landed anywhere in the world. Most of the boats were using one-thirty pound tackle, he said, because they were after the giants. "We're trying to catch the one that will beat the fifteen-hundred-and-sixty-pound world record," he said. That one had been taken off Peru. "We've had ours on a few times, but we haven't caught him yet. One of these days, though, it's going to happen."

Marlan passed a line of shallow green water over a reef marking the outer edge of the Barrier, and then we were out in the deep blue Coral Sea. I stayed with skipper Allan Collis up on the flying bridge. The white awning kept off direct sun, but did nothing to reduce the diamond glare of the water. Collis was wearing a wide-brimmed straw hat plus sunglasses. He was standing in the position he was to keep for much of the trip – a flexible side-on-to-the-wheel stance which allowed him to come close enough to looking in all directions at once. This feat was necessary if he was to do what he was supposed to do, which was navigate the boat, watch the sky and the sea for clues to the presence of marlin, keep his eye on the baits travelling behind the outriggers, alert the anglers the moment a marlin surfaced, and then manoeuvre the boat so that the fish couldn't get off the hook. "This is where we catch most of our fish," he said, as the engine noise died and the boat dropped back to an idling speed. Without the breeze whipped up by a fast-moving boat it was suddenly very hot. The awning was no protection from the enveloping glow. "It's something you never get used to," Collis said. "My lips still burn unless I put a special cream on them." The temperature of the water around us, he guessed, would be eighty degrees.

At a quarter past ten we were still rocking gently along on the hot calm sea. For half an hour the baits had been trailing from the outriggers, which were fine lines of white above the cobalt water. The boatman swung up on to the bridge to watch the baits. One was moving awkwardly, and the boatman, looking dissatisfied, climbed down to bring it in again. Collis said a man like that was valuable. A fish was really caught by three separate efforts, that of the skipper, that of the boatman and crew, and that of the angler. The fish was credited to the angler, but his share of the work was about fifteen percent. A great deal depended on the manoeuvring of the boat, he was saying, when he broke off, straining to see something in the water behind us. Then he shouted. Instantly the men below went into action – action which was at first confusing, since it was aimed, not at hooking a marlin, but at getting rid of it. It turned out that everybody wanted to save the carefully prepared bait for a bigger fish than this one which was speeding towards it. This was a mere two hundred, two-fifty pounds. "It's just a little feller," Collis was calling down to the cockpit. "Wind it in," someone implored as the marlin gained, "wind it in!" Collis was saying prayerfully, "Ah go away, go *away*!" The fish leapt. For an instant there was about ten foot of marlin, gleaming dark, hanging in the sky. Then the fish fell back. "He's *on*," someone lamented. By now one of the fishermen was in the chair with the rod, leaning forward and winding, then leaning back, leaning forward again and winding, and leaning back – and then the action stopped, the shouting died. The marlin was off the hook. It had stayed just long enough to ruin the bait.

We idled on over a sea which reminded me of the brilliant ink-blue I'd seen the starfish divers swim through off Green Island. Today's sea, though, was a denser colour – you couldn't see far down into it. It was a good colour for game fishing, Collis said. With the sea that colour, there could be big fish around. Why? There just could be.

Something which I took at first for a small bird, blue and shining, rose in front of the boat and flew. As I watched it speed on and on for a hundred yards or so I realized it was a flying fish. Launched by a tremendous underwater tail-beating, it was now riding the air with fins outstretched like wings. These fish were supposed to fly only when trying to escape a predator. When Collis saw the flying fish, he began to search the sky. "No," he said finally, "no frigate birds around. I thought there might be. They come down after the flying fish. Yesterday we saw three or four of them. They have this habit of sitting above a marlin while it's travelling. The marlin isn't chasing anything, just travelling, but the flying fish don't know that. They see it and get scared. They fly up out of the water, and the frigate birds are there to catch them. So sometimes a frigate will lead us to quite a decent-sized marlin." There were other stories about these big, dark seabirds. Their presence over a Reef island was supposed to be an infallible sign of rain. And they were airway robbers. Superb flyers, they would lounge around the sky while small birds below worked at catching fish and then, swooping, would force a mid-air surrender of the catch.

Collis shouted again. It was another ten-foot marlin making for the baits. "Oh you *stinker*, you!" he groaned. Down below there were despairing cries of, "He'll grab the bait!" and "Wind it in, quick!" But the marlin kept coming. And now I saw him, and he was one of the most beautiful things I could ever see. His colour had changed. He was lit up with the feeding glow. His dark tail and fins had turned to a luminescent blue, his black body to a rich brown. The vibrating blue of the fish made the blue sea pale. He swam in his own blue glow, and came at the boat so fast, so excitedly, that as he closed on their bait the men began to laugh. The line snapped out of the outrigger, the boat almost stopped, and a fisherman was in the chair with the rod, winding. "We're going to get rid of him in a hurry," Collis said to me. "Catch him, or lose him, or *something*. He's only about two hundred pounds." Losing him might be achieved through the movement of the boat, Collis said, his eyes on the engagement below. If the catching took too long, the boat would be manoeuvred to help the fish get free. The boat could be made to work with or against the angler, which was one of the reasons the skipper was so important in the catching of a fish. No angler, he said with a sudden grin, could catch a fish the skipper didn't want him to catch.

In this case the fight was over quickly. Near the boat the wire broke and the fish, no longer glowing, took off with hook and bait. "Ah well," said Collis, as the boat started up again, "we were only going to tag him." The tagging programme, he said, had begun this season. It was aimed at getting information about these fish whose life was still a mystery. Nobody knew where they were born, how fast they grew, if and where they migrated. It could be that they bred somewhere around the Reef, because this seemed to be the only place in the world where black marlin weighing only twenty pounds or so were caught. In future, tags recovered from marlin might help fill in the mystery. "The Japanese will be on the lookout for the tags now," Collis said. "They catch the most marlin out here, on their long lines."

When I climbed down into the cockpit for a cup of coffee with the anglers they were discussing the little marlin that got away. The talk came around to the subject of bringing in a big marlin, and the use of the flying gaff to do this. The detachable hook, or gaff, fitted on the end of a handle about seven feet long. There was about thirty feet of rope attached to the gaff. After the instrument was thrust into the fish the handle came away and left the rope and gaff in the fish. "You just get rid of all the rope in the boat and leave him thrash around about thirty feet away," one of the anglers said. A big fish, he said, could straighten out a steel gaff about eighteen inches long. I was looking at the immense hook when one of the men, smiling, said, "Fish are cold-blooded. They don't feel things like animals on land."

This matter of a fish's capacity for feeling poses some interesting questions. On the answers to them depend the justification for excluding fish from the laws of humane killing extended to other animals. After spending a good deal of time on the Reef I found I had developed a feeling for the fish, and a sensitivity to the way they were often treated after capture. I had watched a man who wouldn't have thought of cutting a slice of flesh from a living bird not bother to kill a fish before cutting a piece out of it for bait. The fish lived on for what seemed a long time, but it didn't matter, the man said – fish don't feel. On a tourist fishing boat another man worked for over five minutes by my watch trying to force a piece of wire with his name on it through the head of his catch, a beautiful pink fish with veils of blue spots. He tried to thread the wire through the gills and up through the top of its mouth. When the convulsed animal leapt from him he grew indignant, as if it were being deliberately tiresome, and said he'd take a knife, then, to the bugger. He did that, but even then he didn't kill it. He poked around with the knife making holes for this wire bearing his name, the fish still squirming and thumping. Eventually I took this question of a fish's capacity to feel to Professor James Thomson, professor of Zoology at the University of Queensland. Thomson had been giving public lectures on "Animals of the Sea". "I suppose the general theme I was plugging," he told me, "was that life arose in the sea and that we ourselves are – if you believe the theory of evolution – direct descendants of sea creatures. The animals in the sea should be rather familiar to us. They *are* animals – they're not something quite different. They take in oxygen, they put out carbon dioxide, they do all the things we do. Except they stay in the water. Cold-blooded simply means that they cannot control their own temperature. Their temperature fluctuates with the environment."

Would there be as many grounds for thinking that a fish could feel, I asked, as for thinking this of other animals which couldn't communicate with us?

"Oh yes," he said. "They certainly have a well developed nervous system. Apart from sheer intelligence, reasoning power, they're probably better developed in many ways than human beings are. Their sense of smell is far better, their reaction time to light stimulus is far better, they can respond to wavelengths of pressure and sound that we can't respond to. We don't hear some of the things they hear." The failure to regard fish as other animals were regarded came down to identification, Thomson suggested. "Primitive man looked on other animals as a source of food and a source of clothing. It's only as we become sophisticated that we start having any sympathy for them. We extend that sympathy first to the animals that look most like us – the hairy ones, the fur-bearing ones, and then the feathered ones. I suppose," he said, "it's a logical extension that eventually people will feel consideration for all sorts of animals, including fish."

Out on the Coral Sea, *Marlan* trailed baits from white outriggers over indigo water. No marlin came up to take them. Not far away there was another game boat, moving slowly backwards. Collis, who had been talking to this boat on the wireless, said, "He's backing up on a fish. We'll see it fly out of the water soon." The angler on the other boat, he was saying, was out after a record on a fifty-pound line – and then the marlin jumped, very close to the boat that was hunting it. As the boat travelled backwards in a circle, quite fast, Collis said, "That fish is pretty close to the surface, and pretty close to the boat. They're trying to scare him to make him jump a bit more. It'll tire him." If a marlin weren't tired, he said, he could be too hard to handle when it came to bringing him in within gaffing range. The fish jumped again, fantastically high this time, and arching as it fell back. Down in the cockpit one of the men whooped admiringly, and another gave a little cheer. I realized I was smiling. The fish was putting on a good show. In this sunny atmosphere you found yourself believing that the fish, too, was enjoying the day, playing up to an audience which understood it, respected it. Big-game fishing seemed to be rather like other sorts of hunting – the quarry was held to be of legendary cunning, and to *like* matching wits with the hunter. A black marlin, I had been assured, was a tremendously intelligent adversary. This conviction co-existed with another, that it could feel nothing. A couple of hundred yards off the other boat continued its back-tracking tactic, but the fish didn't jump again. As we drew away Collis said, "They could be another five minutes with that fish. Or another two hours." I asked him if he had ever had the experience which Leahy had mentioned, of seeing a hooked marlin throw out its stomach. He had, he said, very often. The marlin leapt, and there was its stomach, flapping around in the air in front of it. "If the hook is in the stomach lining and the lining goes straight out of his mouth – well, on one-hundred-and-thirty-pound tackle the hook just tears straight through." He had also known marlin to swallow the stomach again. When he'd pulled them in and cut them up, the stomach had been back in place.

Marlan continued her slow patrol to the south. The white boat idled on the deep, opaque, blue, solid blue, sea. It was peaceful, and very hot, and you could hear the slap and surge of the water. The big fish did not appear. At half past two Collis said, "Well, that's it for today", and the lines were pulled in. The boat began to travel faster and made a breeze, but up under the white awning we burned in the glare from the water. The way back to Cairns was through the Grafton Passage, past Euston Reef, marked by colours which might have been spilled out on the ocean by overturned paint tins. Streams of bright green-blue flowed around pools of yellow, rivulets of turquoise ended in sudden deeps of purple splashed with azure. The colourings, Collis said, were produced partly by corals, partly by changes of depth, partly by the reflections of sky and water-covered sand. *Marlan* passed over a long blue grotto, and then Euston Reef was behind us. Looking back at its colours, at the immense sea-washed palette of the Outer Barrier, I felt the same exhilaration I had felt earlier, encountering the beauty of the blue-glowing marlin.

It was around here, Collis said, about a month ago, that his boat encountered an oil slick about a hundred yards wide. One of the big ships using the Grafton Passage must have released it. "We couldn't go through it," he said. "It would have been all over the boat. Filthy oil. We had to go way to heck around it. They hadn't even bothered to wait until they got out to sea. They'd dumped their oil right here in the Reef area." His experience was not uncommon. More and more oil slicks were being reported in Reef waters, which were used in a year by about fourteen hundred trading ships of all classes.

Marlan's journey in to Cairns on this afternoon was without the drama of its return a couple of days before, when, flying the flag with a marlin on it, it had hauled a fish weighing more than eleven hundred pounds down the long bay to the town wharf. The flag had told people ashore that the catch was coming in, and the game-fishing buffs among them had rushed to the waterfront to see it. Today another boat had drawn the crowd. When we arrived a marlin had already been hoisted high above the wharf, head down, and fifty or more people stood looking up at its gallows. The great back had ragged tears in it, as if raked by the gaff, and its blood dripped on the wharf. The party from the boat which had caught the fish posed in front of it for pictures. It turned out to be the fish we had watched battling the fifty-pound line. It looked huge. In fact it weighed only a little more than three hundred and fifty pounds, which was certainly the weight of two men, but still not much for a black marlin unless it happened to have been caught on fifty-pound tackle. A fish normally hanging here would have been caught on one-hundred-and-thirty pound tackle, and would have been much larger – about, say, the size of a horse. This fish was only the size of a pony. If it had been a pony, of course, the scene would hardly have been acceptable to anybody involved in it. But it wasn't a pony, or a horse, or even an animal, really. It was just something hauled from the sea. And when it came to the sea, we were out of our element. There were impediments to our understanding.

CHAPTER 5

"Controlled Exploitation"

✳

THE sea off the coast of Queensland, and the riches it contained, were the subject of a plan with the heading, "Proposals relating to the Conservation and Controlled Exploitation of the Great Barrier Reefs".* It was a plan that recognized that man was on his way back into the sea. After aeons of dependence on the land, he was about to re-enter the ocean, perhaps to live in it, but certainly to take from it what he pleased. The Proposals were set out over eight and a half foolscap pages, were signed by the Chairman of the Great Barrier Reef Committee, and were designed to be put before "the Ministers in charge of relevant Queensland Government departments, the Managers of mining and exploration companies, the Managers of tourist resorts and the Director of the Australian Conservation Foundation".

"Exploitation of the mineral resources of the area has scarcely begun," said the Proposals, "but exploitation on a large scale is imminent ... several oil companies are amassing geophysical data in the region.... High grade lime for building, manufacturing and agriculture is present in enormous quantities. High grade silica for glass manufacture is present in quantity in some areas. The nature and extent of submerged mineral deposits are not known." There was also the fact that the potential of the area to provide food had not been explored: "In view of the phenomenal increase in the world's human population which is now occurring the time is fast approaching when all available protein resources must be exploited.... It seems inevitable that, in the future, some elements of the flora and fauna will be cropped to provide food."

The Proposals, based on an assumption which some conservationists felt themselves bound to reject – that the Great Barrier Reef would inevitably be exploited – called for scientific research to gauge the least harmful way of carrying out the exploitation. Accepting that the role

* See Appendix A.

of the scientists of the Great Barrier Reef Committee was not to oppose exploitation but to supervise it, the Proposals pointed out that "The Committee has no political affiliations and has a worldwide scientific reputation. Hence it would be an ideal body to handle the formulation of an overall plan for the conservation and controlled exploitation of Barrier Reef resources. Moreover, it could act as an advisory or referee body in contentious matters relating to the Reefs (e.g. applications for mining leases contested in Mining Wardens' Courts, applications for new tourist resorts, etc.) and as a buffer between the government of the day and vocal parties affected by legislation dealing with Great Barrier Reef matters".

A scientific research programme would require funds. Bodies which might support the work included:

"The Department of Mines. This department would benefit directly from the carrying out of the projects envisaged. It would benefit as a result of the obtaining of scientific data on the effects on the fauna and flora of coral reefs of dredging activities associated with the removal of coral rubble in mining operations. It would benefit from having at its disposal an assessment of reserves of coral reef detritus on accessible reefs. It would also benefit greatly as a result of the formulation of an overall plan for the conservation and controlled exploitation of the Reefs, the same way as the Premier's Department would benefit.

"Oil Companies. From the viewpoint of fostering good public relations oil companies holding prospecting rights over areas of the Reefs or carrying out exploratory work in the area of the Reefs would benefit greatly if they contributed towards the cost of obtaining the scientific data necessary to formulate a plan for the conservation and controlled exploitation of Reef resources. There is undoubtedly opposition from several quarters to the activities of oil companies in Australia's major tourist area and it will help their cause considerably if their support for conservation of the fauna and flora of the Reefs were announced to the general public, particularly if this support took the form of assistance for the carrying out of the projects outlined.... Also, oil companies would benefit from having access to data on water currents, tidal amplitudes, etc. in Barrier Reef waters obtained by scientists....

"Companies interested in exploiting coral reef debris as a source of lime for agricultural and industrial use. Obviously, such companies would benefit greatly if a survey of reserves of coral reef debris in accessible areas were made and if a plan for conservation and controlled exploitation

of Reef resources were formulated. From the viewpoint of fostering good public relations it would seem to be in the interests of these companies to provide financial support for at least the project involving the effects of dredging activities associated with exploitation of coral reef debris on the fauna and flora of areas affected."

That these were the attitudes of the Great Barrier Reef Committee executive was not generally understood. Naturalists thought of the Committee as a body existing primarily to study the Great Barrier Reef, not as one which included in its Memorandum of Association, in one of its statements of aims, a significant last clause: "to carry on marine biological and other scientific research generally and to protect and conserve the said Reef and to determine and report upon and advise on the proper utilization of the said Reef".

Utilization. The word was anathema to the old musician on Green Island, the man who remembered Pavlova, as it was to an artist on the coast who was ultimately to lead the defence of the Reef. But to many scientists, both inside and outside the Committee, it had for years appeared to be a respectable, even an exciting, aim, this of showing that the area they studied was not merely beautiful but useful. Collaboration with the new technology was seen as a service to the community. Utilization practically demanded that the scientist get along with the government and the industrial powers-that-be – how else could things be utilized? From such a viewpoint, it was not so extraordinary, for example, that the Scientific Director of the Committee's research station at Heron Island should use a Gulf Oil plane for his work on currents. The oil companies were, pre-eminently, utilizers. But many conservationists were unaware of these attitudes, and when they did become aware of them they were outraged. They even suspected that they were themselves the "vocal parties" against which the Committee was offering in its Proposals to protect the government. But that was some way on in the battle for the Reef. When the battle opened – with an application by Donald Forbes, secretary of the Cairns District Canegrowers' Executive to take lime from Ellison Reef for agricultural use on the canefields – naturalists strung out along the Queensland coast looked to the Great Barrier Reef Committee, with its powerful membership of scientists, to oppose the application. They had not even considered the idea of controlled exploitation. They had a simple expectation that the Great Barrier Reef Committee would defend the Great Barrier Reef, and to them that meant opposing this application to mine it. The Committee did not oppose it. The defence passed to an artist. This was John Busst, who lived on the coast not far from the threatened reef, and was president of the Wildlife Preservation Society of Innisfail, a group with a cash reserve of approximately five dollars. In organizing the campaign against lime mining, Busst eventually opened up the whole question of whether the Reef's resources were to be exploited. The debate he launched broadened out from a consideration of whether lime should be taken from one area, Ellison Reef, into one of whether the search for oil and minerals throughout the entire Reef should be tolerated. He and the conservationists he rallied made the question a national, and eventually an international, issue.

CHAPTER 6

John Busst, Conservationist Leader

✳

WHEN I went to see John Busst, he drove in from the coast to the little station about fifty miles south of Cairns to meet my train. As the train stopped and I began to get down with my luggage, a very thin man with tanned skin and grey moustache appeared out of the white sunlight and said he was John Busst. He would take my cases. The car was just over here. In the dry, quiet voice, the understated manner, there was something which suggested not the artist but the colonial administrator. He might have helped preside over the last years of the British Empire in the East, catching malaria in the line of duty (he had indeed caught malaria, I learned later, but during a painting trip in New Guinea). He stowed my cases in the back of his polished cream station sedan – or rather, he placed them there with the sort of deft care which turned out to be characteristic of him – and then we started the drive to his house at Bingal Bay. The journey was through country of a violent tropical beauty. Where the glossy green rain forest had been cleared the earth was red, sometimes almost purple. This was the country which had attracted a group of Dutch and Germans who had been forced to leave Indonesia. Back in Europe they had made the discovery that they were no longer Europeans. Emigrating to this coast, they had found in these lavishly coloured landscapes and this humid air an assurance that they were home again. Busst was driving now across a sun-flooded plain of green sugarcane, with occasional stands of forest rising from it. Approaching one of these islands of trees he slowed the car. "Rain forest," he said. The dazzle of sun died against the green cliffs of foliage, and I looked through a gap in the leafy wall into a glistening dimness. Splashes of sun falling from a high opening in the forest illuminated a rope-screen of vines and tall green fountains of ferns. Coolness flowed out on to the hot road, and with it the sound of birds. There was a call like the single note of a bell, repeated, and a silvery whistling. Then there was a rush of red through the greenness and a parrot's screech.

"You get seventy percent of all Australia's species of birds in the rain forest of this coast," Busst said, starting up the car again. But, he added, there were only remnants of the forest left, and those remnants were under almost continuous attack. There had even been moves by the Army to use the rain forest for testing defoliants intended for Vietnam. He had protested and been given assurances, so perhaps the defoliants wouldn't be used. As we drove on he continued to talk about the preservation of the rain forest, for which, he said, a committee he belonged to had for many years been working. He had first been inspired to interest himself in the forest's survival by the scientists who had come to the island of Bedarra, where he had lived and painted from 1941 until 1957. The island was located off this coast, not so far, as it happened, from the reef which the canegrowers' secretary had chosen as the subject for his application to mine. Busst's island of Bedarra was close to Dunk Island, which in the early decades of the century had captured a large away-from-it-all readership for E. J. Banfield, the Englishman who settled there and wrote as "Beach-comber". Islands such as Dunk and Bedarra were not coral cays but seagirt hills, and like the coast from which the ocean had separated them they supported forest. Scientists who came to Bedarra to study the forest extended the artist's admiration for its beauty into an awareness of it as a botanical marvel. Busst left the island in 1957. By then he was married, and it did not seem such a good idea for a woman to be cut off from the mainland by Reef waters. There were violent storms and even, in those days, the chance of a whale surfacing under a small boat crossing to the coast. "Besides, you know," Busst said, as we drove towards his house at Bingal Bay, "the days for living on tropical islands have gone. Half Bedarra now is a tourist resort. And there's no privacy out there any more. Speedboats everywhere, buzzing all around you." When he moved to Bingal Bay, he said, it was to a rain forest setting much like the one on the island. "On this coast," he said, "there are patches of land which are the only places in the world where eucalypts grow in conjunction with rainforest. We're battling to preserve them for the botanists. They're unique." The survival of such uniqueness was by no means unconnected with the survival of the Reef, he added, since the clearance of vegetation affected the coast's relationship to the Reef waters alongside it. The river estuaries, the mangrove swamps, the shallow waters close to the coast supported life which was part of the whole marine system. These waters must be affected when vegetation was cleared and torrential rain stripped earth from the coast and dumped it in the sea. "To make way for sugar, for cattle fattening, for bananas," Busst said, "they fell the rain forest. They cut it in July, and they burn it in December. Then down comes the rain of the Wet season – and this is one of the wettest areas in the world – and there's no cover on the ground. I see rich red topsoil every season pouring out into the ocean.

"Here's where I live," he said, as we turned into a landscaped park. After we had driven through acre upon acre of lawn and trees I said, "You must be rich." He smiled and denied it. His father, a mining warden, had made some money from investments and had left him independent, that was all. He had bought this land when prices were more reasonable, and he did all the work on it, the lawn-mowing and the cultivating, himself. There were acres of rain forest he intended to leave to the nation, and six acres of cultivated land. He had put in twenty-five different eucalypts which were strangers to the district. He was growing the trees for scientists who wanted to know how they'd make out in this lush climate. They were doing magnificently, Busst said, and might turn out to be a good source of hardwood.

The white house stood on its own cliff, the rain forest behind it, and in front the satin shine of blue water stretching away to where the reefs of lime lay hidden. It was the traditional Australian country house, a core of rooms surrounded by wide verandahs, with a roof like a shady hat pulled down over the lot. Like the grounds, it was the creation of its owner. Busst had built it. The white walls, the dark blue posts, the long, airy verandahs gave the house a pleasantly light look. In fact it was a fortress, built of brick and reinforced concrete to outlast the cyclones which periodically smashed through this coast. Busst's level, administrative voice explained, "I am not interested in making anything that won't last for a thousand years. I build," he reiterated, "for a thousand years." We stepped off the verandah through the long window into a room with ceilings lined in a sort of bamboo parquetry. There were three long bamboo couches with pink-red upholstery, and bamboo armchairs and bookcases. The furniture, like the ceiling parquetry, was made from local bamboo and was Busst's meticulous creation. Around the walls were his own land-scapes and portraits, painted in a representational manner which looked back for its inspiration beyond the characteristic styles of the twentieth century. "I was taught to paint, and to build, by Justus Jorgensen," he said.

Justus Jorgensen, of Montsalvat. It was surprising. On the one hand there was this presence with something of the inexorable about it, this thin man with the even voice who would hold the fort, man the life-boat, go down with the ship. And on the other there was the man who was not only an artist but an artist from Montsalvat, that colony of Bohemians who, on the outskirts of the southern city of Melbourne, had raised a Gothic château as a fortress against the philistines. The château, dating back to before World War II, was still there. It had been built to the design of Justus Jorgensen, artist and theoretician of the good life. Its construction had been the work of the students who, with something approaching a medieval relationship to the master, apprenticed themselves not only to painting but to a building craft. Jorgensen had urged his students to live simply, to be self-supporting, to try to keep themselves free of commercial entanglements. Later, when I looked up a 1950 press interview with Jorgensen, I found that it named his two most successful students. One of them was John Busst, who, it was reported, had gone off to live the admirable life on a Reef island, growing his own food and painting, in the style approved at Montsalvat. But before he left Busst had been an important character in the life of the colony. He had helped to build the château, specializing in the craft of stone-cutting but also giving a hand wherever it was needed, which might be in the raising of a pisé wall, or the carving of a door, or the making of a wrought-iron hinge, or the adapting of parts of old buildings demolished by Whelan the Wrecker. When it was complete the Gothic château rose on its hill like a shrine to non-conformity, to non-machine-age man. Inevitably, the neighbours called it the Temple of Love. Melbourne, a conservative city, a capital of finance, tended as a matter of policy to look to the future with shining eyes. There must have been something irritating about being looked down upon by a Gothic château facing so firmly back to the Middle Ages. And now, for the apostles of the new technology, the utilizers, it was not simply irritating, it was the wildest bad luck that as they moved in to exploit the Great Barrier Reef there was waiting for them there a graduate of Montsalvat – a graduate who was not simply a romantic artist but John Busst, at once a man of emotion and a wickedly cool organizer.

Busst's wife Ali came in through the long window of the living room and announced there was a meal waiting on the back verandah. A tall woman, wearing printed tangerine and yellow shorts and shirt, she preserved in middle age a long-legged coltish elegance. Like her husband, she had an understated manner. No, she hadn't done much in the Reef campaign. Just typed John's letters, really. With one finger. How many? Oh, about four thousand. Well, there were people in Europe and England and America to be written to, too, you see. One of her more memorable throw-away lines described her part in cooking the superb chicken we were eating: "I simply dropped it in boiling water." ("She can cook in about nine languages," Busst said. "I can't eat very much but I adore good food.")

Eating good food, drinking cold wine, we sat on the verandah and looked out at the hot brilliance of the grounds. Butterflies larger than swallows, their wings an enamelled blue, or an iridescent green, fluttered and floated between shade and the sunlight splashed with hibiscus reds and pinks. "The strangest thing I've ever seen here, I think," Busst said, "was a battle on a scarlet canna flower between one of these big blue butterflies and a little sunbird. They were competing for the same flower, for the nectar. The fight went on for about ten minutes. They chased each other around and around above the flower. Eventually it was the butterfly that won. The bird flew away." I said I kept hearing of butterflies flying out to the reefs, and even resting on the corals at low tide, as if they were migrating. "Oh, that is so," Busst said. "I've seen swarms going out to the reefs. I haven't seen them coming back. There isn't much information about their movements in this part of the world." All around the house there was the singing and whistling and calling of the birds which treated these grounds as their own. A sunbird, perhaps four inches long, flashing yellow and green and blue, hovered like a hummingbird over a red hibiscus and then buried its curved beak in a flower. A dove from the rain forest strutted the grass and watched us brightly. A kingfisher flew down, dark blue and azure and white. I rather hoped for one of the cassowaries which were a feature of the Reef coast, but none came. Instead we talked about them – how they hounded the dogs, and raided the bananas – lazily eyeing the rain forest in which they lived, and where later I was to see them passing through walls of leaves: forbidding, ostrich-like birds, with blue feathers on their long necks and dark helmets. Our bird-watching broke up when Ali Busst rose.

She had an arrangement to visit a friend nearby – Zara, the widow of the late Prime Minister, Harold Holt. Busst and I went inside. Soon, in the house built to last a thousand years, the fortress against time and the wind, he began the story of the battle to save the Reef.

CHAPTER 7

The Reef Defended in Court

✳

THE move to take lime from Ellison Reef, Busst said, had been defended on the ground that the reef was dead – that because its corals had died off the reef was of no importance. But it happened that for years on the island of Bedarra he had lived beside a reef which might also have been described as dead. It had been damaged in a cyclone. Corals smashed in the turbulent waters or smothered in the stirred-up sand had not grown again. And yet that reef was full of life. Herbivorous fish came to graze on its algae. Myriad organisms lived on its shelves and in its crevices. The coral polyps were dead, but their skeletons had become part of the life of other creatures, part of their environment. Busst's memories of his island life told him what scientists who later joined him in the fight were to assert – that to mine a reef was to destroy the habitat of a great variety of animals; that since these animals were all part of the Reef's chain of life, a disturbance on one reef could produce a chain reaction, the results of which could be estimated only after years of research.

Having taken his decision to oppose the application, Busst launched his campaign. Isolated at Bingal Bay, hundreds of miles from people he needed to consult in southern cities, he began to run up a phone bill which eventually reached seven hundred and eighty dollars (he paid it from the sale of some land). Even so he was unable to organize much in the way of a defence before the hearing opened. The case was being heard by a mining warden in the small town of Innisfail, not far from Bingal Bay. Between the high cost of transport from the cities where the scientists who might have given evidence were located, and the scientists' own commitments, it became clear that Busst would be unable to present scientific witnesses against the application. Instead, he decided, he would have to present himself, quoting from scientific works. Prepared to do this, he arrived at the Innisfail courthouse on 29 September 1967, with an armful of books he had swotted up and marked for quoting. With him was Bill Hall, a local naturalist, and

Les Arnell, the solicitor who throughout the case gave his services without charge. In addition, Busst had the support of a number of written objections to the application. Professor L. C. Birch, Challis Professor of Biology, University of Sydney, wrote in his letter to the Mining Warden at Innisfail, "Anything that in any way destroys the Reef – no matter how profitable for commerce – is an act of vandalism. I do not think it could be contemplated by anyone who knows the uniqueness of this biological wonder of the world". Associate Professor A. K. O'Gower, School of Biological Sciences, University of New South Wales, wrote, "The raping of Australia's resources and scenic birth-right has progressed at an exponential rate over the years without heed for future generations of Australians . . . the removal of coral for the production of lime could have such far reaching effects as to be catastrophic for the future of the Great Barrier Reef".

The Great Barrier Reef Committee wrote, "we have not lodged an objection to the present application as we have no information at present which would suggest that the Ellison Reef under consideration is significant biologically".

The Committee's letter to the Mining Warden at Innisfail went on:

"We are, however, concerned that the granting of the present application should not constitute a precedent for the granting of mining rights where they might interfere with the viability or potential of the Great Barrier Reefs.

"We are at present giving consideration to an overall plan for the controlled conservation and exploitation of the whole area in relation to the scientific work which the Committee has largely sponsored there since 1927."

As it happened, this overall plan of the Committee's incorporated an assumption which turned out to be one of the points of dispute in the Ellison Reef case, and later in the debates on oil drilling and other forms of exploitation – the assumption that it was possible to isolate one part of the Reef and exploit it without damaging other parts.

The Proposals of the Committee spoke of a planning, co-ordinating and advisory body being required to gather data and "recommend that certain areas of the reefs be reserved as marine national parks, that certain islands be reserved for future tourist resorts, that certain reefs be opened for mining, etc." But, said the critics of such plans, the reefs were most of the time underwater. How was it possible to divide off areas of water for exploitation? How was it possible to run a fence through the sea, put a wall across tides and currents? How could you set aside an area of water for, say, mining, and limit damage to that area? What about the flow of eggs and larvae through the water, the interchange of life between the reefs, the imbalance which would follow from animals being killed in a mining area and so removed from the Reef system? Later, when another body put forward a plan for marine national parks, to follow much the same pattern as terrestrial parks, marine biologist J. H. Choat, of the Queensland Littoral Society, suggested that the scheme to cut up the Reef into areas was an impossible one.

"It seems reasonable," he wrote in a letter to the *Courier Mail*, Brisbane, "to consider many of our terrestrial national parks as islands ... movement beyond the park is curtailed and the whole complex becomes (we hope) a self-sustaining biological unit.

"In the marine environment the situation is quite different. On coral reefs, most animals and also the plants have a planktonic episode in their life cycles. That is to say, numerous eggs are cast into the surface waters at the mercy of the currents.

"We know very little concerning the movements of currents within the Great Barrier Reef except that they are complex. It is impossible to predict where eggs shed on a particular reef will begin adult life.

"*This in our view constitutes the crux of the Great Barrier Reef conservation problem.* (My italics.)

"All previous thinking on conservation and national parks seems to be based on 'island logic'. Set aside geographically limited areas and predict (or hope) that they will be self-sustaining. Such logic cannot be applied to the conservation of the Great Barrier Reef. . . .

"The essential patterns of larval recruitment in the various populations of animals and plants on the Great Barrier Reef are still completely unknown. . . ."

Considerations of this sort were behind the opposition to the lime application, to the idea that one area could be isolated and destroyed without affecting, perhaps catastrophically, other areas of the Reef.

The Ellison Reef case began with a challenge from the Busst party to the court's authority to conduct the hearing. With an eye to the confused legal position of the whole Reef, their solicitor suggested that the Queensland government had no jurisdiction over Ellison Reef. The point was not allowed by the mining warden. The hearing proceeded, and Busst began to quote from his authorities. "But the barrister for the applicant objected," Busst recalled. "He said my references to authors were not permissible as evidence because the learned authors were not present in court to subject themselves to cross examination. The mining warden upheld the objection. So I was torpedoed in one."

There was still Bill Hall, the naturalist who had come to court with Busst to defend the Great Barrier Reef. "Bill would be about seventy-six now," Busst said. "He and his wife were running a caravan park in Townsville before they came to this area. He's retired. He has devoted a large part of his life to studying the Reef. He has tremendous knowledge of marine biology, but no academic qualifications. His evidence was very good, but it lacked the authority of a degree. I knew I had to get an adjournment, I had to have time to get scientific support from the south. I said to the solicitor, 'If we run out of time before five o'clock the whole case is lost'. Somehow we got through to five o'clock and secured an adjournment. Then I shot south."

In the south, one of the people he sought out was Australia's most eminent skin diver, the Prime Minister, Harold Holt. Not long afterwards, Holt was to disappear while swimming alone off the southern Australian coast. Before that happened, though, he was to play a part in Busst's struggle to protect the Reef. He and Busst had been friends since their schooldays in Melbourne. Holt had often stayed with Busst at Bedarra Island and later at Bingal Bay. He loved to dive in the waters of the Reef, and Busst spent a lot of time sitting in a boat watching for sharks while Holt was somewhere underwater. On a typical day there were no alarms. Once, though, there had been a bad shark scare. Busst was sitting in the boat when Holt surfaced with a crayfish. He tossed it over the side and then, before Busst could stop him, swam off to capture another. Busst was left remembering the warning of the Torres Strait islanders who used to call at Bedarra in the days of the pearling luggers. Never take more than one crayfish, they'd said. Take one, and then get out of the water as fast as you can. A captured cray sends out some sort of alarm which always brings the sharks. In normal circumstances a shark might not attack a man, but it would always attack a man with a crayfish. It liked crayfish. When Holt came up to the boat with his second cray Busst was relieved, and then horrified when he realized that after dumping this specimen, too, Holt was making off to catch a third. Busst tried to tell him about the Torres islanders, but it was a long story and Holt hadn't time just then. There were crayfish down below, and he needed just one more. He swam off. A little later, a shark duly appeared. It swam to the spot where Holt had taken the first cray, circled as if it were trying to locate something, and then dived. It came up again and swam to the spot where Holt had taken the second cray. It disappeared again. Busst and the boat met up with Holt and the third cray just ahead of the shark.

When Busst turned to Holt for assistance in the Ellison Reef case he was turning to a man who understood the Reef. But he was also turning to a Prime Minister no longer on holiday. It was remarkably hard to corner Holt for a private talk, even after Busst had accepted an invitation to stay with him in Canberra. "I stayed at the Lodge six days," Busst said. "He'd get up at six and shoot off to work. He'd be in the House all day long. I'd sit next to him at lunch, but there'd be other guests, and it would be impossible to talk to him. I'd sit next to him at dinner – again, impossible to talk to him. Then he'd disappear into the House again and mightn't be back until three in the morning. Gone again at six." It ended with Busst gathering up his papers, marshalling his arguments, and accompanying the Prime Minister on a flight to Melbourne. The plane took off, and Busst, prepared to talk, turned to the Prime Minister. He was already asleep. Busst considered his old friend's fatigue, and he considered the situation of the Reef, and then he shook the Prime Minister. "Harry," he said, "you've got to listen." It was the merest statement of fact. Before they parted at the end of the flight, he had an important undertaking. Behind the scenes, the Prime Minister would give any assistance he could. This was a State rights matter, and States were jealous of their rights. The mining warden's hearing would have to go on. But if Busst lost, or if the Reef were endangered by Queensland's actions, Holt would step in. "I will promise you personally," he told Busst, "that the federal government will take over the Barrier Reef."

Another ally Busst found when he went south was the president of the Wildlife Preservation Society of Queensland. This was Judith Wright McKinney, one of Australia's leading poets. Her immediate response to Busst's appeal for help was to put him in touch with scientists and divers whom she knew through the Wildlife Society to be in sympathy with the conservationist outlook. The result was the formation of a team willing to travel north, examine Ellison Reef for signs of life, and then go into court and testify on its condition. There remained the problem of finding the money to pay for transport for the team, and this Busst solved by putting before an airline a depressing estimate of its future dividends from tourism if mining were allowed to ruin the underwater gardens of the Reef. The airline agreed to carry Busst's witnesses free of charge to and from Innisfail – an undertaking which involved the transport of hundreds of pounds of excess luggage in the form of diving equipment for the examination of the Reef. When the airline set the party down they were to be picked up by a hire-car company, which had also accepted a discouraging view of its future if mining were allowed to interfere with tourism. Eventually the team would be delivered to two boats supplied by friends of the Bussts and taken to Ellison Reef for the survey.

And so, when the hearing reopened, Busst was able to produce witnesses calculated to dazzle the court with science. "I am a Bachelor of Science of Sydney University, a Master of Arts and Doctor of Philosophy of Harvard University," said Donald McMichael, Director of the Australian Conservation Foundation. "From 1951 until earlier this year I was on the staff of the Australian Museum in Sydney, first as Assistant Curator of Molluscs, then as Curator of Molluscs, and later as Deputy Director. The work on molluscs concerned the scientific study of shells and the investigations of their classification in biology and, more generally, studies of marine organisms in relation to them.... Altogether I have collected on, and studied the biology of, some twenty or thirty separate reefs." McMichael went on to inform the court of an extraordinary coincidence – the fact that in 1965 he had done a survey of this reef which was the subject of the mining application, and had found that it supported a species of shell which had been located nowhere else. This was a species of *Cymbiolacca*, a genus which was itself unique to Queensland waters. Ellison Reef therefore had great scientific interest, and if only for that reason should not, in McMichael's opinion, be disturbed. But there were other reasons – and he went on to describe the visit he had made to Ellison Reef the day before this hearing with Peter Brockel, a member of a diving survey team from the Queensland Littoral Society, to see how dead the reef was: "In company with Mr Brockel, I swam over the reef, using both snorkel and aqualung equipment at different times. They enabled me to submerge, particularly the aqualung, which allows one to stay on the bottom and examine the reef in detail.

"I would say that Ellison Reef is a typical coral reef of this part of the world and that it is just as much a living coral reef as any other coral reef I have examined. Any coral reef consists of living and dead material. It consists of patches of coral sand and detritus interspersed with patches of living coral and other marine organisms including fishes, molluscs, and algae, and the sand itself is the home for a wide variety of different kinds of marine organisms. . . .

"I do not believe this sand could be mined in the manner described without causing serious damage to the life of the reef, and in particular I am concerned that removal of the sand would also lead to the destruction of the animals which live in it, including the species of *Cymbiolacca* which I went to collect in 1965.

"My observations of the reef yesterday indicate that even a slight disturbance of the bottom material generates clouds of fine silt which stays suspended in the water for a considerable time and I consider that the silt would be widely distributed over the reef flat by the currents which have been shown to occur there."

Then there was Dr John Barnes, medical practitioner, senior research officer of the National Health and Medical Council, and marine research consultant to the Department of Harbours and Marine. He had come down from Cairns to warn that the mining of Ellison Reef could lead to an increase in *Ciguatera* poisoning, the mysterious and occasionally fatal ailment likely to afflict humans eating tropical fish from a disturbed habitat.

"From 1958," Barnes testified, "I have been actively engaged in the investigation of marine animals causing injury to humans. This involved the study of both inshore and offshore sections of the Great Barrier Reef waters. I have published thirteen works in this regard and have made contributions to the works of many other authors. . . ."

In other parts of the Pacific, Dr Barnes said, a great deal of work had been done on *Ciguatera*, especially by the Americans and Japanese. The particular organism responsible for the production of the poison had not been definitely identified, but it was generally conceded that it was a small vegetable form living on the sea bottom and showing a preference for raw or freshly created surfaces.

These surfaces need not be large. In other parts of the Pacific, surfaces created by the dragging of the chains of ships at anchor, or the dumping of war-surplus materials, or the sinking of a small vessel, had provided areas for colonization by the primary sources of the toxin.

"The areas where disturbance is likely to create a *Ciguatera* problem,"

Dr Barnes said, "are confined to tropical waters of relatively shallow depth and in the vicinity of reefs.

"The toxic organism is absorbed by fish during their normal feeding and the active principle of the poison is stored without deterioration or change in the tissues of the fish. As larger fish eat smaller, each predator acquires the total lifetime toxic experience of its prey, so that eventually the concentration builds up to a high level in the flesh of large fish, which are favoured by man as food.

"Quite commonly these large predatory fish are caught in an area adjacent to, but not actually at, the site of the original damage to the sea bottom. Progressive removal of surface material by mining would create a continuous new exposed surface on which the toxic organisms could grow without effective competition from other organisms. These toxic organisms are known to exist in the area, because of their effects, and could be expected to colonize the surface so created. Because there would be always new raw surfaces available, multiplication and possibly population explosion is likely."

Dr Barnes said he had accumulated detailed information on two hundred and thirty-two cases of *Ciguatera* intoxication, of which approximately half were cases treated by himself. "*Ciguatera* poisoning is quite widespread in Barrier Reef waters and has been so for many years," he said, "but in its present form the toxicity is low and the illness is unlikely to prove fatal. In other Pacific areas, where conditions have been favourable to an increase in toxicity, the illness has a fatality rate of two to five percent."

Dr Barnes opposed mining operations which would create the surfaces on which *Ciguatera* in Reef waters could increase. "I believe there is a serious risk," he testified, "that the proposed mining operations could precipitate a massive and dangerous outbreak of *Ciguatera*."

In court to present the evidence gathered on Ellison Reef by the diving team from the Queensland Littoral Society was Edward Hegerl, a twenty-three-year-old American. Hegerl had brought with him to Australia in 1963 a memory of the beauty of the Florida reefs, on which he had dived from childhood, and of the damage done to them by spear fishermen and coral and shell collectors. These experiences had led him to organize the Queensland Littoral Society, a group with a membership which included a number of divers and younger scientists willing to act as a sort of underwater vigilante force in tracking down sources of pollution or other threats to marine life. The evidence collected was brought to the attention of those government authorities with power to take action, and/or to the attention of the newspapers. As a result, the voluntary efforts of the Littoral Society were becoming a force in the politics of coastal ecology.

On Ellison Reef, Hegerl told the court, he and two other members of the Littoral Society, Ross Robertson and Peter Brockel, had carried out a five-day survey. On this supposedly dead reef they had identified one hundred and ninety species of fish, eighty-eight species of live coral, and ninety-five species of molluscs. On the south-eastern face of the reef, in one ten-minute period, four species of fish were observed spawning.

Large schools of parrot fish and surgeon fish were feeding on plant matter in the proposed lease area. "If mining were permitted," Hegerl said, "this would disrupt one of the major food chains of commercial and tourist importance, for the surgeon fish and the parrot fish are the main source of food for the cods and gropers that I observed in the deeper water of the outer reef . . . direct interference with the reef flat area would disrupt these food chains."

Like Dr McMichael, the Littoral Society divers had observed very fine silt on Ellison Reef, and this, if disturbed by mining, would choke both plant and animal life.

The applicant's lawyer did what he could. In Hegerl's case, he asked for academic qualifications. Hegerl admitted he had none. But at the age of twenty-three he claimed sixteen years of underwater experience. He worked for the University of Queensland, collecting marine animals for venoms research. He had done surveys with the Queensland Littoral Society. "The type of thing I have submitted," he said, "is not taught directly in University classes but is acquired through extensive field work." The lawyer insisted, "You are not a marine biologist?" Hegerl replied, "I consider that I am. I have two publications pending and have contributed much of the material for a paper that is in press."

For Dr McMichael there were questions covering such matters as the effects of silt disturbance on reef life. "The silt caused by the operation of heavy seas and high winds," the lawyer suggested, "would be much greater than any created by the mining." But Dr McMichael replied that the effects of the occasional storm were not like those of a protracted mining operation. "I believe that the silt which would arise from mining operations of the type envisaged," he said, "would be in great volume, widespread and persistent."

Dr Barnes, along with questions about *Ciguatera* poisoning, was asked to answer questions about a telephone call he had made to the applicant for the lease, Donald Forbes, who also lived in Cairns.

"You are pretty hostile to Mr Forbes?"

"I don't know Mr Forbes."

"You spoke to him on the phone before the last hearing."

"Yes."

"You threatened him."

"I did not."

"You threatened to punch him on the nose."

Barnes, a short man with a long chin and a thin face likely to split crossways in a grin, said, "I did not. I deny that. I am only a little man."

Later the lawyer asked, "What induced you to call Forbes if you didn't know him?"

"I thought then, as now, that he was unaware of the possible consequences of his proposed mining. I had hoped that he would listen to suggestions of its danger to the welfare of the Reef, and perhaps not continue with his application."

"Did you become a little annoyed when he wasn't receptive to these ideas?"

"I can't recall. I was disappointed, I think."

"Do you think you might have said this: 'I suppose there is nothing else to do but put the phone down and come around and punch you on the nose'?"

Dr Barnes felt certain he hadn't said that.

With the testimony complete, the mining warden, J. W. Ashfield, retired to consider his verdict. When he delivered it, on 8 December 1967, it turned out to be a partial victory for Busst and the team which had gone to Innisfail to testify. But there were some heart-stopping preliminaries:

"On the evidence adduced, and strictly from a mining viewpoint, I know of no reason why the lease applied for should not be approved, subject to survey," the mining warden stated. ". . . In my view the area in question is subject to the Mining Acts and Regulations, 1898 to 1967 by virtue of The Mineral Resources (Adjacent Submarine Areas) Act of 1964.

"However there are other factors to be considered. Many objections have been lodged, and appearing objectors have been heard. Letters and telegrams of protest have also been received by me as warden.

"... on a careful consideration of all the evidence adduced I recommend to the Honourable the Minister that in the public interest, and in the interest of probable preservation of the Great Barrier Reef, that the application should be refused and that the deposit of survey fees and rent be refunded to the applicant."

It was then a matter of waiting for the Minister to arrive at a decision, a process which was to take nearly five months.

CHAPTER 8

Canefields and Coral

✳

AMONG the invisible figures in the Ellison Reef case were the cane farmers for whom the lime was to be mined. While I was in Cairns I set out to meet some of them. First I called on Donald Forbes, who was both the applicant for the lease on Ellison Reef and the secretary of the Cairns District Canegrowers' Executive. Forbes turned out to be a big dark man who laughed easily and heartily, his brown eyes lighting up so that they actually seemed to twinkle. He laughed like that in the Canegrowers' office when I said apparently he had been encountering some rather strong opposition to his plans. "Yes," he said. "One character even rang me up and offered to come around and punch me on the nose." His own view of his application was that he would do no harm to the Reef. Giving his side of the Ellison Reef case, he argued that the lime he wanted to take was not living coral but coral which had been beaten down into sand. It was lying all over the place out there, just waiting to be gathered up. Well yes, I said, but what about the animals which lived in it, what about the whole – "Ecology?" Forbes asked, and laughed that hearty laugh. "Ecology – that's the word now, isn't it? Everything's ecology. But you know, it's ecology in your back garden, too. Say you go out in the garden and take up a handful of earth. You don't think of all the little mites that you're disturbing – such a multitude of them you don't even realize they're there. But then somebody gets up and says, 'This bloke is destroying the valuable little such-and-such and so-and-so'. And people think, 'what a wretch!' But if they were just told that this bloke had gone out into the garden and picked up a handful of dirt – it would seem different, wouldn't it?"

He hadn't been upset by all the abuse, nor had his wife and their four children. They'd found the situation pretty hilarious, too. "Basically we're rather a well adjusted family. We've been through some pretty dry gullies at times, and it takes a lot to upset us." In World War II, Forbes had been a leading seaman in the Australian Navy. Afterwards he went back for a time to working in a bank. But the land had always attracted him, and he had decided to take a risk on buying a cane farm. Since he wasn't rich the soil wasn't, either, and his main profit from the enterprise was an understanding of how tough canefarming could be. It was good experience for this job as an executive for other canegrowers. When he had thought about the lime enterprise he had consulted a geologist at a southern university. He felt he had acted responsibly, and he had tried to explain his viewpoint to the conservationists. He showed me the long letter he had written to the Wildlife Preservation Society of Queensland, in which one of the points he had made was that mining Ellison Reef would have some value as an experiment. ". . . results of my trials would at least provide a guide to what might or might not be able to be done when oil and mineral-sands people really begin to move," he had written to the society. "There is very little area not already involved with these interests in some form or other and the big people are the ones who will really make inroads if something goes wrong and there is no previous experience for guidance." He regretted that apparently his letter had not changed the views of the conservationists. He feared a lot of these people had the wrong idea of him because of distorted publicity, which had made them think, "This bloke's a ratbag."

But in fact that was not what these people thought, or not the conservationists I had met. The fear of many of them was that Forbes' application was really the beginning of a campaign to open up the whole Reef to exploitation, that if he succeeded with the Ellison Reef application then much bigger interests would move in. Almost a year after Forbes' letter to the Wildlife Society, conservationists at a Reef symposium in Sydney in May, 1969, seemed to hear an echo of his argument for experimental limestone mining in an address given by the manager of Conzinc Riotinto Exploration. The company was part of a mining group dominated by Britain's Rio Tinto-Zinc Corporation Limited (R.T.Z.), described by *The Australian* newspaper in 1969 as "the largest and most diversified mining group operating in Australia". At the Reef symposium the exploration manager, D. S. Carruthers, delivered himself of the cheerless news (for conservationists) that quite apart from limestone and oil and gas, the Reef probably contained "mineral commodities of value." Mainly, he thought, these would be siliceous sands, heavy mineral sands, tin and phosphate. "The principles involved in their exploitation," he said, in a sentence which reinforced the fear that experiments in limestone mining would open up the Reef to many sorts of despoliation, "would be substantially the same as for limestone."

He felt that "it should be possible to carry out mining operations in restricted parts of the Reef province without interference to actively growing parts of the Reef". And he stressed that there should be "no complete ban on mining on the Reef because of the great difficulty in having such a ban modified in any way later". What was needed, he told the symposium, was a definitive study which would show what the effects of mining would be. "It may be necessary," he said, "to carry out some experimental or carefully controlled mining before such a study can be regarded as complete."

Forbes had been candid enough in his letter to the conservationists about the fact that he was willing to have his enterprise regarded as an experiment. Still, when he said he thought bad publicity had made people think of him as a ratbag, and I replied that I thought the hostility was based on something else, that his project was thought of as a flyer for bigger interests, he seemed unhappy. "Yes," he said sombrely, "yes, that has been suggested, too." Afterwards he gave great emphasis to the point that nothing he contemplated could harm the Reef, that after all everybody in his family was keen on Nature. "One of the things my wife and I have always remembered is that we are living in an era when a lot of Australia is being reduced from its natural state," he said. "We have always made a point of getting out into the bush and saying to the kids, 'look at this and remember it – because by the time you grow up all you'll be able to do for *your* children is tell them about it'."

I was surprised into saying, "You just accept this?" And he on his part looked surprised and said, well, what could you do but accept it? Everybody knew it wasn't going to last much longer. How could it, the way everything now was being developed?

It was Forbes' offsider, Allan Antcliff, assistant secretary of the Cairns District Canegrowers' Executive, who drove me around the sugar district and introduced me to some of its problems. The sky was blue, the hills were bluer, the cane sprang green from red earth, but many of the farmers, it transpired, were in deep trouble. They, and through them the Great Barrier Reef, were among the world's unlikeliest victims of the Cuban revolution. Because of the disorganization of Cuba, and because the United States government had no palate for Castro sugar, and because these circumstances were thought to present an opportunity for Australia to step up from second to first place among the world's raw sugar exporters, there had been a great and uneconomic expansion of cane growing in Queensland. New farms had been opened up in the sugar districts along the Reef coast (so that more insecticides and fertilisers had found their way into Reef waters) and men with big mortgages had worked incredibly hard to produce more sugar. They had produced it at about the time it became clear that other countries had also observed Cuba's difficulties, and had also produced more sugar, and that in any case Cuba was still managing to market sugar, and that as a result of all this world prices for sugar were beginning to slump. On the Reef coast, the worst hit were the new farmers, the men who not only had mortgages to meet but, being latecomers with last choice of the land, comparatively poor soil from which to meet them. Some of these farmers were struggling to raise their crops in "white earth", a variety noticeably paler than the rich soils of the older farms. Most of the soils benefited from the use of lime, but the white earth almost demanded it. And the farmers who owned this earth couldn't afford the lime they needed at the price it cost after a long trip overland. These men had naturally given some thought to the argument that water transport was cheaper than land transport and that just out there in the sea were thousands of tons of highly suitable lime. Don Forbes talked of Ellison Reef supplying the farms around Innisfail, but there were plenty more reefs to supply other areas. The farmers didn't want to harm the Barrier Reef (and weren't there many assurances that mining wouldn't harm it?) but if somebody like Don Forbes could get them cheap lime by floating it in from the reefs, well then, they wanted to see him do that.

As well as troubles, these canefarmers had certain things they were proud of. Several times it was mentioned to me that their sugar industry was, in a way, unique, since it was the only one in the world run entirely on white labour. The curious emphases in these remarks were a reminder that in the last century there had been racial trouble on this coast, much of it connected with the sugar industry. The early opponents of the White Australia concept were not always the liberal-minded people who now opposed the policy barring non-white settlers. Often, the opposition had come from men who were by nature slavers, working to establish in Queensland an old-southern-plantation type of society based on sugar, cotton, and the labour of South Sea Islanders. Many of the ships which sailed through the Reef in the second half of the nineteenth century belonged to the black-birders, the kidnappers of island labour. The trade they conducted in kanakas, as the islanders were called, was often as violent as the African slave trade. The men they brought to Queensland ostensibly came under indenture freely entered into, but actually, in many cases, as prisoners. Some had been lured on board the ship with offers of presents and then locked below until the ship cleared their island. Others had been run down in their canoes and grabbed out of the water. Others had been handed over by their chiefs in return for assorted considerations from the blackbirders. The brutality of the trade, along with its effect in depressing the wages of white labourers, aroused a strong opposition in other states, and in the first years of the twentieth century, following federation, it was ended. One of its legacies was an often fanatical support for a White Australia. Another was this habit of pointing to white achievement in the sugar industry – to the fact that all those men out there slaving in the heat of the canefields were white. People said it showed that a white man could stand up to the tropical sun as well as anybody. And there was no reason anyone could think of, offhand, why Northern Queensland should hold the world's record for skin cancer.

One of the new farmers growing cane in poor earth was Vic Hussey. His house stood in front of a field of young sugarcane, the foot-high plants leading back in green rows towards a chain of trucks piled with cut cane going to the mill. The earth wasn't really white. It was, in fact, quite brown, but without the incredible red to purple tinges of the richer soils. Hussey came in from the field to greet us. He was a large, blue-eyed man. He had on a wide-brimmed hat, and he also had a stubble of beard protecting his fair skin. He'd had what he called sun spots – skin cancers – and had had to have radium treatment. He took us out of the glare into the shade of an iron awning over farm machinery and a 1942 truck, and then on into a very neat, light, suburban interior, with a china cabinet and a dark velvet lounge suite and vases of bright plastic flowers. On the long dining table were laid out the four varieties of cake which his wife Tina had baked for us. She was a slight, dark, pretty woman, the daughter of a Sicilian who had come to Queensland forty years ago. Pouring tea, she said with a little smile that she supposed things then had been even harder, in a way, than they were now. Her father had worked as a cane cutter, and he'd had to walk between farms looking for jobs. The farms were far apart then, too. Still, eventually he managed to buy a bicycle, and then he managed to bring his wife out from Sicily. And then he leased some land and they started to raise vegetables. And then Italy entered World War II, and he was interned. He had no politics, but they mixed him up with someone of the same name who did have. There were thousands of Italian migrants in the sugar areas, and it got to be confusing. It was hard on the women in the family, because while the father was interned the son was in the army, and that left the women to keep the farm going. There had been one good, easy time in her life, Tina Hussey said, and that was early in her marriage. Vic Hussey had been driving a mobile crane for the council, and they were very comfortable. But then everybody started talking about there being money in sugar if you got in now. Hussey had cut cane as a boy, and he knew that a successful sugar farmer was a rich man. He and Tina decided that a cane farm could give their children a future. In 1963, when Hussey bought his land on mortgage, sugar prices were phenomenally good. In 1964 prices slumped, and the hard times began which were to outlast the decade.

Not eating, crumbling the cake in front of him with sun-bitten hands, Hussey said, "If I had lime, I could get more out of this ground. Definitely, I could get more to the acre. The experimental station near here says all this white soil ought to have lime. But I don't have it. I can't afford it. When I came into this business all I wanted was a fair living, but by gee I'm not getting it. My average earning per hour, I'd reckon is about thirty-five cents. The man I bought the ground off – he has let me owe him the money at interest. But for his goodness I wouldn't be here."

"And yet he's doing three jobs," his wife said. "He works on another man's farm as well as his own. He goes down there in the morning. Leaves here at a quarter to six, comes in about quarter past eleven, gulps down a lunch and goes off again at twelve to start hauling cane. When he comes back about half-past four, five, maybe later, he's down in the paddock trying to catch up on his own work. And it's weekends, too. It's the whole week, it's not just five days a week. It's Saturdays and Sundays." She laughed. "And I'm getting crankier every day."

Hussey said, "I have no alternative". He added, slowly and carefully, "If I don't do it, we walk off". His wife sighed and smiled and said "Oh dear" – something she continued to say at intervals, without appearing to notice.

"Lime," said Hussey, "it's a sweetener. And I reckon all this fuss about it is because Don Forbes is just a little man. The oil companies are drilling the Reef, aren't they? Nobody'll stop the oil companies." Well, I said, the conservationists hadn't realized the oil companies were drilling until quite recently. Now there would be moves to stop them. "I'd like to see it," Hussey said, smiling. "It's the battler that loses out. They want oil, they get it. We want lime, we can't have it." He had to get back then to his three jobs. Walking away down the canefield he wore his big hat, but no hat could keep out this heat which seemed to strike through fabric and skin to the bone.

Perhaps half an hour later I met up with him again in a neighbouring field, and he introduced other men who shared his opinion of the lime issue. One of the men, an Italian, said, "My land, they say it needs lime. But the lime's too dear. We don't want to harm the Reef, but we want lime". Forbes was popular with all of them. He was a battler, they said, and he was also, in the words of one, "a gentleman and a half, that Forbes".

Later, Allan Antcliff (of the Canegrowers' Executive) drove me around the sugar fires, showing me what might be the most stupendous fireworks display on earth. He had heard there was to be a burn at a certain farm at about a quarter to six, but when we got there it was over. There would be others, he said, and we drove on for a long time, seeing nothing between high walls of cane. These fires were lit, Antcliff said, to clean out the fields for the next day's harvesting. The fire didn't hurt the cane, but it got rid of the undergrowth, and the snakes, and the rats, and the *spirochaete leptospira*, which was spread by the rats and could cause a serious infection called Weil's Disease. When we emerged from the green corridors of cane, some of them ten feet high, there was still just a little light. The hills were mauve-dark above the canefields, which were a geometry of bare red earth, and young green plants, and tall plumed canes. Yellow grass ran in lurid ridges up into the hills, and in places the jungle-black of rain forest divided the fields. The light faded, and a pyramid-shaped hill showed dark against an only slightly less dark sky. At the left of the pyramid there was a small, orange-gold glow. "That's a fire now," said Antcliff, and began to drive for it. We drove into a smell of sugar cooking, as if all over the plain people were making jam. Ahead of us there were dark clouds underlit with gold, and then a long rectangle of the night went up in flames. We got out of the car to watch. We were a quarter of a mile from the fire, but it was impossible to talk. You could hear nothing except the crack and roar of the fire, which was now five to ten minutes old, and near its last surge. It ended with a column of orange flame flung into the sky and gone in seconds. "We'll find you another one to watch from the beginning," Antcliff said obligingly, and we drove on through the smell of jam, the sky dark, the earth occasionally spurting a far-off plume of flame. By good luck, we came on a field just as a fire was about to start. Stationed well back from the field, we waited as men walked through the dark with kerosene burners to touch it into flame. A glow spread out in a line and began to rise, to gain height, to move like a molten wave along the whole width of the field, a front three-quarters of a mile wide. In this huge wave of fire other fires started. Pale gold bubbles rose up through the flame as if through water and sank again, and rose, and then began a rapid bouncing. Fountains of red fire spurted out of gold. As the canefield screamed and roared and cracked, stars rained upwards on the sky. Then all the fountains and stars and bubbles rushed up together into a toppling wall of flame that collapsed on the night. There was just a faint glow now behind the palisades of stripped cane. It lit the figures of two hurrying farmers and then, dying, extinguished them.

CHAPTER 9

Lime, Oil and Other Resources

※

CONSERVATIONISTS were growing anxious over the decision on Ellison Reef to be handed down by the Minister for Mines. Why was he taking so long? By April of 1968 it was four months since the mining warden had made his recommendation that the application be rejected. Surely it should not be such a hard decision to make. The position of the canefarmers was that they needed lime to grow sugar which, sadly, wasn't needed. The solution, at least to the lime problem, was to subsidise or in some way adjust the price of lime available on the mainland, not to despoil the Reef. But were there other considerations to be weighed in the precedent-setting application to mine Ellison Reef? Commenting on the case, the Queensland Littoral Society Newsletter said, "It is known that extremely large supplies of limestone are available on land in the Townsville area" (of northern Queensland). "We understand, however, that major Japanese and American companies may be negotiating for mining rights on large areas of the Barrier Reef." Why? To be economic, limestone supplies had to be cheap to exploit. Could it be a proposition to take a ship from a far country into the Reef area, and then, with a minimum of handling charges, load the uniquely pure sand straight on board? "I know why they're going into the Barrier Reef," said Professor Gordon McKay, Professor of Civil Engineering at the University of Queensland, in a general comment on moves to mine the Reef. "Think of this. A box of oranges can double in price every time it's put down and picked up. Now, if you want to haul stuff, say, to Japan, you've got to put it on a ship. So if you can get it straight out of the ocean, that's the obvious way, isn't it? It's the cheapest way of getting stuff out."

Sometimes even the mystery of the crown-of-thorns explosion looked easy to solve alongside the mystery of which mining or oil concern was planning to do what where. The conservationists worked on hints, passed each other clues. Even so, it was impossible to keep track of all the developments. Few people realized, for example, until the Conzinc Riotinto Exploration manager referred to the matter at the 1969 Reef symposium, that in 1967, before the Ellison Reef application had been fought out, North Australian Cement Ltd. had checked on bottom sediment in Reef waters as a source of limestone. The investigation had taken place in an area east of Magnetic Island, and had suggested that "it would be technically feasible to dredge such calcareous bottom sediment".

In May of 1968 the Queensland Minister for Mines, the Honourable Ronald Camm, gave his verdict on Ellison Reef. He had considered the mining warden's recommendation, and he had decided to reject the application to mine. But before the conservationists could send up a cheer he had added a *however*:

However [said the Minister] the decision does not mean that the position cannot be reviewed at some future time if the current objections to the proposal can be proved to be incorrect.

The Queensland government regards the Great Barrier Reef as a valuable national asset and no member of the present government would favour, for one moment, any action that would be harmful to the Reef. . . .

No mining activity based on the harvesting of dead coral is permitted at the present time on the Great Barrier Reef and this state of affairs will not be changed unless overwhelming evidence is produced to suggest that there could be some limited exploitation that would not adversely affect the Reef in any way.

However, the decision does not mean that the position cannot be reviewed. With that *however* sounding in their minds the conservationists pondered the fact that the government had engaged an American, Dr Harry Ladd, to report on the conservation and exploitation of the Reef, and that he was even now reporting on it. Dr Ladd was an eminent scientist, but he was not a marine biologist. He was a geologist. Not a biologist but a geologist had been chosen to advise the government on the future of an area containing one of the world's most marvellous communities of animals. To gather material on which to base his recommendations Dr Ladd had arranged to visit the Reef and make a survey, and incredibly this survey was to occupy one month. "We are extremely concerned about this matter," said the Queensland Littoral Society in a newsletter to its members, and listed the reasons:

1. We do not see how it is possible even to gain adequate geological

impressions in one month that would be of any value in formulating a conservation policy.

2. Dr Ladd stated during a television interview that nearly two-thirds of most coral reefs in the Pacific were dead, thereby implying that such areas (i.e. reef flats) were of no biological significance. Dr Ladd is a geologist.

3. We question whether even an eminent geologist, together with an equally eminent biologist and perhaps also an economist could make a significant assessment in twelve months of intensive study, let alone a one-month trip.

4. Mr Camm* has stated that during his visit, Dr Ladd will be constantly accompanied by Mines Department officials and will not have time to meet representatives from local groups.

When the Ladd report was released, it was prefaced by a summary. This included the observation that, although neither oil nor gas had as yet been discovered, "the outlook for such discoveries is promising". The summary continued, "As a source of agricultural lime and lime-stone for cement manufacture, parts of the reef that do not now support living coral can be developed, if sites are carefully selected and operations rigidly controlled".

Early in the report there was a statement on the events which had brought Ladd to Australia. It appeared that in March, 1968, during that period when the Queensland Minister for Mines was suspending judgment on the Ellison Reef case, I. W. Morley, the Queensland State Mining Engineer, was in Washington having talks with J. Cordell Moore, the United States' Assistant Secretary of Interior for Mineral Resources. According to Dr Ladd, "Mr Morley spoke of his govern-ment's need of certain advice regarding the mineral potential of the Great Barrier Reefs and their future exploitation, having due regard to their conservation. Secretary Moore suggested that Mr Morley discuss the matter with Dr W. T. Pecora, Director of the Geological Survey. This was done, Dr Pecora recommending that the writer be sent to Queensland for a rapid survey. . . ."

From Brisbane, Dr Ladd set out on a tour which did not in fact take a month. It began on 3 May 1968 and ended with his return to Brisbane on 26 May. In the intervening period he examined reefs and

* The Minister for Mines.

islands by plane, launch, and on foot. In his acknowledgments of help given him in Queensland, Ladd wrote, "I am especially indebted to Mr J. T. Woods, Chief Government Geologist, who planned my itinerary and accompanied me during parts of the survey, and to Mr Peter Ellis, geologist with the Queensland Survey, who is familiar with the land geology opposite the Reef and who accompanied me during my entire trip, giving me the benefit of his knowledge as well as making arrangements for travel by launch and plane".

The report which resulted struck an optimistic note. "The reef must be protected from serious and widespread damage," it said – seeming to suggest that there was such a thing as unserious and localized damage – "but some of its resources can, nonetheless, be exploited, if such operations are controlled." The report warned that, "In the case of drilling for oil and gas, the selection of drill sites will not be governed in any way by the richness of the surface reefs but instead, by the location of underground geologic structures". In a reference to something called "excessive pollution" (could there be on the Reef any other sort of pollution?) the report said easily, "Control of excessive pollution can be exercised during the drilling process and, after discovery, pollution can be held to a minimum".

The report's recommendation was for an overall survey of the Reef preparatory to exploitation. The first step would be to make an adequate base map, since none existed. To obtain the information for such a map, the Reef should be photographed from the air. The cost of the photographs would be around four hundred thousand dollars.

"Before discussing the kind of field work to be done on the newly mapped areas," the report said, "it might be well to consider what agency should be responsible for planning the survey and actually seeing that it is carried out." Ladd listed agencies as various as the Department of Mines and the Wildlife Preservation Society of Queensland, and then concluded that "the Government departments and the Great Barrier Reef Committee are, perhaps, the most broad-minded of the organizations named. They are well aware of the need for conservation but they also believe that controlled exploitation is possible and, indeed, desirable." He suggested how activities in the survey might be farmed out. The geologists should be in control of plans to study and exploit the shelf that lay beneath the Reef – that is, beneath its corals, its fish, its dolphins, the whole of its life. "This, it seems to me, is a field where the Queensland Geological Survey should be in control," Ladd wrote. "The Survey is already co-operating with oil companies, using Survey data to assist in the selection of drill sites and receiving logs and cores obtained during drilling. This is a mutually beneficial exchange. If and when oil and gas resources are discovered the Queensland Department of Mines (and its Geological Survey) will be in a position to recommend regulations that will permit development without excessive damage to the existing reefs." The role to be assigned to the marine biologist in the research on mining, that activity which would so intimately affect the living Reef, seemed to emerge from the recommendation that "Survey personnel assigned to study potential mining areas should include a geologist with training in sedimentary petrology and shallow water oceanography; a biologist should be available at least on a part-time basis. . . ." The Great Barrier Reef Committee might be called on for advice: "Personnel assigned to study conditions in much used areas should include a geologist and/or sedimentationist with basic training in reef biology. If unusually difficult biological problems are encountered the survey group should ask the members of the Great Barrier Reef Committee for advice and, if needed, for active participation in field surveys." As for the time to be allowed for the study on which action governing the fate of the Reef was to be based – "It is estimated that at least two years will be required for an overall survey of much-used areas and areas where mining has been proposed or where prospects for such activity appear promising."

At least two years. But two years would go nowhere in marine biology. Two years wasn't enough to uncover the basic facts about one species such as the crown-of-thorns starfish, much less the thousands of species which would be affected by exploitation of the Reef. Dr John Barnes of Cairns compared the period mentioned in the Ladd report with the time it had taken him to study the killer jellyfish without coming to the end of its mysteries. "This jellyfish thing has taken me ten solid years," he said. "I've broken it open but I haven't tied the ends of it. And this is relatively a small problem, just one little aspect of Reef life."

There were, of course, various estimates of the Ladd report. At the Reef symposium of 1969, the manager of Conzinc Riotinto Exploration was to quote it with respect in support of his feeling that it should be possible to mine parts of the Reef without overall damage. He pointed out that Dr Ladd had said as much after that visit which the manager referred to as Ladd's "comprehensive reconnaisance in 1968." But "comprehensive reconnaissance" was not what a number of other people called the twenty-four day visit. "It's purely a political move," said John Busst, at northern conservationist headquarters at Bingal Bay. Dr Ladd, he said, had been brought in by the government in the hope that his report would allow it to go ahead and mine. "Dr Ladd has said strict controls should be established," Busst pointed out. "What sort of controls? How can you stop siltation and pollution on a mining site on the Great Barrier Reef? What do you do – put a canvas fence around it?"

In a sense, the report might have been interpreted as a defeat for Busst and the forces which had defended Ellison Reef. However, it would by now be extremely difficult to act on such a report. Busst and Monkman and the Wildlife Preservation Society and the Queensland Littoral Society and the citizens ranged behind them had raised such a furore that people all over Queensland and beyond were catching their concern. Even among scientists who had supported controlled exploitation of the Reef there was some rethinking. In the Great Barrier Reef Committee a resolution was proposed which included the very important words, "The Committee is opposed to mining". It was a resolution which, as one Committee member pointed out, was not in agreement with the statement submitted to the State government on conservation and exploitation. In fact, it seemed to move a long way from the spirit of the Proposals. Still, members such as Dr Patricia Mather, the honorary secretary, were for it. Dr Mather said there were strong moves for conservation throughout the community and the Committee would be avoiding their responsibilities if they did not support these moves by stating policies for the maintenance of faunal balance. Another argument put forward for the resolution was that there had been criticism of the Great Barrier Reef Committee when it had not publicly opposed the application to mine Ellison Reef. In the end a meeting carried a complicated resolution which differentiated between the renewable and non-renewable resources of the Reef – that is, between fish, say, and minerals. The resolution contained the vital words, "The Committee is opposed to mining as an operation designed to remove resources which are not renewable, until such time as it can be shown that mining does not adversely affect the renewable resources of the reefs."

Among conservationists at the beginning of 1969 there was a feeling that after all the forces which had fought for Ellison Reef had won a victory. And they had, too. But it was a victory like many others, good only until the next challenge. This challenge was to develop through 1969 as the government struggled to force public acceptance of oil drilling on the Reef. One of the warning shots of the new battle was to be fired off in February by the State Mining Engineer (late of the Washington talks to arrange the Ladd visit) when he suggested that certain oil experiments could be carried out at the lovely island where the Great Barrier Reef Committee had its research station – Heron Island, at the southern end of the Reef.

CHAPTER 10

Heron Island, with Reptiles and Researchers

✳

THE night sky over Heron Island seemed very high and black beyond its veils of diamonds. The sea around was shining dark. Somewhere out there in the smooth blackness of the water, and possibly at this moment coming in over the corals towards the beach, were the turtles which had swum perhaps a thousand miles down the Reef to lay their eggs on this island. Lost in the darkness of the beach, observers were waiting for them. The observers included Dr Robert Bustard, who was engaged on a turtle research programme, and later this evening would be collaborating on a film about the turtles being made by the Australian Commonwealth Film Unit. Invisible behind the curve of this almost oval cay, the unit was setting up its cameras and lights. Suddenly, away on my right, there was a movement in the shallows. Something huge was rising from the dark water – something like a boulder was beaching itself on the pale sand. *Chelonia mydas*, the great green turtle, the carapaced reptile weighing perhaps three hundred pounds, was coming ashore. It pulled itself up to the shining line which marked the end of the sea and the beginning of the land, and rested. Even now, it seemed, it might refuse to go on with this visit, might turn back into the ocean where it could swim fast and be reasonably secure. On land it would be helpless – a slow, heavy animal without defences. And yet it was compelled to come ashore, because it was compelled to deposit its eggs in sand. Its ancestors, deserting the land, had adapted to the sea in everything but their method of reproduction. A young turtle had still to hatch from a shelled egg, had still to struggle up out of a sand-covered nest and scramble down a beach before it could become a dweller in the sea. And the mature female turtle, defenceless on land, had still to leave the sea to perpetuate the cycle.

At the wet rim of the beach the turtle put out its flippers, jerked forward, rested. Again the flippers moved, again the boulder jerked as it began its advance up the beach to find a nesting site. The track it was leaving was like that of a huge tyre, deep and clear even by starlight. A hunter had only to follow that track to take both the animal and its eggs. This was one of the reasons why in many parts of the world the sea turtle had come close to extinction. On the Barrier Reef, too, it had been headed that way. This turtle landing on Heron in the nineteen-twenties would simply have been delivering itself to the soup cannery which then operated here. Now its instinctive nervousness was unjustified. Turtles had been declared protected in Queensland waters, and except for the traditional Aboriginal hunter no one was permitted to kill a turtle or take its eggs. The worst that could happen to this specimen was that a numbered tag would be attached to it, making it a contributor to the data from which Dr Bustard was filling in the story of its species in Reef waters.

An aspect of that story was the long swim the turtle had made from the north to lay its eggs. The mystery was not only why it had made the journey, but how. "Why" was probably answered in part by the fact that, like green turtles in other seas, it had found that its rather specialized requirements both in feeding and in egg-laying could not be satisfied in one locality. The green turtle was largely herbivorous. It found good feeding grounds in the north, but encountered there a coastline and islands with a great deal of mangrove frontage, useless to an animal needing a beach in which to bury its eggs. And so the turtle swam south – but not just to any beach, it was suspected, but to one particular beach, a beach to which it would probably return in another four years to lay its eggs again. The question was, how did it select this beach? And how did it find it? Similar questions had fascinated scientists in other countries where the migrations of the green turtle had been noted. The Brazilian green turtle, for example, regularly travelled fourteen hundred miles to nest on Ascension Island, in the South Atlantic. How did it find that island in a wilderness of water? It had been suggested that a sense of smell might be involved, an ability to nose out substances which were signposts on the journey. So might an ability to navigate. Dr Archie Carr, Florida's eminent authority on sea turtles, had written in *The Reptiles*:

> When the known facts of the life history of the green turtle are carefully examined, the conclusion that it is able to navigate seems almost inescapable. The Brazilian green turtle colony that makes regular nesting migrations to Ascension Island in the middle of the South Atlantic is obviously guided in its travel by some incredibly

sophisticated means. The most likely theory now seems to be a hybrid one: that the guidance mechanism is a combined sun-compass sense and olfactory capacity to detect Ascension substance washed downstream in the equatorial current.

It was with some feeling of awe, then, that I followed along behind the huge migrant jerking its way over the Heron Island beach into the cover of the trees. I walked behind it into a forest growing from sand. It was dark among the trees, but the sand made a pale floor to the darkness – a very uneven floor, much of the sand being cratered as if from a bombardment because other turtles had been digging nests here. The turtle I followed jerked like an old tank over the craters, half-sliding down one side, heaving itself up the other. It rested near a tree and I thought that perhaps it would stop and dig. But it started up again, possibly having calculated that the tree roots would ruin its excavations. It jerked on over the bombed-out sand, pushing deeper into the trees. Suddenly the forest seemed to be full of cranky babies, all crying at once. In the darkness the protests began with a tight-throated wail, opened up into a steady bawling, died away into a sob, and then started all over again. This was the song of the shearwaters, the birds which, like the turtles, dug their nests in the sands of this island, and travelled even greater distances to get here. Every year they flew down from Siberia, finding the island in the southern ocean by means about which there was as little certainty as there was about the turtle's methods of navigation. The shearwaters burrowed out nests in the sand, raised their young, and then deserted them to return to Siberia. The young followed up to a couple of months later, so that it could not even be argued that they found their way across the world under the guidance of older, experienced birds.

As the turtle advanced, looking for a nesting site, the wailing song of the shearwaters rose just ahead of us. The turtle went no further. It pushed in under a low, leafy branch and rested. Then it began to dig, scooping up a flipperful of sand, the first of perhaps a ton which it would displace during the making of its nest. The sand rose in the air and fell with a thud. The turtle's flipper scooped again, and again there was a thud.

A sleepy whistling began up above in the trees as another group of the turtle's neighbours registered its presence. These were the noddy terns, which also used Heron as a rookery. They left the cratered ground to the turtles and the shearwaters and in their thousands took over the trees. In the darkness, as the digging turtle sent the sand flying, more and more terns were awakening with complaining whistles. A tern investigator flew down. All that was visible in the dark was the white cap of the head, disembodied as it circled the turtle, making small indignant noises. Indifferent, the turtle went on heaving sand. The tern gave up. The white cap ascended, and in a little while the whistlings died away and the dark trees went back to sleep.

The film unit, I realized, would now be about ready to start work. The turtle's excavation would go on for a long time, and I didn't think I'd wait. It would go on digging until it sat in a pit with the top of its carapace about level with the ground. Then, with its rear flippers, it would dig a second hole, the egg chamber, extending down from the first. Into this chamber it would drop its round, rubbery eggs – about one hundred and ten of them if the clutch was an average one. It would cover the eggs with sand and then, since this was Heron Island and it had no enemies here, it would make massive tracks down the beach and swim out over the reef. But that event was hours away, and the film unit would now be starting up work on the beach. I decided to leave the turtle to its excavations.

Walking across the island, flashing a torch now to avoid the turtle pits and bird burrows, I saw the shearwaters I had been hearing. They were solid, dark birds with downward-hooked beaks and something the look of small ducks. They sat around in groups, some on the cratered sand, others among the gnarled roots of the pisonia trees. In these roots there were caves which were obviously the habitat of gnomes. The shearwaters, though, had taken them over, and stared from them as I passed. Their singing never stopped. In trios, quartets, quintets, they sat and made complicated songs, the low "whoo" notes held against a rising wail, a short quick bawling cutting through a sound like an angry sob.

As I walked through the last trees behind the beach I came on Dr Bustard, a large figure crouching in the shadows with a bucket of baby turtles from his research hatchery. He was waiting to empty them out on a wide stretch of sand which had been turned into a floodlit stage. A camera was stationed down near the water, facing up the beach. Floodlights on lofty tripods beamed down on the sand, which hadn't a turtle track or a footmark on it. The film crew, Bustard said, had been guarding this stretch of the beach from intruders. When they filmed it they wanted a picture of the little turtles racing across otherwise unmarked sand. It was an uncomplicated scenario the film-makers had devised for this scene – release the turtles beyond range of the camera, then film them as they rush down the beach – and now they were ready to shoot it. The producer gave a signal. Bustard tipped his bucket. Turtles about two inches long poured out, hesitated, and then began to row down over the floodlit sand. The four flippers worked together like those of the large turtle, but immensely faster. Behind them were the small straight tracks the producer wanted. They had only to move a little further down the beach and he would have a perfect sequence. The turtles rowed on, pointing for the horizon. Even on a night without moon or stars they unerringly found their way to the sea, responding to a radiance out there which attracted them like moths to a light. You couldn't see the radiance, but it was definitely there – Bustard had an assistant on the island measuring it. It drew the turtles straight from the nest down to the sea. Or rather, it drew them provided they did not encounter a stronger light on the way. Now, having encountered the film unit's floodlights, the little turtles were slowing down. They were beginning to turn in circles, to wander, pointing now towards one tripod and now towards another. Eventually there were groups of turtles fanning out toward each of the lights and some, reaching the tripods, were trying to climb them. The confused tracks in the sand made it look as if it had been worked over by a particularly disturbed doodler, and from the film unit there was a low moaning.

The turtles had to be retrieved and the shots done again. Walking out and picking them up meant that footprints would be added to the mess of tracks in the sand. Eventually a couple of the crew danced out on their toes, scooped up turtles, and then tiptoed off backwards, smoothing the sand as they retreated. For the next attempt, it was decided, a larger batch of turtles would be emptied out on the sand. Some of their number, surely, would remain loyal to that radiance in the sea.

Perhaps half an hour later it seemed that the unit would at last get the picture it needed. But it seemed so only briefly, because it was at this juncture that another party of turtles came marching into focus to ruin the take. The new arrivals looked much the same as the stars of the film, but they were not the same. They were loggerhead turtles invading a film about green turtles. Somewhere beyond the top light they had just scrambled out of a nest. Now they, too, were on their way towards the radiance in the sea. The trouble was that instead of rowing as a green turtle would, they were using their flippers to walk like quadrupeds. Instead of being white underneath, they were dark. It wouldn't do. Green turtles would have to be separated from loggerhead turtles, and the shots done again. There was a rather long session then of sorting greens from loggerheads. When you picked up a two-inch turtle the flippers went on rowing or marching on the air. The little turtles felt like soft leather, and they had dark, gentle eyes. The greens were returned to buckets. The loggerheads were taken to the water and dropped in with the suggestion that they get on with the business of swimming for the horizon. Filming began again. Buckets of green turtles had been emptied out on the sand, and a fair percentage of them were holding their course for the sea, when marching up out of the water and back on to the sand stage came squads of loggerheads. The floodlights had proved stronger than natural radiance. The loggerheads had been drawn backwards on to the beach. Again, the loggerheads and the greens had to be separated, and this time the loggerheads were imprisoned in buckets to await the end of shooting. This did come at last, with the film unit's decision that it must have some decent pictures by now.

Shooting the next stage in the hatchlings' life turned out to be no easier. The aim was to record the small turtles' first few minutes in the sea. Again, an action which normally took place in darkness had to be done under floodlights. This time the film men waded out over the reef shallows with camera and lights and positioned them underwater, pointing up to the beach where Bustard waited with a bucket of turtles. To operate the equipment the technicians had to bend over it, their heads in air and their hands underwater. The lights came on, making the dark water bright as lime jelly. On the edge of the beach Bustard emptied out the turtles, and they began to swim for the camera. For a few seconds there they were, dozens of small oval silhouettes rowing over the bright green. And then the whole reef seemed to explode. Fish leapt, white gulls screamed, things rushed underwater and plummeted down from the air. Somebody yelled, "They're eating our turtles – *eating* them!" The film crew straightened and stared down at the water, looking for their subjects. One or two of the turtles were left, but that was all. The lights had shown them to every enemy they had.

The film men were standing there, the illuminated green water between them and the beach, and at their backs and all around them the blackness, when someone called, "Shark – look out for the shark!" The men moved forward into the lighted water and faced back, straining to interpret the passages of shadow that seemed darker than the darkness. One of them shouted, "Yes – there!" But then another said something, and they began to move back to the equipment. "Don't think it's a big one," someone shouted back to the beach. They turned their backs on the darkness again. Bustard with another bucket of hatchlings waded out through the shallows. The plan now was to empty out the turtles nearer the camera, thus increasing their chances of reaching it. With the dark water all around them, Bustard and the unit conferred. The producer's wife was standing near me on the beach, watching her husband out in the water. She remarked that she didn't much like these night scenes. She was scheduled to do some herself soon, and she wasn't looking forward to them. She was an actress, and her current role was to swim among the corals and fish as the unit filmed them. Some of the scenes were to be done at night because the colour came up so well under the lights. A diver with a knife would be down there with her, just out of camera range, but she still didn't feel especially happy about being in a sort of illuminated aquarium without the glass, every movement visible to predators in the surrounding blackness. You probably wouldn't see a shark, she reflected, until it rushed you. I agreed that I shouldn't have liked the assignment either.

There is something uniquely fearful about a shark. In millions of years it has changed little, possibly because its original arrangements for survival turned out so nicely for it. Unlike other fish it has no bones, only cartilage. It is covered not in ordinary scales but in teeth – in thousands of small, sharp denticles which, as they brush against a swimmer, can shear the skin away. The outpouring of blood which follows can drive some sharks into a feeding frenzy, in which they will tear at everything they can reach, including other sharks. In a species such as the tiger shark the mouth is a variation of the skin, lined with rows of teeth. Some of the teeth are in use, others are spares, ready to move forward as the old teeth wear. In ten years a tiger shark might use more than twenty thousand teeth. Divers don't strike up friendships with sharks as they do with almost any other sort of fish, including the massive old groper, the Reef giant with a mouth big enough to take a man's head and torso at one bite. Gropers can behave like bemused cats, turning up to be petted and to receive presents of fish they are certainly capable of catching for themselves. Sharks don't go in for that sort of thing. The shark is fast and supple, it moves beautifully in its bonelessness, but otherwise it is unappealing. I didn't think I'd like to be out in that water on Heron Reef with even a small shark circling in the darkness. When the unit signalled that they had their picture and started wading back to shore with the gear, the producer's wife said in a heartfelt way, "Oh, good!"

I decided then to go back to my cabin. I was tired, and sleep seemed a fine idea. When I got there, a squirming heap of small turtles blocked the doorway. There was an outside light, and they were trying to climb the wall to get to it. If I turned off the light, I calculated, they would head out to sea – wouldn't they? This cabin was near the retaining wall above the beach, and to get down to the sand they would have to descend a flight of steps. Could baby turtles descend steps? I wasn't sure, so I gathered them up and put them in the washbasin while I considered the question. If they did get down on to the sand there would be ghost crabs waiting for them. I had seen a couple of these crabs, like large pale spiders, watching from just beyond the floodlights as the turtles performed for the cameras. How did the crab kill a turtle, I'd asked Dr Bustard. Usually, he said, the crab carried the turtle to the mouth of its burrow before it began its meal. It started on the head, often with the eyes. I remembered Noel Monkman carrying the turtles out past their enemies. Then I turned out the lights, took my torch in one hand and a water jug of turtles in the other, and walked down the steps. At the edge of the sea I emptied out the turtles, waited until they were well afloat, and then turned back up the beach. When I turned around automatically for a farewell look, flashing my torch over the sand, there were the turtles, marching and rowing after me. Up above, I saw now, the lights of the shower block were on, and they would stay on for much of the night. I fled up the steps, shut my cabin door, undressed in the dark, and refused to contemplate turtles hunted by ghost crabs as they sought a way up the wall to the shower block. Next morning it was apparent that many of them had found a way up, or around, because there they were in the showers, and people were collecting them and taking them down to the water. I delivered a couple of them myself, watched by casually floating gulls, and then I left the beach to walk through the island.

Almost immediately, I encountered yet another turtle in need of help. This one, though, weighed at least two hundred pounds. It was jerking along past a line of tourist cabins, escorted by four speckled guinea hens, all screaming at it. When the turtle stopped and rested its head on a step, they formed a half circle around it and scolded. It took no notice. It had lost its way, missed the tide, everything was too much. It wanted to be put back in the sea, all two hundred pounds of it. Its need of help was great. The carapaced body, which weighed comparatively nothing when supported by water, was on land an intolerable burden – a crushing burden, for like a stranded whale this turtle would eventually die under its own weight. It simply had to be taken back to the sea. Since this was Heron Island, it would be taken back. A truck would come for it, two or three men would heave it aboard, and it would be chauffeured back to the water.

I left the great boulder with the hens screaming at it and wandered on past the tourist cabins, which looked rather like small coloured garages set down among the trees. Around the gnome caves of the pisonia trees there were no longer gatherings of shearwaters. At first light some of the adults had flown out to fish, and the others had gone into hiding with the young birds until evening. I walked through a stand of pandanus, their trunks rising out of an openwork pyramid of prop roots towards foliage like shaggy bouquets of reeds. Then there was the beach, and on the beach – well, yes. This time the huge turtle was stranded behind a low rock wall. There should have been water to float it over this wall and out over the reef beyond. At high tide there would have been water. Now there was only rock, and the turtle lay there and baked in the sun.

A brownish, long-legged, long-necked bird as tall as a pony came stalking along the beach, its head in a cloud of gulls. This was the emu, an import from the mainland. When it stopped to look down at the stranded turtle, the gulls rose and waited. When it stalked away from the turtle's problems the gulls descended around its head. They seemed to be there for amusement. They were not pecking, only hovering and screaming. The emu evidently found this unsettling, for every so often, hopelessly, the head on the long neck struck upwards at the gulls. The emu was unable to fly. In self-defence it kicked – but how to kick a hovering gull? The gulls seemed to know the answer. Eventually the emu seemed to know it, too, for as it paced away into the distance it held its head unmoving in its wild halo of wings.

9. Expanded coral polyps of *dendrophyllia*

10. Polyps of true coral

11. Coral almost completely destroyed

12. Soft coral

Now the turtle was backing out from the rock wall. In a little while I saw what it had sensed, that the tide was coming back. A finger of water reached in around a rock, and then there was a trickle, and then there was a small stream lapping at the shell. The turtle veered sideways to meet the incoming sea, which was filling a canal parallel with the rock wall. When the water was high enough the turtle half swam, half floated along the canal until it reached the end of the wall and swung around it. Obstacles gone, it moved slowly out over the reef, through the hydrangea blues of the shallows, towards the creaming circle of breakers. Approaching that circle the heavy, cumbersome animal seen on land would begin a sea change. As the water deepened under the great body it would become lighter, swifter. Swimming out from the reef with the corals below sloping away into the depths, the turtle would raise its front flippers like wings, and lower them, and raise them, and lower them, until finally, speeding through the blue underwater sky above the coral gardens, it would be flying like a bird.

Why had the turtle come to this particular island? How old was it when first it came here? Both these questions were among those which would possibly be answered by the results of the tagging programme launched by Dr Bustard. There was a feeling that the turtles which swam down from the north to lay their eggs on Heron Island had themselves been hatched here – that they were returning to their own birthplace to lay their eggs. This feeling would be confirmed if hatchlings tagged on Heron Island returned as mature females and laid eggs. Their age at the time of their return would be calculated from their date of release, which could be read from a system of coded marks on the shell. This quest for information about the habits of Reef turtles had involved the marking of thousands of hatchlings. Young turtles had so many enemies, and so few could be expected to survive, that for a research project great numbers had to be tagged and released into the sea. The turtle hatchery on Heron could accommodate fifty thousand eggs. Eggs were gathered as the turtles laid them and transferred to a sand enclosure where there were egg chambers dug to the pattern of those made by the turtles. The result was a handy supply of hatchlings for marking and release.

Besides his work with turtles, Dr Bustard was planning a research project on another reptile, one he had already worked with in New

Guinea, the crocodile. Reptiles had held his interest for about twenty-seven years, ever since, at the age of three, he had become attached to some lizards he encountered during a stay in Western Australia. His home was in Perthshire, Scotland. He had fair skin, dark, brushed-back hair, a faintly Byronic look and a manner of speaking for the reptiles as if he were one of them. When, talking with him at the Research Station, I asked how it was that a nesting turtle could lose itself in the middle of Heron Island, he replied as if it were perfectly obvious, really, "I dig, but I strike a tree root. So I think I'll go around to the back of the tree. I wander on. And then I am lost." The voice of the turtle had a light Scottish accent. When the same voice came to speak for *Porosus*, the estuarine saltwater crocodile which inhabited the Reef coast, and which never had managed to learn that eating people is wrong, it said mildly, "It's not a question, you see, of a taste for flesh. It's a matter of eating a thing that's a convenient size. As you grow bigger you can't go on catching small fish – they're not worth the effort. When you're a small crocodile you can eat water bugs and even jump out to catch nice insects sitting on branches, or on the leaves over the water. But when you get bigger it wouldn't be much use eating a grasshopper, would it? Besides, you'd be inclined to miss it. So you eat food as large as you can reasonably manage at any size. It just happens that after you're too big to eat invertebrates and you're getting a *bit* big to eat frogs, fish become useful. As you get older, of course, you become much more cunning. You learn to lie in wait in places where there is suitable food. And you have a stage when you go on to birds. Waterfowl. They're quite nice, but again they're not terribly large. If you're pushed you can always eat a few waterfowl, but you'd much rather eat something bigger still. So – you go after mammals. There's a shortage of large game, though. And it's even worse in New Guinea than here, because there there are no large kangaroos. But the introduction of pigs has been a big asset. Pigs are *very* good eating."

With the support of the Great Barrier Reef Committee, Bustard had been working for the protection of the crocodile. The animal had a tremendous pedigree, going right back to the dinosaur. In fact, it was a sort of dinosaur, survivor of the age when reptiles ruled the world. Now that a species with a gun ruled it, it seemed that the day of the dinosaur might really be over at last. In two Australian States, Western Australia and the Northern Territory, there was legal protection for a freshwater species, the slender-snouted Johnson River crocodile ("a gentle, shy creature," Bustard said, and indeed that was the general reputation of an animal which figured in idyllic tales of Aborigines and crocodiles romping together through the waterlilies). But even in the states which protected it this crocodile was still being netted and bludgeoned and shot because poachers could send its skin for legal sale in Queensland, where there was no protection for crocodiles of any sort. The great saltwater crocodile, *Porosus*, said to be the largest crocodile in the world, had almost disappeared. It had once been common in Reef waters. At twelve to thirteen feet long it weighed a ton, and it grew to be about twenty-five feet long. It had a roar like – well, like a speedboat, which it had been known to attack, possibly because it mistook that boat's unlovely noise for the challenge of another crocodile. It was probably inevitable that it would be hunted out of settled areas, but it had been hunted out of isolated areas, too. Along the northern Reef coast there were mudbanks which once had been packed with basking dinosaurs, eating nobody. But the safaris of tourists and skinners had found them, and now the mudbanks were deserted. *Porosus* had even been gunned down at sea. "I've seen crocodiles many miles from land," a safari master once told me. "One day sailing up the coast we spotted something a long way off, in absolutely smooth, glassy water. We got out the binoculars, and it was a crocodile. This croc deliberately swam almost a mile to come and have a look at us. When we knew it was a crocodile we just sat quietly on deck with our rifles, and when he was about fifty feet away we shot him." Bustard's estimate of the crocodile's future in Queensland was such that he intended to set up his research project somewhere else, probably in Western Australia. He was continuing, though, to urge legal protection and the formation of national parks for the crocodiles. He argued that if their numbers could be rebuilt they would justify their existence economically, both as a tourist attraction ("these gigantic reptiles inspire awe in people," he pointed out) and, under strict controls, as suppliers of skins.

I asked him whether in the natural world there was any role left for a dinosaur. It appeared that there was – that in fact it was so important to fisheries that its extermination was likely to have serious results. The young crocodile's role in the scheme of things was to eat water-bugs which were enemies of fish eggs and larvae. Without the crocodile the waterbugs thrived and fish supplies suffered. The crocodile had a further role in fisheries. When it had passed from the waterbug stage to a fish diet, it tended to eat the coarser fish which humans didn't care about. The result was that when it was no longer there to eat them these coarser fish multiplied, to the detriment of the fish which humans did care about. In parts of East Africa, where fish were important in the diet of the people, the decimation of the crocodiles had caused serious problems. In Australia, where there was not the same interest in fisheries, the decline of the dinosaur had, as yet, gone unregretted.

Scientists and students who came to work on Heron Island, the Scientific Director, Peter Woodhead, said, were accommodated here – and he indicated the long, low buildings of the Great Barrier Reef Committee's Research Station. The buildings stood around a sandy quadrangle with some of the island's forest left on it. The trees must have been packed with terns, because their whistling cries made a racket in the sunny air and followed us when we entered the buildings. Inside, the accommodation was plain and pleasant, in rooms that had panels of louvres as tall as a door. The people who came here, Woodhead said, made their own beds and cooked their own meals. The kitchen was at one end of a very large room where everybody gathered to eat and talk. There was refrigeration, and a stove which worked on bottled gas. In fact the only real problem was the one which occurred so often on the reef, a shortage of fresh water. There was a desalination plant, supplying limited water for tourists, but the research centre depended on rainfall collected in tanks. And there had been no worthwhile rainfall to collect for quite a while. A fortnight ago people at the station had had to start using sea water for dish-washing, even for cooking vegetables. The vegetables tasted – well, salty. And there was one other point about the island's water. "As you can hear," he said, and paused, so that I became aware again of the terns' voices, "there are a lot of birds on this island, and that sweetens up the water no end." He laughed exuberantly. He was a burly, grey-eyed Yorkshireman whose home ground was not the tropics but the Arctic. Working for an English fisheries laboratory he had sailed north in winter for eleven years to study Arctic fish. Sometimes he had made two or three trips a season to study migration and other aspects of fish behaviour. Since coming to this station on the Reef he had retained his interest in fish, but his main work had been with the corals, and with an investigation of the currents. In his work on sea surface drift he had had the co-operation of Australian Gulf Oil, which had financed the project and undertaken the clerical work connected with it.

We walked across the sand into another building – long, single-storied, with more trees and terns beyond its louvres. This was the main working building of this station which the Great Barrier Reef Committee had created as an on-the-reef study centre. It was the base which scientists from many countries used when they came to work in what was perhaps the world's greatest marine laboratory, the waters of the Great Barrier Reef. The equipment varied from a high-powered microscope to live-specimen tanks fed by water pumped straight from the sea. The Royal Society, the Rockefeller Foundation and the Australian Academy of Science were among the bodies which had contributed towards the cost of buildings and equipment. Now there was a need for more contributions to add to the buildings and to acquire sophisticated new equipment. But still, the Director said, even with limited resources it was a valuable base for marine scientists, and it had an incomparable facility in the fine reef on which it was built.

Woodhead's own interest in working at Heron had come originally from his feeling about an early and by now celebrated expedition to the Reef. This was the English-Australian expedition of 1928–29, organized by the Great Barrier Reef Committee. "There were about twenty people on the expedition, and they lived at Low Isles, north of Cairns, for one year," he said. "Later many of them turned out to be very eminent scientists, quite apart from the work they did at Low Isles when they were relatively young. To my mind, it was one of the most successful and one of the most romantic of marine biological expeditions." When this post of Scientific Director at Heron Island was advertised around the world, he thought of the appointment as something which would be, as he put it, "a thing which might come once in a lifetime, and in very few lifetimes at that." He decided to try for the appointment on the basis of his general marine experience, and he got it. He became the Scientific Director of the Heron Island station (and, through an affiliation arrangement between the Committee and the University of Queensland, an employee of the University). He was installed on the island when a ship carrying a Belgian expedition called in. With this expedition was Woodhead's hero, the leader of the 1928–29 expedition to Low Isles, C. M. (now Sir Maurice) Yonge. Woodhead joined the party. "And so," he said, looking very happy at the memory, "on my first visit to Low Isles I actually went with C. M. Yonge. It was a bit like going to Mecca and getting Allah to show you around."

There had been other interesting visitors to Heron during his term of office here. Sixty Russian scientists, for example, had called in on their own ship. They stayed at Heron for a couple of days mainly to investigate the small marine animals which give out phosphorescent light. To avoid disturbing the animals, and to observe them luminescing, the Russians dived at night without lights. "I would have found that a little off-putting," said the Director, who dived himself to make his observations, but not without light. Eventually, he said, the Russians would send him detailed analyses of the animals they had observed. Their ship had no suggestion of the fishing vessel about it. "They were pure biologists, much like myself, just looking at fundamental aspects of the sea. Though as one might expect with the Russians, and perhaps with most people, there were commercial undertones. In the sense that increasing your knowledge of the sea enables you to exploit it more efficiently." On this cruise, for example, the Russians had gathered information which had begun to change their outlook on tropical plankton. Since plankton was the basis of production in the sea, their new knowledge of it could eventually have some effect on the way they fished.

Another visitor to Heron had been "a very charming old man", Professor Eguchi, Japan's leading expert on corals. "Professor Eguchi was collecting on behalf of the Crown Prince of Japan," Woodhead said. "He had just been working on the imperial collections of corals. The Japanese royal family have always been very interested in marine biology, and have made quite significant contributions." Eguchi spent a week working on Heron Island, and then he and Woodhead joined the Japanese submarine expedition which was surveying the Reef. This expedition had caused some worry in conservationist circles. The Japanese had invited Australian scientists to do a series of exploratory trips, sharing facilities and costs. The reason for the conservationists' alarm was the announcement that Australia's bill for this exploration of the Reef – in a submarine equipped with a claw hand to pick up samples from the depths – was to be paid by the Commonwealth

Bureau of Mineral Resources. In the Queensland parliament a member had asked whether the decision that the Bureau would pay the costs indicated that the excursion aimed at an assessment of mineral potential rather than an increase in knowledge of marine biology. He received a non-commital reply. Perhaps the answer really was that the distinction hardly mattered. As the Scientific Director said, practically all knowledge could be used to make exploitation easier. And as an oil company executive had remarked, almost any research into corals or the sea bottom could reveal matters of interest to his industry.

"On the trip I was on," Woodhead said, "we went from Heron to the Swain Reefs. Perhaps eighty, a hundred miles. It was fascinating." His happy look as he recalled the trip emphasized an impression which kept recurring – how much he enjoyed this area he worked in. "We lived on the mother ship, an ocean-going tug that had been modified. It towed the submarine behind to the spot where the diving took place." The submarine was really a submersible, he added. It could dive deep and stay down three or four hours before coming up to be recharged. The trip had filled in considerable detail for him at depths he had been unable to reach in his own diving. The submarine's magic hand had picked up samples from the seabed and from the bottom of reef cliffs. As well as the Japanese, there had been two Australian geologists on board. For a marine geologist, Woodhead explained, a submersible like this, with its large viewing portholes, was a great improvement on the old method of tossing a dredge overboard and hoping it would bring up something useful. "That method is very much like closing your eyes and making a grab. You never know to what extent your samples are typical until you've made a large number of grabs to see if you get the same thing time and again. With a submersible, you can just go down and look for yourself." It was a most impressive facility, and the Bureau of Mineral Resources would be using it quite frequently.

Speaking about his study of the currents, he said it was connected with his interest in a number of questions about the life of the Reef. For example, Heron Island had an extremely rich growth of reef-building corals, yet not far to the south these corals suddenly cut out. Apart from variation in temperature, he wondered what the reasons were that they stopped so abruptly. "It's a puzzle," he said, "why they should stop suddenly, on the dotted line, almost." Then there were the other questions: "What happens around here, anyway? Where do we get our water from? Where does it go to? The eggs and larvae of animals breeding on the reefs, and of the corals themselves, are released into the sea, and settle elsewhere. Just what happens to them? Where have they come from, where do they go?" He felt he had been fortunate in obtaining for his work the support of the Gulf Oil Company. "They were interested in surveying the area, too, to see whether there were oil prospects here. My work wasn't going to tell them about oil prospects but it would tell them about the water circulation. If they were to get any washouts, say, from a well – though they didn't expect to have any – they wanted to know at least where the oil might go. I think it is fair to say that they wanted to make sure they had more traps, in case of an accident, than is required of them by law. Well, they backed me. They paid all expenses for developing a new type of drifter which I made up, and we released these things from an aircraft." He brought out one of the drifters standing in a corner of the room. It resembled an open parasol made of red and black plastic. It had a yellow tag on it, bearing a number and the offer of a reward of fifty cents for its return to Australian Gulf Oil. "This," he said, "is the larger brother of a thing called the Woodhead Seabed Drifter which I developed while I was working in England. It is still used extensively by the Russians and Americans and English and Yugoslavs and Canadians. It – uh – drifts along the seabed, you know? I released tens of thousands myself around Europe and in the North Sea. They were released at a certain place, at a certain time, and when they turned up so many months later at some other place, we could work out the overall movement across the seabed. We wanted to know what the bottom currents were doing – it had implications for fisheries and for general oceanography."

On the seabed, he said, the drifter looked rather like a travelling parasol, with the plate on top and a weight at the bottom. "It just hopped along the seabed," he said, moving it in hops across the floor. In Reef waters, for work on the surface currents, the design was reversed. Now the parasol floated upside-down just under the surface of the water, with the tip of the rod protruding. Floating this way, the device was protected from the effects of the wind. "The more deeply you can float your plate, your drogue," he said, "the more truly you get a reflection of surface water movement." The device was more reliable than, say, the plastic drift envelopes with a message inside which had been released by the thousands in Europe. The envelopes had moved across the water surface, but the wind had had a great part in moving them. A surface drift bottle, too, could be much affected by the wind. "That is why," Woodhead said genially, as he returned the drifter to its corner, "I hold that this is much better than the traditional method. Which is, of course, to take a bottle of whisky, drink the contents, put a message in it and throw it over the side."

When it came to releasing the drifters in Reef waters, he had gone up in the Gulf plane himself to help throw them out. The drifters were tied up in bundles with a water-soluble plastic. In the sea the plastic dissolved away, releasing them. The plane had distributed the drifters over a southern Reef area of fourteen thousand square miles, taking in the Capricorn Channel and the Saumarez Reef beyond the Swains. When reports of stranded drifters came in they were from as far north as Mackay and as far south as Bateman's Bay. A couple of drifters were also reported from New Zealand.

What did all this imply about the spread of escaping oil in the currents? There could be more than one opinion, as there was more than one opinion on the probable spread of oil by the tremendous twice-daily movement of tidal water through the Reef. This movement was described by one geologist as likely to spread pollution rapidly, but also as likely to take it away rapidly. This in his mind made the Reef safer from pollution than Santa Barbara had been. A conservationist, on the other hand, might hold the opposite conviction – that the tidal movement, having forced the oil through the Reef's thousands of passageways, depositing a coating of it in crevices and under ledges, could not simply reverse the action and suck it all out again. There was also the point that if the oil dissolved on and around the reefs it would dissolve into such substances as benzine, toxic to fish in a concentration of a few parts in a million.

The oil-spreading effects of the currents also seemed likely to be interpreted in various ways by various people. One implication of Woodhead's work surely was, though, that any oil spilling out in Reef waters would be most thoroughly circulated. Reefs standing in a current, Woodhead said, acted to some extent like rocks in a river. They created eddying and considerable mixing, increasing the rate of diffusion at all levels in the water mass. There was quite a complex pattern, or rather, number of patterns. The feature that came out of his work, he said, was the high degree of dispersion occurring. "Drifters from the same release position turned up at times in very different places," he said. "It seems unlikely that stuff will remain in the one place."

His own interest lying not in the movement of oil but in the movement of marine life, his results led him to ponder again the ways in which reef animals made their journeys through the water. He could not as yet say why the reef-building corals ended so abruptly south of Heron, but he did find himself with some stimulating thoughts about the general distribution of reef animals. "I was led to think more, for instance, about what happens on central Pacific atolls – which are very isolated – and the mechanisms by which the reef populations arrive at these places or remain at these places." The atolls were pinpoints in vast areas of ocean where the animals couldn't possibly settle. Their chances of finding these pinpoints and of hanging on to them were connected, he thought, with the swirls and eddies which occurred around reefs. These movements would help keep the animals circulating in the vicinity of a reef, giving them a chance to settle. If they were swept on, he saw them travelling over the ocean in repetitions of the circular movement. Instead of going in a straight line, he said, "there they were, eddying through the ocean. They're going around in a spiral – and so they covered a bigger area, and had a higher chance of hitting on something, than if they were just travelling directly from A to B". He added, "One starts thinking this way because one sees what happens to one's drifters, and begins to consider what happens to the animals one is living with on the Reef".

Some of the results from the drifters, he said, could have implications for other scientists – for Dr Bustard, for instance. From the distribution of stranded drifters and the location of turtle nesting sites it did seem there was a possibility that the currents had some influence on the travels of the turtle. But this would have to be looked at in more detail. Then, too, there were government mining authorities with an interest in the results, because they, like the oil companies, wished to know the answers to such questions as where an oil leak would end up.

Eventually I asked if he had ever had misgivings about co-operating with an oil company. He laughed tremendously. "The oil companies!" he said. "These days everybody wants to blame the oil companies. They're the great sinners. Look, I'm a conservationist, too, but when it comes to these people who put 'Save the Barrier Reef' stickers on their cars – tell me, what do their cars run on?" Only half-laughing now, he added, "If people didn't want petrol there'd be no oil companies. The oil companies are just the handmaidens of the public".

My visit to Heron was in February, a month which was fine for seeing the migrant turtles and shearwaters but a little uncertain for seeing the corals. This was because February is a stormy month on the Reef, and coral-viewing requires reasonably calm weather. Glass-bottomed boats do not put out into rough waters which might force them on to a reef and which, in any case, blur the undersea landscapes. On Heron, a couple of trips by glass-bottomed boat had to be cancelled because of strong winds. Instead, the hostess suggested, why not go for a walk on the reef, and perhaps snorkel in a calm pool out near the edge? A small party gathered to make the excursion and I joined it.

Standing on Heron Reef on that windy February day felt rather like being at sea on a waterswept raft of coral. Crossing it often meant wading almost knee-high in water. You prodded ahead with a long stick, and then you put your foot forward on to the spot you had prodded, reasonably sure it would support you, and then you pulled the other foot out of the water and brought it up to the first. You then prodded ahead again, and in this way you progressed for the wind-buffeted half hour or so it took to battle your way out to the edge of the reef. Some of the daisy-like polyps were out feeding, but mostly they were concealed in their skeletons waiting for the night. Several times just ahead of our probing sticks something like an outsize pancake with a tail shot away. This was a stingray, you realized, as it flopped down again on the sandy bottom. The wind roughed up the watercolours of the reef, the pools of indigo and the aquamarines over the passages of white sand. Near the reef's edge, where the Coral Sea foamed against the rocks, there was a large basin of calm water called the Blue Pool. Two of us put on goggles and snorkels and entered it. Down in the blue light the fish hardly moved. Dreamily, a pretty wrasse with a long pig snout floated back a foot or so to let me pass. Tiny blue-enamelled fish drifted in a cloud. There were two silver-pink fish swinging like baubles under a little tree of coral. I went close to look at them and they looked back, swinging gently beneath the branches. I had been told that the fish around Heron were unusually tame because people on the island had been making a serious effort to enforce the regulations protecting reef life. The result was fish like these, practically without fear. Swimming among them in the Blue Pool you had a feeling of being in a paradise of animals, of looking back through a blue corridor into Eden before the Fall. As I waded through the long return journey to the white beach and the green forest, I reflected that Heron, with its birds and its turtles, its pools and its fish, must be one of the most fascinating of all islands.

"Yes, I'd say so too," Bob Poulson agreed when I mentioned this conviction to him. Poulson ran the Heron tourist business, and had the reputation of being a sincere conservationist who had worked hard to preserve the island and its animals. When he and Dr Endean had realized the quantities of corals and shells which were being taken away, and the extent of the hunt being carried on by spear fishermen, they had moved to obtain legal protection for the marine life around the island. "We got that through all right," he told me. "But I don't know what's going to happen to the place now. Not if they're going to pour oil over it."

I said, "*What?*" and he said, "Pour oil over it. Oil. That's right. Oh," he said, "you probably haven't seen the paper," and he handed me a newspaper brought by the helicopter. In it was a report on the evidence given by I. W. Morley, Queensland's State Mining Engineer, to a Senate Select Committee investigating offshore oil exploration.

The Santa Barbara oil blowout off California of some weeks before had not affected marine life, Morley had told the Commission. He had suggested it was problematical whether escaping oil would kill coral polyps. It would affect the "air-oil-sea interface" of a reef, but not the living coral beneath. No experiments had been carried out by the Queensland Government on the effect of oil on corals, he said. However, there was a marine science laboratory on Heron Island which would be a suitable site for such experiments. Drums of oil could be taken to the island, a slick poured out, and the effect on the coral measured. He had also said that other witnesses before the Senate Committee, including members of the Great Barrier Reef Committee, did not seem to be fully aware of the precautions against pollution demanded by the government.

The wireless, Poulson said, had also been carrying news of Morley's statements. The Australian Broadcasting Commission had reported him as saying that oil companies had contributed greatly to the present scientific knowledge of the Reef. (Later, when I was able to check on the A.B.C. report, I found that it ran, "Mr Morley said some people who had already given evidence had not been fully aware of the value of the work done by oil companies in this field. He said his Department did not consider that the university-sponsored research into the Reef was sufficiently basic to contribute significantly to an overall study of the Reef. He said the work was usually done by young graduates seeking post-graduate degrees and it would appear that a number of their projects were directed to abstruse features of the problem rather than to direct contributions to increasing the basic knowledge of the reefs.")

So in view of all that, Poulson wondered, what was going to happen? It was a question to which he might have to wait some time for the final answer, since that could only become clear from the scientific work eventually undertaken on Heron. But the interim answer was a furious debate on Morley's evidence. Back on the mainland both the chairman and the honorary secretary of the Great Barrier Reef Committee were protesting against his statements. And those statements were indeed extraordinary, not only for their suggestion of an experiment suitable for Heron Island, but for their disparagement of university-sponsored research work, much of which was associated in some way with the Heron station. It was an odd situation, because previously there had been quite a degree of accord between the Committee and State mining authorities. The Chief Government Geologist, Alan Denmead, for example, had written to express his approval of the mining section of the Committee's proposals for controlled exploitation. He had studied this section, he said, and so had the State Mining Engineer, and neither of them would suggest any modification. Since then, of course, some people would consider there had been a modification. The Committee had passed its resolution recording that it was opposed to mining, "until such time as it can be shown that mining does not adversely affect the renewable resources of the reefs".

Another protest against the State Mining Engineer's statements came from the visiting American marine biologist, Dr J. F. Grassle. He wrote to the Brisbane *Courier-Mail* pointing out that the effect of oil pollution on coral was already known from a report that eighty percent of the corals in an area of Eniwetok Atoll had died of pollution from a wrecked tanker. This was reported in 1954, and a check in 1967 had shown that coral had not grown again.

Dr D. W. Connell, Brisbane research chemist and an activist of the

Queensland Littoral Society, also attacked the idea that the effect of petroleum spilt on the Barrier Reef could not be known. He pointed out that oil destroyed marine life not only through direct contact when it floated on the surface but through the poisons it released when it dissolved. A high proportion of oil dissolved in sea water, he said, releasing such toxic substances as benzine, which would kill fish in a concentration of a few parts per million. In his letter to the Brisbane *Courier-Mail* Connell wrote: "The effect these substances have on coral has not yet been determined, but since the substances have been demonstrated to be poisonous to a wide variety of creatures ranging from man to fish, there is little reason to believe corals will not be affected in the same way. It should also be pointed out that the use of detergents, floating booms and all other slick control measures are completely ineffective against dissolved oil constituents in sea water".

Around Heron Island the sea became a little calmer, and the glass-bottomed boat made a journey over the deep corals. It passed close to a wrecked ship, crewed now by tall herons. The birds stood in line, some in grey-blue plumage, some in pure white. The wind was strong, but down below, under the glass, visibility was good. We looked deep into one of the finest reefs in the world. Fish were everywhere among the corals. Above the wind the hostess shouted that there were eleven hundred sorts of fish around this island, and it seemed a reasonable estimate when you looked down into the carnival processions of spots and stripes, of georgette fins and painted armour, of colourings ranging between the delicacy of a pale rose and a poster boldness. Here, I remembered, was where the big turtles dawdled after their journey down from the north, waiting for the night to go ashore on Heron. What would be the effect, I wondered, of an oil spill on a turtle? One knew what would happen to the migrant shearwaters if ever they had to dive through oil to catch their fish – they would simply never rise again to commute between summers. And it wasn't hard to say what would happen as benzine mixed down among the inhabitants of the Blue Pool. But the turtles – what would be the effect on turtles and their hatchlings as they surfaced through oil to breathe? Soon – either through a tanker being wrecked on a reef, or a blowout occurring in an offshore well, or simply through an experimental oil release on Heron Island – the answer might be made very clear.

CHAPTER 11

Scientists, Politics and Starfish

✳

DR ROBERT ENDEAN, Chairman of the Great Barrier Reef Committee, marine biologist in charge of research into the crown-of-thorns
starfish, sat behind his desk at the University of Queensland. In front
of him, beside a pile of papers, was a thorny wheel with many spokes:
the crown-of-thorns starfish. He wasn't talking about the starfish,
though, because the government had not yet released his research
report and he didn't feel free to discuss its contents. For the moment
he was talking about bird-watching, lamenting the difficulties in really
getting close to wildlife now that everything in Queensland was
becoming so fenced in. The birds you were interested in, he said,
always turned out to be on somebody else's property. "Disagreeable
aspect of this age," he said, with the sigh which often punctuated his
remarks and conveyed a sort of resigned amusement. "Here in
Queensland you can drive five hundred miles west and just not find
many places where you can even pull in off the road and have a look
around. If you do, you're trespassing." He found it handy to keep up
the miner's permit which he'd taken out years ago. It conferred the
right to go through properties. He never seemed to strike gold, but his
prospecting did uncover some interesting specimens of – he smiled –
the king parrot, for example, and the white-crested rosella, and the
black cockatoo. There was a feeling of the world closing in, he thought,
even in this relatively young city of Brisbane, where he lived in an
outer suburb. You could try to keep a bit of land around your house,
but in the end the rates went up so much – his own rates had increased
sixfold in 1968 – that eventually you had to give up and move on. He
shook his head, half smiling. "Sign of the times," he repeated.

This man who was regretting the way things were, was an
Australian, young-looking at forty, broad-shouldered, with a quantity
of not especially tractable brown hair. His white shirt was unbuttoned
at the neck under a loosely knotted tie. He was equable and un-

pompous, he smiled easily, and it was difficult to see anything about him to suggest that he would be in sympathy with the iron aim of utilization of Reef resources. But then, all sorts of unexpected people did seem to be in sympathy with that aim. Dr Don McMichael, for example, who had given evidence against the mining of Ellison Reef for lime, nevertheless approved of exploitation controlled by scientists. When, after the Ellison Reef case, John Busst had attacked the Committee's attitudes, McMichael had explained to him that he considered he was being unfair. He said he thought Busst should realize that the Australian Conservation Foundation, of which he was then the Director, would take the view that utilization of resources was an aspect of conservation. McMichael's own view was that there was room for controlled commercial exploitation, provided it was done with full knowledge of the consequences. It would seem, in fact, many more marine scientists agreed with controlled exploitation than did not. It was in general only the simple conservationist-in-the-street who let out an anguished roar when he heard about the plans to mine and drill the Reef, and realized that the beauty of the Great Barrier Reef was the latest thing his affluent society couldn't afford to leave alone. The attitudes of many of the scientists tended to be more complicated, and there could be surprises for the layman encountering them. There had been for me, for example, an element of the unexpected in the reply given by a marine scientist when I asked him what he thought about a mooted plan to ship minerally valuable beach sand from Whitsunday. He was not disturbed. You had to remember, he said, that beaches were formed in the first place by the depositing of sand derived from somewhere else. And so he supposed that if you took a beach away it would leave an unattractive foreshore, but eventually the sand would be replaced – in a thousand years, perhaps, but it would be replaced. There was in such a man an ability to take a long view, to make a balanced appraisal, which was often absent in the more emotional conservationist.

It seemed less in character for Dr Endean, though, to be committed to controlled exploitation than for some other scientists. Yet his name as Committee chairman signed the Proposals. Eventually I raised the subject. Did he ever feel, I asked, that it might have been a good idea from the beginning to oppose mining and drilling? After a rather long pause he said no, he hadn't felt that. Despite all the agitation, in the end exploitation would be inevitable. He still thought the proposals

13. Newly hatched baby turtle swimming frantically
from the beach to deeper water

14. Female turtle digging nest

15. Sunset – Heron Island

for exploitation under scientific control had been the best answer. He didn't feel that an operation in one part of the Reef would ruin the whole. "It's only human nature to exploit natural resources," he said. "What else are we going to do?" Leave them alone, I essayed. "Yeah. Well. Then we're in trouble. Because pressures upon us are such that we can't leave these resources alone and maintain the standard of life which seems to be accepted. I'm not happy about the present situation but apparently most people are – or they wouldn't have it, would they? And with population pressures, higher standards of living, we must get more oil." But the alternative, I suggested, was perhaps to question this, to ask whether this *was* what we had to do. "I certainly do question it, yes. But I don't think mere questioning, at this stage at any rate, is going to achieve very much. After all, there are several eminent people who do question where we're going. But they don't seem to carry much weight. They don't seem to influence the attitudes of people generally." Sometimes he had a curious chagrined smile, and it was there when he said, "I just think it's a good thing one has lived when one has".

And yet later, when it came to campaigning to save the Reef from the starfish which he maintained were destroying it, the note of resignation was not there. In his demands for action there was nothing of this feeling, so much like that expressed by the Scientific Director of Heron Island Research Station, that the fate of the Reef had already been decided by the demands of the human multitude. In the case of the starfish he asked that the multitude *do* something, or rather, that its elected representatives do something, and he persisted even when its representatives gave a clear indication that they preferred to do nothing. It was July of 1969 before the Endean report on the starfish was at last released. Between the lodging of the report and this release, the starfish spawning season of December, 1968, had come and gone. The most urgent recommendation of the report had been that teams of collectors be organized to gather up the crown-of-thorns before they could spawn. Now, obviously, the aim would have to be to collect the starfish before the December of 1969.

Gathering the starfish would be difficult, the report said. They would have to be individually disentangled from amongst coral at various depths. However, the largely defunct trochus and beche-de-mer industries had involved the manual collection of animals under comparable conditions, and a pool of skilled collectors should be available in Queensland. A great number of collectors would be required, including some with scuba equipment. Local government authorities and citizen organizations might be approached to provide volunteers who could help the professional divers. Apart from action to contain the plague by collecting the starfish, there would have to be an extended programme of research into the various questions still unanswered about these animals and about the giant triton. The programme for one year would cost almost ten times the $26,400 allocated for the original two years of research. It would require $250,000 a year for two years, after which time the costs might be halved.

When the Endean report was released, its recommendations were already old. December had passed without any action to stop the starfish spawning, and so each mature female had released into the waters of the Reef between twelve and twenty-four million eggs. Most of the eggs would have been food for predators – but there were already infinitely more starfish than there used to be, and who knew how many predators there were? Endean began to issue warnings of disaster for the Reef, a course of action which took him into the politics of tourism. What if, as a result of all these statements about the ravages of the starfish, the idea got around that the Great Barrier Reef was no longer worth visiting? An opposition arose to Endean which included divers, tourist promoters, shell collectors. They quoted their sometimes considerable experience of Reef waters in maintaining that the reports of the Reef's peril from the starfish were exaggerated, that either there was no plague, or that there may have been a period of plague but it was now over. At a heated moment in the debate Endean was to say, "The people who have spoken out against the plague so far have been the ones with something to lose by my reports. I have received a number of letters already from tourist-industry people and shell collectors saying that I am damaging the tourist industry by highlighting the damage of the crown-of-thorns." His recommendations certainly did threaten some dislocation of tourism. He thought it significant that the reefs worst affected by the crown-of-thorns were those accessible to shell collectors, who, he reasoned, had removed the giant triton, in his view the chief natural control on the starfish. There seemed to be a definite correlation, he wrote in his report, between the accessibility of a reef to the new predator, man, and the degree of infestation of a reef with the crown-of-thorns. "It is known," he wrote, "that shelling parties from Cairns, Innisfail, Townsville, Port Douglas and Cooktown visit the accessible reefs in the vicinity of these centres frequently. Moreover, commercial shell collectors operate from these centres. . . . Then, too, there has been a spectacular boom in the sales of high-powered outboard motors in Queensland since 1961. Nowadays it is common to find large numbers of outboard-powered craft, many of them carrying shell collectors, anchored at reefs in the area." If Endean's viewpoint prevailed, what followed? Restrictions, perhaps, on the use of power craft in Reef waters? A general policing of tourist trips? It would certainly mean the finish of the shelling trips now offered as a feature of Reef holidays. His report made a specific recommendation for "restricting the activities of shell collectors generally on reefs of the Great Barrier Reef". It was nothing less than the end of laissez-faire tourism.

There were many statements in reply to Endean that the giant triton never had been plentiful in Reef waters and therefore never could have been the predator which had kept down starfish numbers. Endean countered that apart from the depredations of tourists and commercial shell collectors, the giant triton had for many years been taken at the rate of around ten thousand a year by the trochus divers on the luggers. These luggers had operated up to about 1960. His statement drew support from L. Ellis, of Mt Gravatt, Queensland, who wrote a letter to the Press saying that for six years from 1948 he had lived on Low Isles, north of Cairns, and that of the many trochus luggers which in that period had called there all without exception collected giant tritons. Since the tritons counted as the property of the diver who collected them, and the trochus shell belonged to the lugger, skippers had found some of their divers neglecting trochus to collect tritons. During the six years Ellis had been on Low Isles he saw hundreds of triton shells on offer. "Now if this was taking place on these small islands," he asked, "what was happening in the normal supply ports of the north from Cooktown south to Mackay, where the luggers had regular buyers of shells for the tourist industry who would take any quantity?" He agreed with Dr Endean that many thousands of giant tritons had been removed from the reefs. Even so, said Endean's critics, the fact that the giant triton had once been present in large numbers did not prove it had been the most important predator on the crown-of-thorns, nor the control from which the starfish had escaped.

Prior to the nineteen-sixties, the crown-of-thorns had been a rare animal. In 1960 it was still such a novelty that when a single specimen appeared on a reef outside Cairns naturalists made special trips to observe it. Why, then, did it emerge from obscurity in about 1963 to become the plague of the Barrier Reef? And why, from around 1967, did the build-up of its numbers become noticeable in other parts of the Indo-Pacific area, until by mid-1969 infestations had been reported from such places as the east coast of Malaysia, from Borneo, New Guinea, Fiji, Guam, Truk, Palau, Yap, Rota, Saipan, Wake, Johnston Island and Midway? Much of the fascination of the crown-of-thorns mystery lay in the wide variety of factors put forward as possible causes of the explosion – each factor, seemingly, with a good chance of being right, and yet each facing cogent argument against its rightness. It was not impossible there was more than one cause. And there was even a sense in which, after a while, the cause of the plague was the plague. This was because coral polyps fed on plankton, which contained the eggs and larvae of the crown-of-thorns. The corals were thus one of the predators on the early stages of the starfish which as an adult preyed on them. The starfish which ate the coral polyp was destroying the predator on its own offspring, and thus ensuring that more of its offspring would survive. But in Dr Endean's view, a failure of predation at this egg and larvae stage could not have been the *original* cause of the explosion. If it had been, he argued – if, say, predation by corals had failed, or small fish which normally consumed great numbers of eggs had been missing, as in Noel Monkman's theory – then the starfish would have emerged suddenly and in unimaginable numbers. But they hadn't done that. Their numbers had built up slowly over several years. This suggested that the plague had originated in the breakdown of some quite moderate control – in the absence, say, of the giant triton, capable of disposing of about one adult crown-of-thorns starfish in a week, and of a number of large juveniles.

If the removal of giant tritons had led to the population explosion, then it seemed logical to redress the balance by putting giant tritons back on the reefs. Specimens should be imported, Endean suggested, some for research, some for breeding and release. This last suggestion aroused a certain nervousness in people who remembered that on the coast beside the Reef there was a celebrated example of an animal which, having been imported to control something else, had itself escaped from control. This was *Bufo marinus*, the giant toad of Central and South America, brought in to eat the beetle which damaged sugar cane. As it turned out, the giant toad ceased to care about cane beetles once it saw a better way to live. It preferred to hang around houses. In Cairns, as sprinklers played on lawns in the evening, toads up to six inches high and almost as broad squatted under the spray like monstrous garden ornaments. They also sat around under the street lights waiting for insects to fall. They destroyed native insects and were the bane of the apiarists. In the stomach of one toad, three hundred bees were found. No other animal seemed able to win out against them. When a snake caught a toad it was often the snake which died, suffocated as the toad swelled in its mouth. Birds, dogs, cats were killed by the poison in its glands. Meanwhile the job it had been imported to do, controlling the cane beetle, mostly had to be done by insecticides such as Gammaxene and dieldrin. Nobody wanted the equivalent of the giant toad multiplying on the Barrier Reef. And the giant triton was in its habits no more winsome than the toad. The triton immobilized its prey with a toxin, and cut it in pieces with a flexible file-like structure bearing numerous teeth. It made a leisurely, twelve to twenty-four hour meal of the crown-of-thorns starfish, which was too noxious and spiny for other creatures to tackle. Mightn't this triton turn out to be as great a menace as the toad? People with these misgivings might perhaps have found reassurance in the thought that whereas the toad had been a new import, introduced without predators to control it, the giant triton was simply being returned to reefs on which it had always had a place. But what sort of a place, the nervous wanted to know? And who could guarantee that there were now enough predators on the giant triton to stop it setting off its own population explosion?

The same kind of objections operated when, much later, another predator on the crown-of-thorns was reported from Africa. In January, 1970, a German zoologist, Wolfgang Wickler, mentioned while presenting a paper to a scientific conference in Tanzania that the food of the painted shrimp (*Hymenocera elegans*) included crown-of-thorns starfish. The remark was taken up by two scientists present at the conference from the Smithsonian Institution. Interested in the possibility of combating the starfish plague in the Pacific, the Smithsonian scientists asked Wickler to stage a demonstration, and as a result saw in a laboratory a pair of two-inch-long painted shrimps demolish a crown-of-thorns starfish measuring about twelve inches across. The shrimps lifted one of the starfish's arms, attacked its tubular feet so that they released their hold and retracted, and then forced the starfish over on its back. The shrimps fed by tearing at the flesh with their pincers. Their meal was spread out over a day, and at the end of it the crown-of-thorns was reduced to a mound of debris. Excitement at the discovery of yet another animal which, like the giant triton, might offer a means of biological control over the starfish plague was tempered by the realization that painted shrimps were not common around the threatened Pacific reefs, and the introduction of new shrimp populations could have unpredictable results.

Dr Richard Chesher, working from Guam on the crown-of-thorns infestations around the Pacific, looked for the causes of the explosion in the early stages of the starfish's life. He had speculated around the question of what would happen if there were no filter-feeders such as corals left on the reefs to eat the crown-of-thorns' larvae. The answer was that many of the larvae must escape predation to start a population increase. And this had been precisely the situation on certain Pacific reefs stripped of filter-feeders by dredging and blasting. In fact, Dr Chesher wrote, "infestations in Guam, Rota and Johnston Island were first noted near blasting and dredging activities." He had examined the idea that giant tritons were the vital control on the crown-of-thorns but was unconvinced. Giant tritons which he had observed sometimes ate only a portion of the starfish, which occasionally survived to grow into a new whole. His observations settled the point of whether or not a crown-of-thorns could regenerate lost parts, and thus defeat attempts to tag it by lopping off some of its limbs. It could. "Regeneration of small functional arms required about two months," Chesher reported. The chances of the giant triton being the missing predator seemed diminished by his observation that at Palau and Rota, on reefs seldom visited by shell collectors, tritons were common, and yet there were also large populations of crown-of-thorns starfish. (But, Dr Endean countered, for the triton theory to hold "it would be necessary for populations of predators of the starfish to be greatly reduced in numbers on only a few reefs. A plague could be initiated under these conditions". The starfish larvae could be spread by the currents and the adult starfish could travel across the sea floor. Also, he said, in the Australian experiments "we have never observed the survival of a crown-of-thorns starfish attacked by a giant triton".)

And so the debate went on, with Dr Endean providing arguments against the idea that the absence of corals or of egg-eating fish had caused the plague, and Dr Chesher providing arguments against the idea that the absence of the giant tritons had caused the plague. Still, as Dr Chesher pointed out, it was not necessary to identify the cause before taking some action against these starfish infestations which he, like Dr Endean, believed threatened the Pacific with disaster.

In mid-1969, between 1 July and 15 August, teams of scientists organized from the United States fanned out over the Pacific to investigate the crown-of-thorns plague. The Americans saw the starfish as a threat to the islands of their Pacific trust territories. Unless the plague could be contained, the islanders would not only lose the corals which were the basis of their best income prospects, from tourism, but they could also lose their edible fish, which would be likely to desert a reef environment altered by the attacks of the crown-of-thorns. They might even find their islands threatened with erosion as the starfish killed off masses of coral in the protective reefs and these, with their ecological system destroyed, began to break up in storms. The intensive survey of the problem launched by the U.S. Department of the Interior in July, 1969, involved ten scientific teams working under the direction of Westinghouse Ocean Research Laboratory. Another five teams worked under the direction of the University of Hawaii. In the large areas involved, one of the chief methods of locating the starfish was to tow divers behind boats, so that they could make a reasonably fast survey. When a diver located a trouble-spot a scientific team went down to investigate.

During this U.S. programme, Dr Endean visited Guam and conferred with the researchers. Then he went on to Tokyo to talk with Japanese scientists studying the plague. At the end of July, returning to Australia, he urged that the starfish menacing the Great Barrier Reef should be subjected to "immediate holding action". There was no action. In mid-August he went to the southern Barrier Reef and found there, at the opposite end of the Reef from Green Island, the beginning of a crown-of-thorns infestation. His reports of the spread of the starfish made headlines. Everybody in Queensland who could read a newspaper became aware of his campaign for funds to control the crown-of-thorns. Press stories about his researches on the Reef had helped to make him the marine scientist probably best known to the Queensland public. Now his duel with the government on the subject of the starfish rated a lot of space.

Towards the end of August, 1969, he spoke through the Press about another of his problems, that of finding money for the research station on Heron Island. His appeal for government funds for Heron was a reminder that a new marine centre was rising to compete for endowment – the Research Centre in Tropical Marine Science planned for Townsville, on the Reef coast. Putting the case for the Heron Island station Endean pointed out that "its location in the middle of a flourishing set of coral reefs has brought it world scientific recognition for being one of the best possible sites for a marine research centre". The station, he said, had been acclaimed for the past sixteen years by top international scientists. With money, with new equipment, it could become the world's major research centre in its field. But in October 1969, Prime Minister John Gorton confirmed the hopes of Townsville. There would be three million dollars for its new marine institute. "We expect," he said, "that it will become a centre of excellence that will give Australia a world reputation in marine science". One of the first priorities of the new institute would be a general investigation of the Reef and of ways of protecting it.

The decision would have pleased John Busst and other conserva-tionists who, having been alienated from Heron Island and its aspirations by the events of the Ellison Reef case and by proposals for controlled exploitation, had wanted to see a fresh influence in Reef research. And now there it was – a new power in Reef science at Townsville. Nevertheless it was rather hard to tell how far the attitudes of Townsville to Reef exploitation would differ from those of Heron Island. On the one hand Professor Cyril Burdon-Jones, the professor of marine biology at Townsville University College, had spoken strongly for a moratorium on the Reef. On the other hand his pamphlet for the new marine science centre which he was promoting pointed out that "The University College is competent to assist

Government and semi-Government Organizations in such matters as the conservation, development or exploitation of the organic and mineral resources of the offshore islands, the reefs, the continental shelf and the overlying waters in the North Queensland area".

When Dr Endean made his appeal for Heron Island late in August, 1969, an announcement of three million dollars for Townsville was already very close. Still, even if Heron Island was not to obtain the funds which Endean hoped for, there still remained the matter of money to fight the crown-of-thorns starfish. The State Premier had several times asked the Commonwealth to help finance this fight. Now the Commonwealth was about to give three million dollars to a Queensland marine centre whose first task would be a general investigation of the Reef. Would there also be funds available for a campaign centred on one Reef species, the crown-of-thorns starfish? And was such a campaign even necessary? There were many people to say it was not. There was no plague, they said – or if there was a plague, then it was a natural phenomenon, and its cure could be left to Nature. But Dr Endean insisted the Reef was in such danger that he felt, "I must spend as much of my spare time as possible not only investigating the problem but also letting Australians know the actual seriousness of the position". The statement appeared in *The Sunday Mail* on 7 September 1969. On 8 September there was a State cabinet meeting. Afterwards, the Queensland Premier announced that the crown-of-thorns starfish were not destroying the Great Barrier Reef. There was no damage that could not be reversed by Nature.

"In effect," he told the Press, "we are not going to set up a big, elaborate inquiry into the starfish. I am clear in my own mind that there is no real cause for concern. There is no vast plague destroying the Reef. No irreversible damage is being done to the Reef, and recent publicity has presented an unduly alarming picture". State cabinet, he said, had received a report from the chairman of a recent meeting of State and Commonwealth officers who had considered the crown-of-thorns problem. The meeting had decided the situation should be kept under observation. In disagreeing with Dr Endean's estimate of damage to the Reef, the Premier quoted as his authority a veteran skindiver and underwater photographer, and "others in the tourist industry".

There was one further announcement: Robert Pearson, who had done so much research at Green Island and on other reefs under

Dr Endean's direction, was to work in future on the starfish under the direction of a State fisheries research biologist.

Presumably the Premier expected that Dr Endean would now feel that the crown-of-thorns problem was no longer his, and that he would have no occasion to go on talking to the Press about it. That was not the way Endean felt. "I intend to work on," he announced. "I want to prove to fellow-Queenslanders and Australians that there is indeed a plague of starfish on the Reef." He would charter a boat at fifty dollars a day to take an expedition out from Innisfail, to inspect ruined reefs and reefs where the starfish were still active. He would be happy if other boats joined the expedition – he wanted people to see the starfish for themselves. Later it was reported that he had picked up seven hundred and fifty crown-of-thorns in less than two hours, and that he had said, "It would be impossible to count the number of starfish attacking the Reef in this area". There were letters supporting him in the newspapers, and Dr David Noble wrote to say he was appalled at the ruin he had observed while diving only the previous month on a reef south of Cairns. In an area measuring one hundred feet by six hundred feet he estimated there were eight hundred crown-of-thorns starfish.

As Dr Endean receded from official councils on the crown-of-thorns starfish, the Australian Academy of Science began to come forward. On 4 December 1969, a statement* on the starfish problem was released by a committee of the Academy. The committee had found that, "in some parts of the Great Barrier Reef the population of the crown-of-thorns starfish has shown a considerable increase during recent years". The committee had considered several hypotheses advanced to explain the increased numbers of starfish on the Reef without having been able to find any one of them proven. However, the Academy said, "the Committee feels that in the future special attention should be paid to the possibility that destruction of coral by *Acanthaster planci*" – the crown-of-thorns – "is a cyclical phenomenon which has occurred on previous occasions and been followed by regeneration and recolonization with coral polyps".

This recommendation set off a new debate. There was no evidence, Dr Endean said, that the plague was a cyclical phenomenon. All available evidence indicated it was man-induced. To support his view he was able to point to the Final Report to the U.S. Department of the

* See *Appendix B*.

Interior by the teams which had been surveying starfish infestation of the Pacific Islands. This report said: "Some observers who did not participate in the survey advised, 'Let Nature take its course,' or 'It's a natural phenomenon and doesn't need control' and 'Let's study it for a while'. The Trust Territory field teams interpreted all available evidence to indicate that the extensive *Acanthaster planci* (crown-of-thorns) predation is not a natural phenomenon; it appears to be man-induced, and 'Nature's course' would be no more desirable here than in an uncontrolled forest fire...." The field teams had obtained no evidence that similar explosions of the crown-of-thorns had been a repeating phenomenon in the past. On Guam, for example, it would not have been possible for the corals to have developed to their present complex state if a similar infestation had occurred within the past hundred years – "and it is highly improbable that an infestation happened within the past two hundred years...." Again, it had been estimated that "some corals that have been killed represent more than one thousand years of continuous development". The report said that during the survey "participants commented that the conditions were 'far worse than I suspected' ... 'depressing' ... 'fantastic', or some variation of these. Everyone who observed the destruction felt the situation was clearly an important phenomenon representing an extreme unbalance and an unnatural ecological condition". The report did not nominate a definite cause of the plague. The two most promising hypotheses, it was suggested, were that there had been a decrease in predation either on the crown-of-thorns larvae through dredging and blasting of reefs, or on the starfish through giant tritons being removed by collectors. There was, said the report, "no question about the need for further study of the control program, but the institution of limited controls should not be delayed while study of the problem continues; valuable reefs should be actively protected". Like Endean, the Americans urged the organization of teams of divers to destroy the starfish. They also reported on the killing of starfish with injections of formalin. "Using formalin guns, a diver can kill up to 600 or 700 *Acanthaster planci* (starfish) per day, depending on the density of the animals. Six divers can clear about one mile of reef per day in areas of heavy infestation. Divers killed 20,506 *Acanthaster planci* in Guam, eliminating the two major fronts and several large population centres...." (A front was defined as "a massive herd of *Acanthaster planci* [starfish] in the process of migration. Dead coral lies behind the front and live coral ahead of it." Such fronts were also observed on the Great Barrier Reef.)

In Australia, the committee of the Academy of Science suggested interim control measures which might possibly include the use of a formalin gun. It was no part of the Academy's brief, though, to organize those measures. In fact, it was nobody's business to organize them. And now it was December again, and on the Barrier Reef the spawning season of the crown-of-thorns was again beginning. Once more, without any campaign having been launched to collect them, the crown-of-thorns were about to release their eggs. After this, Endean said, any future effort to contain the plague could cost in the vicinity of a million dollars a year.

With 1970 came yet another starfish inquiry, and this inquiry revealed a widening split among the scientists. Dr Patricia Mather, honorary secretary of the Great Barrier Reef Committee, said that the scientists undertaking the inquiry had their own excellences, but they were not experts on the crown-of-thorns. "If it is an expert committee," she remarked, "then there are certain notable absences." One such absentee was Dr Endean, who had done so much work on the starfish.

Underlying the debate which developed before this committee was the question of whether funds should be spent on hunting down the starfish now present on the Reef, or on endowing the work of scientists wishing to undertake further research into the plague. Should the authorities be guided by the Endean report, which recommended action now against the starfish, whether or not the cause of the plague could be agreed on; should they consult the U.S. Department of the Interior report which, drawing on the starfish survey in the Pacific islands, outlined the action which might be taken – or should they in effect ignore Endean and the Americans and sponsor a fresh research programme? One scientist who spoke for a fresh research programme said, "Money should be spent on trying to find out the causes, rather than going on a rampage trying to stamp out what is there now". He believed, he added, that the Reef was not in any immediate danger from the starfish. Dr Endean's reaction was to publicly criticize his statements and say that he had no direct experience of the plague on the Reef.

Not long afterwards a confused public read that it was being held responsible for the state of the Reef by Dr Bruce Halstead, director of the U.S.-based World Life Research Institute. Dr Halstead had come to visit the Barrier Reef and report back to a committee on maritime pollution attached to the United Nations. "That Australians are not doing enough to protect the Reef from the crown-of-thorns starfish is an understatement," said Dr Halstead. Never, he said, had he seen such infestations of starfish – and they were probably at least doubling their numbers each year. "Some people have said starfish plagues are a simple cyclic phenomenon of nature and should be left alone," he said. "I suppose we could have called the bubonic plague a cyclic phenomenon and let it run its course, too." One Press report had him thumping the table as he said, "I cannot comprehend or rationalize the attitudes of the Australian people towards the Reef...." The accused, though discomfited, felt that after all they had a rather strong defence. It was that they had entrusted this matter to the scientists, and in this August of 1970 the scientists were still deliberating on whether funds should be spent on hunting the starfish or researching them.

CHAPTER 12

Threats from a Developing Coast

※

THE past century had brought more changes to the Reef coast than thousands of years preceding it, and in any of those changes might be hidden clues to the disturbed ecology of the present-day Reef. Much of the interference with coast and Reef had been innocent, carried out in the days before many people suspected that the manner in which a new country was settled could alter both the land and the water and affect everything they supported. The typical pioneering scene was one which was enacted in 1864 when a Scotsman named John Melton Black arrived on the Reef coast to make a port at Cleveland Bay. Eventually the port was to be called Townsville, after Black's partner, Captain Robert Towns. Towns was the Englishman who inaugurated the unofficial slave trade in the South Sea Islanders used on the cotton and sugar plantations. Some of these islanders were to help Black build his port. To make the port, Black began as so many pioneers after him were to begin – he cut down the mangroves. Cheerfully, in a letter to Towns of 21 November 1864, he wrote, "The mangrove belt facing the creek on the town side I have nearly got cleared, and have found a most suitable place for a wharf and store". Who could feel then that such industry was not admirable? The trees which grew out of water and mud not only blocked waterfront building but harboured sandflies, mosquitoes, even crocodiles. It was with something like dedication that the pioneers attacked the mangroves, unaware that the trees they were removing protected the land from erosion and processed the water passing through the tangled arches of their roots. The mangroves filtered and purified the water, and enriched it with falling leaves. Among their roots small animals found shelter from predators. They nourished and protected many marine species, some in the early stages of life, before they moved out into the sea, some for a whole lifetime. Plankton in water filtered through the mangroves thrived. In the bays and estuaries, grasses benefiting by the same water flourished, providing more shelter and pasture for marine animals. When the mangroves were cut down the shock ran from the coast far out to sea. Not only were the feeding grounds and the filtering system gone, but the underwater environment itself began to change. Without the stabilizing mangrove roots, mud and silt began to shift, filling and polluting bays and estuaries. The human reaction to this nuisance made things even worse for marine life and scarcely better for humans. Dredges were brought in to get rid of the silt, beginning a task which in most cases was never to end.

A century after John Melton Black all this was understood. "It is well known," wrote Geoffrey Harrison, Queensland's Chief Inspector of Fisheries, and deputy chairman of the Great Barrier Reef Committee, "that the fishery resources native to the continental shelf make up most of the catches landed by commercial and sporting interests, and it has been estimated that at least two-thirds of these fishes and prawns must spend some part of their life cycles in bays or estuaries dependent upon food generated in the mangrove zone. Thus it can be seen that the size of these resources, indeed their very existence, depends upon the food and shelter supplied by the mangrove swamps." Control of the pests in the swamps – the sandflies and mosquitoes – should be possible, he suggested, without any serious effect on wildlife, if non-persistent pesticides were used in breeding areas "in the right places at the right time". But if scientists such as Harrison understood the mangroves' importance and strove to spread their knowledge, there was a certain failure to grasp their arguments among those who had their own plans for the space the mangroves occupied. Waterfrontage space was now the most valuable of all real estate, and to many developers and planners it seemed shamefully wasted if left simply to perform its natural functions. People wanted houses and apartments on the waterfront and would pay high prices for them. Industries wanted premises on the waterfront to cut down handling costs, both on the material they imported and the products they exported. Gladstone, said to be the fastest-growing port in Australia – and incidentally the departure point for Heron Island about forty miles away – was promoting itself on offers of waterfront land. "Hundreds of acres of land are available for industry and are being progressively reclaimed," said the 1967/68 Harbour Board Report. The Report contained pictures of the huge reclamation works going on in the estuary on which Gladstone is located, and announced that, "The Board welcomes inquiries from industrialists (light, medium and major) relative to the leasing of land." And so, although Queensland mangroves could no longer be cut down without official permission, the pressure for the granting of that permission was strong, and mangroves continued to give way to buildings. When the original waterfront had been used up, a new one was likely to be created by filling in of the bay. The new land made a carpark, perhaps, or a road to a marina, or a developer's Venice where once there had been merely a nursery of marine life.

By the nineteen-sixties dredges were perpetually at work along the Reef coast. Their likely effect was indicated by a paper on wetlands by the Queensland Littoral Society, whose members' concern with the littoral extended over estuaries, mudflats, swamps and mangrove areas. The paper said

Dredging and filling is perhaps the grossest and most violent form of attack on wetlands. Dredges rip out benthic vegetation, create perpetual silt storms which blanket large areas far from the site of operations, killing most forms of animal and plant life in a wide area. Erosion may be encouraged and current patterns, often vital in determining salinity and water temperature, can permanently be disrupted, to the entire destruction of the ecological balance in the shallows. Filling (for carparks, industrial lots or housing development) of course permanently destroys all forms of marine life by creating dry land out of a biologically complex inter-tidal area.

At Townsville, the port which grew where Black cut down the belt of mangroves, the dredge a century later was working four and a half miles out to sea. As it ploughed backwards and forwards it also made a channel for big ships, taking a little more off the bottom with each trip. Acres of land near the mouth of the Ross River were being filled – forty-two acres for a fertilizer manufacturing and distributing plant, acres more for an already existing oil storage centre, more still for a roll-on, roll-off terminal for container ships. About three acres were being given over to a boating centre and the parking space for cars and trailers. This last enterprise was thought of as a facility for tourists, Townsville having some ambition to become a tourist attraction in itself and not what it was now, primarily a departure point for Reef tours. It did have a considerable basis for this ambition. Black's settlement had become not simply a port but an attractive small city. Along with its coolly sensible new buildings there was a good deal left of the old Townsville, which had grown with the hump of Castle Hill painted in ochre and copper on the bright blue sky behind its main street. That Townsville had hotels with tiers of iron-lace balconies, and a town hall with an ornamental ironwork verandah four hundred feet long, and tropical gardens where the band played in an iron-trimmed bandstand. This city might easily charm a tourist. So might the common where the wild grey brolgas, or Australian cranes, staged their dances. Long legged, long necked, they would spread their wings and slowly pirouette, the wings waving like heavy veils. For a partner they would strut, and bow three times, and run and pirouette again. Sometimes they would form up into a company of dozens to dance a ballet choreographed for spread wings and swan necks. But then there was the other Townsville, and this place would seem less than charming to anyone concerned with the life of the river and the sea. Townsville's sewage, untreated, emptied into the bay near the mouth of the Ross River. Dissolved oxygen readings from the Ross, into which local industries dumped their wastes, indicated that fish could be having a hard time extracting the oxygen they needed as its water passed through their gills. A reading of 5 was regarded as satisfactory, the level at which fish could live healthily and breed. At one place in the Ross River in 1968, a reading gave the figures 2.1 at the bottom and 3 on the surface. (Low as that seemed, it was better than one of the readings on the Barron, which emptied into the sea near Green Island. On the bottom of the Barron the reading was 1.) For a fish, life was obviously becoming a matter not of finding its own level but of finding any level where the dissolved oxygen reading was tolerable. As for bottom dwellers facing a count of 1, their reactions were as yet unknown.

This work of analysing the condition of the coastal rivers and the sea alongside was just beginning. In charge of it was Leon Henry, chief sewage engineer of Queensland's Department of Local Government. Henry's engineers made regular trips along the rivers of the Reef coast taking dissolved oxygen readings from a Pollution Unit boat equipped with measuring instruments. These readings gave useful but incomplete information about the river's condition. On the Barron, for example, when the engineers got that reading of 1, they were alerted to the fact that somewhere under the waterlilies and the reflections of wild hibiscus was a serious pollutant – perhaps sewage, perhaps organic matter from the cane farms. The reading was a signal that further investigation was required. But neither the alarming reading of 1, nor the satisfactory reading of 6 in other places, indicated anything at all about the presence of DDT or other pesticides. In water giving a satisfactory dissolved oxygen reading there could be a most unsatisfactory quantity of pesticide, measurable only by tests not as yet carried out on the Reef coast. Further south, fish taken from estuaries late in 1969 were found to contain dieldrin, a relative of DDT, and lindain, a poison used in garden insecticides. Fish kills in the Tweed Heads area, just south of the Queensland border, were ascribed to poisoning by the pesticides used in the canefields there. Along the Reef coast there were big fish kills, some of them easily traceable to industrial pollutants. Whether others were caused by pesticides could not be known because as yet there was no programme of investigation. Professor James Thomson, who after working on the fish kills in the Tweed area called for a total ban on DDT, said, "I see no reason why the Tweed River will be the only one affected. This must be happening elsewhere. It's just that no one has been collecting the evidence to show it." The pesticides used on the canefarms of the Reef coast included DDT, dieldrin and aldrin.

Pollution of waters along this coast was complicated by the wet and dry seasons, the alternation of extremes in which the rivers tended either to flood or dry up. In the dry season, wastes had to be released into rivers with little water to carry them away. By the time the "wet" came there was a concentration of pollutants waiting to be swept down to the sea. Not all of this polluted water would reach the sea since an estuary is a semi-closed system, with the water in it tending to move backwards and forwards, almost in a breathe-in, breathe-out motion. But a part would be swept reefwards by the torrents of the "wet", and the rest would wash around in the estuary, distributing itself over the many marine species represented there.

There were also on the Queensland coast examples of dammed rivers contributing almost nothing to coastal waters, and this was probably as bad as contributing pollutants. "We've virtually cut off every river in southern Queensland from the sea," said Professor Gordon McKay, conservationist and Professor of Civil Engineering at the University of Queensland. "Now we've closed the Fitzroy. There's a complete barrage across the Fitzroy at Rockhampton." This was the river which flowed, or used to flow, into Reef waters about opposite Heron Island. "It worries me," McKay said. "What effect is this going to have, for instance, on the Barrier Reef fish? I don't think anybody knows. This is the sort of job where you're always scared about whether what you're doing is the right thing. But nobody will give you the money to find out. We're never able to check up, really, on the effects of what we've done."

One great river which had recently been dammed had already begun to provide some pointers on what might happen around the Fitzroy. This was the Nile River, which as the Upper Nile supplied the Aswan High Dam. Now that silt no longer flowed down the river to compensate for the erosion in the delta, farming land there was being lost. Without the nutrients delivered by the silt to the Mediterranean, fish were disappearing. In 1968, Egypt's sardine haul was not one thirtieth the size it had been in 1965. Instead of the 1965 catch of eighteen thousand tons of sardines, Egypt was now taking five hundred tons.

Another source of coastal pollution which the conservationists worried about was mining. They pointed out that from coal mining, for example, chemical residues could reach the streams and eventually the waters off the coast. At the end of 1968, legislation before the Queensland Parliament seemed to accept that some streams could be too polluted to be worth saving. Sections of this Mining Bill were being opposed by Douglas Sherrington, chairman of the Labor Party Mining Committee and a spokesman for the conservationists. Sherrington had no hope of stopping the legislation, which was sponsored by the government majority, but he was registering the conservationist protest. One of the provisions of the Bill read:

"... Upon the recommendation of the Minister the Governor in Council may, from time to time by Order in Council published in the Gazette, exempt from the operation of this Part such watercourses, lakes and reservoirs (and land adjacent thereto) or such portions thereof as, in his opinion, are by reason of their polluted condition useless as a means of providing a water supply suitable for domestic or stock purposes."

"Does the fact of the stream being polluted justify the further polluting of it?" Sherrington asked, when I went to see him. "One way for a mining company to dodge its obligations would be to pollute a stream itself, so that pollution would give it exemption. I'm not saying this would happen. But there's this possibility, that they could find it more expedient to pollute the stream than to take the necessary measures to prevent pollution."

Mining had always been an important activity in Queensland, and still was. A number of the industrial nations of the northern hemisphere had an interest in the current mining boom. Huge coal contracts were being signed – one with Japan, for instance, for the delivery by 1984 of eighty-five million tons of coking coal. On the Reef coast, beach sands were beginning to yield up their minerals for shipment to the United States. They were being processed at Gladstone. "Part of Gladstone will take off at almost two thousand miles per hour," a beach sands company ran an advertisement to announce. "Consignments of Australian Mineral Sands to the United States will be processed into the space age alloy titanium – the basic constructional material of the Boeing supersonic passenger aeroplane. Titanium will, in fact, account for 85% of the American SST's weight." (From such mining, in which the beach was dredged for rutile, zircon and ilmenite, conservationists complained of damage to the beach and pollution of the sea. They argued that silt collecting off mined beaches was an abrasive material which damaged the gills of fish and affected their respiratory system. It also clouded areas where there ought to have been good penetration of light to encourage the growth of food for marine species feeding inshore.)

Gladstone was also a centre for the treatment of bauxite shipped down the Reef from Weipa. The bauxite was processed with caustic soda and turned into alumina, most of it for export, for the making of aluminium. The consortium running the Gladstone works consisted of Alcan Aluminium Limited of Canada, Kaiser Aluminum and Chemical Corporation of the United States, Pechiney Compagnie de Produits Chimiques et Electrometallurgiques, of France, and a British and Australian interest represented in Comalco Industries Pty. Ltd. A helicopter rising from Gladstone for the trip to Heron Island looked down on a striking landscape. Spread out below were the acres of reclaimed land, the black mounds of coal, the rectangles and cylinders of the alumina works. Down there beside the dancing blue of the Coral Sea were the massive tanks of caustic soda, the red pyramid of bauxite pebbles, the reddish smudge of the waste disposal pond – the landscape, in short, of one of Australia's fastest growing industrial areas, an inspiration to those who dreamt of industrial greatness for Queensland, but a danger area to others who reflected on the pollution which always seemed to flow from such greatness.

Apart from the interference with marine life from farms and industries and towns along the Reef coast, there was the dislocation caused by the tourist industry. This could be surprisingly extensive. In Cairns, for example – in those sunny streets where frangipani came in three colours, yellow and pink and cream, and jacaranda blossomed in purple-blue clouds, and poinciana trees canopied the sky with scarlet flowers – there was an impression sometimes that this was really the tropical equivalent of the fur-trader's outpost, a place where the whole of the local marine fauna was on offer to tourists. The suggestion was there at the town's Fun-in-the-Sun Festival, as smiling people in their summer clothes leant, benign with beer, over the pub balconies, or stood in the sunlight and watched the bands and the floats go by. The bands included tropical Scots in kilts and sporrans and open-necked shirts playing bagpipes as they marched through the palm trees, and chanting Aborigines who had put on clay and feathers to carry a spear for the tourists. The floats passing slowly above the crowds presented many tableaux of girls – girls in beach scenes and girls in boating scenes, suntanned girls in bikinis and leis, girls as festival royalties enthroned in flowers. But then there was a workman-like girl in shirt and trousers, resting her gun on the head of a dead crocodile stretched out beside her on top of a car. The vehicle displayed a hunter's name and the slogan, "Cape York Wild Crocodile Shooter". This float won the Mayor's Cup for the best Fun-in-the-Sun theme. The award was probably a recognition of how important the crocodile had been, and in its last days still was, to Cairns. "In 1966–67," Dr Robert Bustard wrote, "the value of crocodile skins passing through Cairns was said to be greater than for the whole of the Territory of Papua – New Guinea (where the value of raw hides was about $1,000,000)".

Cairns was also the place to buy small crocodiles, stuffed. They smiled out of shop windows from amongst the painted corals and the huge shells made into lamps. Near them might be the head of a small shark, open-mouthed, for sale as a pen-and-pencil holder, and seahorses set in clear plastic to use as paperweights, and big crocodile claws to use as ornaments. Down on the waterfront where the huge marlin hung on their gallows, people would scramble from the reef-fishing launches clutching animals remarkable for their beauty and sometimes for their size. They looked like pictures from the tourist brochures which had brought them here. Typically, these brochures emphasized the point that if you came to the Reef for a holiday you could expect to catch great quantities of fish. The effects of this fairly guileless attitude in the special environment of the Reef had yet to be researched, but they seemed unlikely to be happy. This was not the North Sea, where each species had many representatives. This was a tropical reef area where there were comparatively few fish of each kind, and the individual fish, inhabiting its own niche in the reef, lived – or should have lived – a long time. Dr J. F. Grassle had criticized the idea that the fish of the Reef could help to feed starving peoples. Unfortunately, this was not so. "Most animals of the Reef," he said, "live a long time and reproduce slowly, so that a large fishery could not be sustained." And yet huge numbers of Reef fish were being killed off for amusement. Sometimes spear-fishermen combined sport with business. Even from the isolated Swain Reefs, said J. H. Choat, of the University of Queensland Department of Zoology, early in 1969, there were reports of commercial spear-fishing parties bringing in six thousand pounds of fish. People, he said, were "still labouring under the delusion of unlimited stocks of fish".

The diver Ian Croll thought it would be a good thing if there were a ban on all fishing and spearing on the Reef. Croll, a tall, suntanned thirty-one-year-old New Zealander, had observed the destruction of Reef fish in the course of his work, which was to collect live specimens for public aquariums. He collected for the Magnetic Island Marine Gardens, of which he was part-owner. He had also helped build the Green Island aquarium and had worked on the reefs out from Cairns. Where spear-fishermen went to kill for sport, Croll went to gather fish, corals, anemones for transfer to aquariums in which the non-diving tourist could see close-ups of Reef life not otherwise accessible to him. Croll went below to bring fish back alive. He hunted ornamental fish with mosquito netting, swimming after a butterfly cod, say, and enfolding that fish made of chiffon scarves in the soft mesh. The giant anemone he peeled from its undersea rock and resettled on a rock in an aquarium (or tried to. Usually, he said, it walked around on its stem base and chose its own spot to settle, which tended to be on the glass with its back to the audience). He brought up colonies of corals in a wire cage. The aquariums to which they were transferred were filled with water pumped from the sea and bringing with it their planktonic food. To collect many of the larger Reef fish, such as the highly coloured harlequin tusk fish, Croll used a child's rod. He simply looked down through the crystal water, selected his fish, dropped the bait in front of it, and hauled it in – an operation which did appear to say something or other about the intrepid anglers who caught these animals for sport.

Croll's work gave him a good view of humans hunting underwater, and like Noel Monkman he disliked what he saw. He was particularly indignant about the way Reef fish were being killed off with power-heads. A powerhead, he said, was something he took along himself on Reef trips, but only as a defence against sharks. "It's a pole with a shotgun cartridge that sits on the end. If a shark attacks, you can hit this thing against it and it kills it stone dead. But people now are using powerheads a lot on ordinary fish. They'll use a powerhead on a fish weighing only a couple of pounds. Or they'll go for a record with it. They'll spot a huge groper that's lived on a reef for donkey's years, and they'll come along with this thing and just blow him to pieces. Then they'll get publicity – big diver catches big groper. Such a pity, really. A groper like that would be very old, I imagine." He did not share the common fear of groper, the massive fish with a mouth that could close over a man's head and shoulders. "I've seen a lot of them, including the big ones. I don't think they're dangerous. I think they're inquisitive beasts. They can be affectionate, like dogs. In Fiji when I was there they had tame groper. They came to the beach, got fed, kids swam with them. It was marvellous. Later they were speared by visitors. And there was a reef I used to work on out from Cairns. As soon as I went there one day I realized that divers who had just come up from the south must have been there. The fish were all scared. There had been big groper on this reef, and when I worked they were always around, watching. But they'd vanished, and I reckoned they'd been speared." Summing up his feeling after years of watching the hunt of the Reef fish, Croll said, "It would be all to the good, I think, if they clamped down on spearing or any kind of fishing on the Barrier Reef".

Around Cairns, where tourist fishing was the equivalent of at least a modest fishing industry, the catch in the late 1960's had begun to fall off. "I've been coming up here for ten years," one angler said, "and spending quite a bit of each year here. Up to 1963, say, you'd get three to four hundred pounds of fish on an ordinary day out on a launch – that would be with about sixteen visitors fishing from it. Now on a good day you get perhaps one hundred pounds. Five years ago, night fishing, you'd get a thousand pounds in a night. Now in a night," he said without irony, "all you can get is about five hundred pounds."

As well as the anglers and the spear-fishermen, there were the different sorts of nets which between them were bringing up creatures as various as the shark and the seahorse, the sardine for bait and the ornamental fish for decorating the seawater aquariums now becoming a vogue in private houses. Along with their prawns the trawlers ploughing the bottom between the reefs were bringing up the big shells, and these, with the exception of the giant triton, they could legally sell to the souvenir trade. What effect was all this having on the life of the Reef? Nobody could be sure. The results were not often as clear as they were in the case of the arrowhead fish trap, which had killed off enemies of the lethal *Chironex fleckeri*, also known and feared in Reef waters as the box jelly or seawasp. "At one stage, the coast was dotted with arrowhead fish traps," said Dr John Barnes, of Cairns, an authority on this jellyfish (and on other marine subjects. It was he who had given evidence against lime mining in the Ellison Reef case). These traps, Dr Barnes said, ran for hundreds of yards out from a beach. They caught everything – the fish people wanted to eat, but also the so-called trash fish, which nobody wanted to eat and many of which were predators on the jellyfish. Almost the only species which didn't follow the long directing wing into the trap were the jellyfish. So while the lethal jellyfish went free, the fish that were a natural control on them were hauled in and thrown away. "Arrowhead traps now are almost banished along the Queensland coast," Dr Barnes said, "although there may still be a few of them further north."

Another clear dislocation of marine life came from the shark nets, spread out mainly to cater to tourists who expected their tropic sea served up without its immemorial inhabitant, the shark. One solution would have been to explain the difficulties (these, to be fair, had seldom occurred to the tourists) and invite them to use swimming pools. Instead, an immense effort had been made to arrange a sharkless sea through a series of nets strung out along the coastal beaches. The nets caught the sharks, but they also caught anything else which took a turn inshore, including dolphin, turtles and dugong. It was not possible, after all, to make a net which would hold a shark but release, say, a dolphin. The animals which drowned in the meshes, entangled and held down so that they were unable to surface for air, were often precisely those which the tourist had come to see.

Dolphins were also the victims of sea-hunts in which men went out in fast boats to shoot at them – "or at anything else, really, that raises its head," said Ray Jones, the Member for Cairns in the State parliament. Down in Brisbane he had tried to have the dolphin protected. He had failed because it had been considered that protection was unnecessary. Perhaps it was. There was really no way to take a census of the dolphin population. It was just that these days you didn't seem to meet up with many dolphins around Cairns. Not everybody was sorry. As one fisherman said, people went on and on about the dolphins, but they didn't seem to understand how much trouble they caused, chasing fish and tangling themselves in the shark nets.

What would be the result of the decimation of the dolphin? Or of the shark, for that matter? Or of the crocodile? While nobody knew for certain, it seemed unlikely that these predators could be removed from the environment to which they had always belonged without some effect on other marine populations.

And the dugongs, the sea cows that came in under cover of high tide to graze on underwater grass in the shallows – where were they? The only dugong to be seen around Cairns seemed to be the one in the Oceanarium, and it had been rescued from a shark net before it drowned. It shared a pool with a dolphin which had also been taken from a shark net. The dolphin was not a bottle-nosed type but an Irrawaddy dolphin, a species which local people hadn't even realized inhabited these waters until netting had started. It had blue eyes and a silver skin and was charmingly playful. The dugong was more reserved, a portly creature of aldermanic dignity. As a grazing animal it was usually described as a sea cow, but in appearance it was closer to a huge grey seal or sea lion. There was a curious regulation governing the hunting of dugong. It said not that you couldn't kill a dugong but that if you killed it you had to use all of it. There was so much to use in a six-hundred-pound dugong that this was thought of as a deterrent to its killing. The Aborigines, though, did use every part of it. It was their traditional prey. So if you wanted to know about dugong, Cairns people said, the thing to do was to talk to the Aborigines.

CHAPTER 13

The Aborigines

✳

WHEN Cook sailed the *Endeavour* north inside the Barrier Reef in 1770, he encountered the Aborigines who had established themselves as part of the Reef's life. They lived on some of the islands, and they visited the reefs and cays to hunt. The stingray's tail provided them with a barb for their spears, and the eagle's claw with a hook to catch fish. Seabirds nesting on the cays supplied their eggs and poultry. The giant triton was their occasional trumpet; pierced, the shell was sounded to announce the hunter's victory over a dugong or turtle. Where were the Aborigines now, two centuries after Cook? A few of them were living like white people, others were trying to live like white people, and some were talking of Black Power. Many were in settlements controlled by white administrators. The government spoke of their eventual assimilation into the white community and of closing the settlements, but some Aborigines were not attracted by the prospect. Assimilation, integration – they were words, these Aborigines had come to feel, for a process by which they would be forced off the land and into the slums, to do the sort of work no man, white or black, would do if he could avoid it. They could avoid it, they felt, if they could build their own society on their own land. They were asking for property rights in the settlements, both to protect them against government closure and against the mining company promoter or real estate developer who suddenly found there was money to be made from land the Aborigines had been given when nobody else wanted it. At Yarrabah settlement, isolated on the coast south of Cairns, some of the Aborigines expressed this feeling of wanting a title to their land. "We don't like to think we could lose this," I was told when I visited Yarrabah. "Some of us have always lived here."

Once, so the story went, Yarrabah was a place where strangers' canoes put in when they came down from the north to trade. Now the rows of little houses had the look of a working man's suburb in a tropical setting. There were banana palms, coconut palms, hibiscus.

Behind the houses were high green hills, in front of them the sea. On this evening as I looked out over the water it stretched away through silvered blues and purples towards the Reef. From down near the shore, across the open parkland, came the sound of a piano playing a waltz. It was coming from the big community hall, I realized, as I walked towards the music. Inside the hall, beyond the display of spears and boomerangs and throwing sticks, Aboriginal girls and their partners were moving in decorous circles. They were practising a débutantes' waltz, rehearsing for a ball at which the girls were to be presented to a white official. A social exercise of this sort, the white administration believed, would speed the acceptance of the Aborigines by the local whites. Black sceptics doubted if anything much would do that. Still, here were the young dancers, smiling as they turned in circles, rehearsing to enter society. Watching them were men in open-necked shirts and shorts or trousers and women in print dresses, all of them without shoes. (When the Aborigines went into town they took their shoes in their hands, putting them on as their barge pulled in to Cairns wharf and joyfully kicking them off again as it left.) In the people around the hall there was a variety of skin colour. They came from a number of tribes, and in some cases included among their forebears northern islanders, whites, or the Chinese who had worked along the coast. Typically the skin was dark brown, but it could be anything from a snowfields tan to a rich mauve-black. The eyes were often beautiful, a southern Italian brown, and some of their children might have been taken for Italians.

The music of the débutantes' waltz followed me as I walked across the few yards to the outdoor café. Under strip lighting in red, blue, green and yellow there were tables and chairs, rusting tins of ferns, and a lot of packable chairs, packed. The dugong hunter I had come to see, Alf Ludwick, was in charge of the refreshment counter. There were no customers, though, so he came and sat at a table and talked. He was a half-Aboriginal who looked white, a tall man with brown hair and hazel eyes. He was thirty-six, had a wife and seven children, and had come to the settlement as a child. "My mother, she was coloured, and struggling, so the police to protect her sent her here," he said. "That's how I come here and I'm here ever since." He didn't think life would be better for him elsewhere.

A dugong, he said, had many uses for his family. "We salt it down, keep it. Cook it lots of ways – fry it, boil it, steam it, bake it. Tastes like pork. And dugong oil is good for cooking. Fry scones, cook a bit of beef in it. And we use it for rubbing on the baby after a bath. Any rash or anything, dugong oil heals it. And the chemists in town buy dugong oil from us. People with bronchitis want it. Put a bit of rum with it and drink it down." Unfortunately, though, this useful animal was getting to be harder and harder to find, Ludwick said. He and other people here had always hunted dugong, but in these last years everyone noticed they were disappearing. He hadn't caught a dugong now in three months. "Only me and Johnny Maloney go out hunting here now. He feels the same as what I feel. Sometimes he go out and hunt all night and find nothing." One reason for the dugong scarcity, he thought, might be all the speedboats around now. "Years ago we didn't have any speedboats. Whether these speedboats scared the dugong away, or scared them off breeding, I don't know."

I asked him how he hunted the dugong. "Hunt them at night," he said. "In a flattie – flat-bottomed boat with a paddle. You can get closer at night. In the day, they see the shadow of the boat, they're off." In the dark you located them by the sounds they made, so it had to be a calm night, he said. "You're flat out hearing them, so quiet they come up. Come to the surface to breathe. They blow, but very soft, very quiet. Or they cough. Or you might hear the big kick from their tail. They bring the tail down on the water. That kick, it's a signal to the mob. Might be ten or twenty of them – or used to be – and they kick to come in to feed, and then kick for the mob to move out.

"Well, we wait, sculling with the little oar, three men in the boat, maybe. I'm on the bow of the boat, standing there with the 'wop'. It's more than thirteen feet long. It's got the harpoon on it. We make it, use mangrove or sourplum out of the bush. Make the harpoon out of ordinary fence wire. Four or five inches wire – we sharpen it and tie it together. When you hit the dugong the wop bounces back out and just leaves the harpoon in, and the wop just floats along with the rope running through the ring on the end of it. We got about seventy-five yards of rope.

"See, when the dugong get up, I'm standing on the bow with the wop in my hands, held across me, pointing the way you expect him to get up. You might have to throw to get him, or he comes up right alongside and you just hit right down. When the dugong get up to blow, his hide is loose. Soon as you spear him he tightens up. He tightens his hide up, and the harpoon bends. That's it, you've got him.

He tightens up and pulls." Then began the wild dash of the harpooned animal pulling the boat after it, sometimes for half a mile and more to sea. "But he gets tired," Ludwick said, "and then we pull him in. Give him a second chop then, spear him again." But still the dugong didn't die. It had to be drowned, its body weighing perhaps six hundred pounds hauled tail first over the boat, with men straining back on the other side to keep the boat balanced, while the hunter struggled to force the dugong's head underwater. You couldn't shoot it, Ludwick said, because then it would go to the bottom and it was too hard to get it up again. "He struggles. I been thrown in the water couple of times. Longest I been drowning one was a quarter hour, but I heard from old timers, they was out half the night, pretty near, trying to drown him. Very wild."

A girl came in to buy something and Ludwick went to the counter. The girl had a ponytail and a bright blue dress and no shoes. Richard Hyde, an elderly Aboriginal I had already met, wandered in and sat down at the table. After the girl went out Ludwick came back and began to talk about turtles, which Aborigines retained the right to hunt. If you harpooned a big green turtle, he said, it would pull a boat with four men in it. The wop was used with a different type of harpoon, and mostly the harpoon went through the shell. If the wound it made was too large or became infected, then you couldn't keep the turtle alive, which was the easiest way to store its flesh. "If we haven't got any beef we kill him straight away, soon as we get home. Otherwise, turn him on his back. You get some turtles, they live a long time on their back. Live for weeks. Not in water, just on their back. But too much infection in the shell, the air get in or something, and kill them." The turtles also were less plentiful than they had been, he said, and again he didn't know why.

Over in the hall, the piano began another waltz. It was the theme from the film of "Doctor Zhivago". *Somewhere*, the piano mourned, *somewhere, my love*. In the warm hall, the dark dancers would be turning, turning, to a memory of unimaginable snow. Ludwick got up and went back to the counter. Richard Hyde and I sat on, listening to the piano.

"That's all they want now, the young ones," Hyde said. "Elvis Presley, things like that." Under the strip lighting of the cafe he was like a shadow made solid, his eyes no more than a shine in the dark skin. He was about sixty-three, and he had the reputation of being one of the keepers of his people's stories. Now, as if to counter the Zhivago lament, he began an anecdote of the eighteen-seventies and the Chinese who had come to this coast for the Palmer River goldrush.

"The Chinese," said Richard Hyde, "he had a flavour to him. That's what they say, in the tribe that ate them. Now my people, they had a try at white man's flesh. But they said, you know, not salty enough. My grandfather and some others, they killed a white, a sailor. Near Cairns, on an island."

I finished the cool glass of cordial and then said, "Why?"

"That's what I'm tellin' you. They want to taste what sort of flesh they got. If it was worth eatin'. But," he said, indulging I thought in a rather special brand of racial prejudice, "they killed one white and tasted his flesh and they said, 'No good'. So they didn't kill any more. That's what the story was."

Mournfully the waltz went on, around and around in circles. *Snow. Sleigh rides. Tender. Splendour.*

"They can tell you about that Captain Cook," Hyde said, looking fiercely towards the hall of the waltzers, and perhaps beyond them to the plans to celebrate the 1970 bi-centenary of the voyage which had brought the white invaders. "They learn about Cook. But they don't know about Damori. Quial and Damori, they come before Cook. Long time, many days. And never got wrecked. The Reef, it wrecked Cook." It had, too. Cook was forced to put in for repairs at what is now the Endeavour River. Damori and Quial were never wrecked, Richard Hyde pointed out. Yet who knew about Damori and Quial? I admitted I didn't, but should like to know. And so he told me the story of the two brothers who came down from the north, one to produce a son rather in the manner of Zeus, and to marry a woman who rose up from the waters of the Reef, and the other to devote himself to bad works, such as putting teeth in the crocodile.

"Damori and Quial, they two brothers. Come from Solomon Islands, in a canoe. And mind, they wasn't very small men. They were hefty, oh, big lump of man. They was travellin' men, they came all the way down through many, many islands. Namin' the places as they come down, callin' it in their own language. This was the greatest story our fathers told. The first story we got to learn.

"There was a good brother, Quial. He was a great gentleman. Damori, he was a man made things hard. The olden-day people, they reckon he was the cursed brother in the family.

"Yet Damori, his word never fall to the ground. It brought fruit.

"In the days to come, Damori said, this place here would be a home. And so it happened. Today, Yarrabah is a home." he paused.

"Yes," I said.

"And Cairns is a home. People live there." He paused.

"Yes."

"His word never fall to the ground."

"No." Making the responses, I remembered that Hyde had been brought up by missionaries.

"All them places that he named, all inhabited today."

I decided to pass.

Hyde waited some little time, and then went on. "Quial, he was a good man. Gentle, kind, loving. People believe he got married to a fairy woman, came out of the water. But before that he got a son. He had a big boil on his leg. They open up the boil, out comes the little boy. Quial says, 'I got a little boy of my own. The likes of me!' And he said, 'Where I gonna find a mother now?'

"He started carryin' the child feed, wild shrimp and things from the sea. One day he leave the child on the beach. When he come back he find the child asleep, and milkstain all over his chest.

"Quial said, 'Eh, woman been here – given milk my little one'. The old custom was, when a mother want to go away a good distance, she always spread the milk all over the child. That child, just like anaesthetic, it go to sleep. So Quial said, 'Woman been here. But where she come from?'

"Tomorrow he go down the beach. 'Now,' he said, 'I find who's this feedin' my child'. He put that little boy on the beach, made a little shed for him. He said, 'Now, I go away, hide'. The little boy started to cry. 'Go on,' says Quial, 'Keep cryin', keep cryin' '.

"Next thing this pretty lovely woman come, gettin' out of the water. Quial is hiding. She go up and she lay near that child, givin' that child her breast.

"And Quial says, 'Oh yes, that's the one! Oh,' he says, '*well!* I must ketch this one for my wife. Want to marry 'em'.

"He chose the best spear out. And he let go that spear. He nailed her right through like that – right through behind the knees. That woman let out one squeal and rear up. She couldn't move.

"He come and hit her across the back of the neck. She didn't have a tongue. Quial hit her across the back of the neck, make her tongue grow long. So she could talk.

"Then quick he make a big fire, to take all that slime off her, slime she got on her like an old eel fish.

"Took the slime off with the fire. Made a big bush fire and stand her near it and see it dry off. Wiped her with a sort of grass.

"He say, 'You'll be all right. You gonna be my wife. You gonna look after my child'.

"After this, Quial say to Damori – the cursed brother – 'Well, brother, I'm goin' to go away. I'm goin' to leave you. I'm gonna leave you now.' Damori said, 'where you goin' to go?' Quial said, 'Well, I don't know where I'm goin' to go, but I'm goin'. And he went with the fairy woman and the boy.

"People here never heard no more about them. Went into the west. We never heard again.

"But Damori said, 'Ah, I'll stay here. Place seem all right to me. Start up a bit of mischief'.

"He think about the crocodile. Early days, crocodile didn't have any teeth. Just like, bare. Damori got the crocodile, said, 'Here, try bite my leg'. The crocodile tried, couldn't. 'Ah, that's no good,' Damori said. 'You want something so you can have a good feed.' He made him teeth, like dog teeth, all way along the mouth. 'Now,' he said. 'You have a try now.'

"Crocodile tried again, bit Damori's leg, took it off.

" 'That's *right*,' said Damori."

Just one question, I said. Why was Damori so anxious to help the crocodile? Why did he worry about him?

"He worried about *everything*. He was a clever man. And he was a man of, sort of, mischief, and not satisfied. Didn't have a wife. He was a bachelor. Single all the way. Really, he didn't have sympathy for nothing. Damori wasn't a man most people'd put trust in.

"Quial was different. You'd never hear anything about Quial. There isn't a word uttered about Quial. He was gentle. He helped the poor. He helped anybody who was stuck. Real kind and mild and gentle man.

"But Damori, he was just a man to himself. Every time he hears a crocodile knockin' some kind of animal out, Damori have a good laugh."

The crocodile was such a clever animal, Hyde said, because Damori taught him his cunning. "Now you can eat a man," Damori told the crocodile with the new dentures. "Now you can eat any animal." The crocodile learned well from Damori. A thing Hyde had seen for himself, he said, was this cunning big crocodile swimming in from the sea with a dead turtle on its head. The turtle was balanced on those spikes at the back of its neck. The crocodile was swimming under the turtle and bringing it back to land, to be stored in the swamp until the flesh was right for eating. Oh, a cunning animal, said Richard Hyde. A clever animal.

Ludwick was closing down the refreshment counter. The music in the hall had stopped. What about the whales, I asked Hyde. How long was it since he'd seen a whale?

"We seen 'em," he said, "but not in these times. They'd play, they'd have good fun. I saw the mother playin' with the little ones, takin' them trainin'. See those little ones way up in the air – " he began to laugh " – not so little, too. They'd leap way up. Our people take notice of that. They said, if you see a whale play, when it's calm, you number the days. In seven days there will be a blow, a wind, a terrible wind. It's so. But not seen a whale in a mighty long time. Except," said Hyde, "those two we got up on that hill." He rose to go, apparently finished with the subject.

"Which two?" I asked.

"That time when the world was flooded," he said, "they left two whales on top of the hill. They was stuck on top. When the flood waters go, they couldn't get down. Still there. Turned to stone." You could see them on a hill back there, he said – back there, west, the direction Quial had taken with the fairy woman, and the boy from his leg, when they all went away from the people of the Reef. Those whales, he said, were there to this day. Those whales couldn't ever get back to the sea.

CHAPTER 14

Oil, Politicians and International Law

✳

In 1969, oil drilling in Reef waters became an issue in two elections – the Queensland State election in May and the Australian federal election in October. The government in each case was a coalition of the Liberal and Country Parties. There was, though, a considerable difference in style and outlook between the State and federal politicians. In the federal coalition the dominant partner was the Liberal Party, representing largely the city man, the manufacturer, the investor, and with some members accessible to the ideas of conservation. In the State coalition, the party with the greater number of seats was the Country Party, which in the form it took in Queensland posed special problems for conservationists. Based on the land, the Country party was held to be lacking in understanding of the sea. "That's why we have such a battle in this State," said one conservationist. "When it comes to the sea and the Reef, these politicians have no understanding at all. They just want to exploit them like the land and animals and minerals. It's automatic with them." If there were, to begin with, differences of attitude between the state and federal politicians, there was also a real clash of interest when, after the state politicians were returned to power in Queensland amidst cries of "gerrymander", they proceeded to disclose a willingness to open Reef waters to oil drillers. Their federal colleagues were left to campaign for their own re-election against the cry of the Labor opposition that they belonged to the same party grouping as that which in Queensland had promised to protect the Reef and then, after its return to government, had forgotten its promises.

In this period before the federal election, the federal Labor opposition could not but benefit from the way state Labor in the Queensland parliament kept the issues of Reef exploitation before the public. The State Labor politicians revived, for example, the question of the seven hundred thousand dollars' worth of shares alleged to represent the Queensland Premier's interest in oil drilling. The Press carried reports that a Labor member, Colin Bennett, had pointed to the new United States ambassador as an example of probity in share ownership: the ambassador was disposing of his shares in all companies having any dealings with Australia. Bennett was sad and disappointed, he said, to see the Queensland Premier "sitting there concealing his holdings", which Bennett understood were worth seven hundred thousand dollars. Referring to drilling on the Great Barrier Reef, he said that parliament was "entitled to know if a person had a pro-curatory action in the deal". He also said, "The day people can't know the shareholdings ministers have is the day democracy will end". Still, next day Johannes Bjelke-Petersen was still Premier. And this fact pleased quite a number of people. The Premier was a Lutheran Sunday-school teacher, clean cut, close-barbered, non-drinking, non-smoking. "With leaders such as you, prepared to stand up and acknowledge God," one woman wrote to him, "our country is destined to great things." The occasion which inspired this letter, and others like it, was that on which the Premier spoke, through a newspaper, of the spiritual strength he derived from the Bible, which he always carried with him in a pocket-sized edition. He read the Bible in the morning and in the evening, and sometimes he also managed a lunchtime reading. "It is a rare thing," a Queenslander wrote to his Premier, "to see men in such high positions moulding their lives around the word of God." The Premier's Labor critics were a little out of countenance. After all, when one considered to Whom the Premier applied each day for guidance, mightn't it be some sort of heresy to suggest he was misguided? They seemed able to push the thought aside, though, to continue a campaign which, while it did not appear to disturb the Premier, was something of an embarrassment to his electioneering federal colleagues.

The Reef issue was a particularly difficult one for the Prime Minister, John Gorton. An Australian who had taken a Master of Arts degree at Oxford, he gave the impression of being altogether more interested than the Queensland Premier in the things of this world. And yet he was not so interested in exploiting the Reef. In fact, when he visited Queensland in August of 1969 for a Liberal Party convention, he said that he was opposed to the Reef being drilled for oil. For a while it seemed that his statement might influence the convention against the policy of the state government. But state politicians of his own party spoke up for the coalition of which they were a part, and eventually it was their viewpoint which prevailed. The State Parliamentary Liberal Leader took the opportunity to remind his Federal Liberal Leader and Prime Minister that despite any personal opposition the Prime Minister might feel towards oil drilling, in fact both the state and federal governments were involved in the oil agreements. Under the Petroleum Submerged Lands Act of 1967 it was necessary for the state to obtain Commonwealth approval of an offshore lease. And it had obtained this approval, often. This was true. But the federal government now seemed to be regretting its part in the contract. With the federal election still to be fought and agitation against oil drilling increasing, a rumour started that the federal government was offering to find the money to buy off the oil companies – to pay them compensation for expenses so far incurred – if the state government would agree to repudiate the leases. A Labor member rose in the state parliament to ask whether, if the Commonwealth was willing to meet claims for compensation, the State government would ban further drilling in Reef waters. The State Premier replied that it was for the Commonwealth to decide how it exercised its powers, but "my government will not be a party to repudiation".

Labor's Douglas Sherrington kept the issues alive by addressing to the state parliament a speech which was largely a resumé of the past and present attitudes to conservation of this government now presiding over the fate of the Great Barrier Reef. Sherrington, a big man with backswept grey hair, rose to remind the honourable members of a whole series of governmental shortcomings. He began by complaining about Queensland's loss of a conservation minister who, he asserted, had been sacked for over-zealousness: "Let it not be forgotten that it was the Premier who said during the election campaign, 'We are the first government to have a conservation portfolio'. Not only did the government drop any reference to conservation in portfolio titles; to make it more obvious, it lopped off the head of the Minister for Conservation in the previous Parliament. I do not believe that he left the Ministry because of ill health; I believe he was sacked because he opposed the views of certain other ministers who wanted to exploit without end many natural resources of the State". (*Interjection:* "There is no charity in that remark".) To illustrate the attitude of the Minister for Mines to conservation, Sherrington quoted a statement the Minister had made in 1962 on the proposal to revoke the declaration of an area of land at Cape Conway as a national park reserve. Referring to an occasion when the Minister had been discussing "scrub" (a colloquialism for rain forest which effectively masks the magnificence of the thing being destroyed), Sherrington said, "The Minister said, and I think this is indicative of his attitude – 'From the point of view of walking in the scrub to view its natural attractions, I can assure hon. members that if one gets into the centre of eight acres of scrub one sees just as much as it is possible to see from the centre of a forty-eight-thousand-acre area of scrub'."

When it came to the Great Barrier Reef, Sherrington charged that the government had "imported an American geologist to provide it with an alibi and an excuse for its decision to grant permission to drill for oil on the Reef".

Oil exploitation, he said, "will not be a matter of isolated rigs off our coast, although the government is trying to create that impression. If oil is found near the Barrier Reef, and if the pattern is similar to that off the Louisiana coast, we will see about six thousand oil rigs off the coastline. We can well imagine the damage and devastation to the Barrier Reef in such circumstances". He said that the Minister for Mines had been reported as saying, "I have been told by a world authority that the risk of an offshore oil rig blowing out is about the same as a meteorite hitting a city". Yet the Red Adair company (which specialized in the control of blowouts) had been called on in one year to attend eleven major blowouts in various parts of the world. Sherrington also quoted figures supplied by John Busst (that artistic organizer made his representations to the Liberal-Country Party government in Canberra and to the Labor opposition in Queensland). The figures came from a letter from Professor Gus Swanson, of the University of Colorado, who had written that "in the area of Cook Inlet, in Alaska, there have been in the offshore oil drilling operations, between the period June 1966 to November 1968, no less than seventy-five oil spills".

Sherrington issued the conservationist call for a moratorium. "I emphatically reinforce the decision made by the Australian Labor Party," he said, "to call on the government for a moratorium of at least ten years, or a State-wide referendum – not on the present gerrymandered electoral boundaries – relating to the future of the Reef". (*Interjection:* "That is unfair".)

Worse, at the federal level, it was embarrassing. The federal politicians facing an election contest with the Labor Party had somehow to disown the Reef policies of their State colleagues without disowning their State colleagues, who mightn't like it. They had to pit such statements as that really it was not within their *power* to do anything about oil drilling, that the decision was entirely one for the Queensland government, against the Labor Party's assertion that if it won the election it would suspend all drilling and mining on the Great Barrier Reef. Ironically, the Labor Party (led by a lawyer, Gough Whitlam) proposed to do this on the opinions formulated by two eminent lawyers who had been non-Labor politicians. One was Sir Garfield Barwick, the Minister for External Affairs from 1961 to 1964, and now Chief Justice of the High Court of Australia. The other was Sir Percy Spender, former Minister for External Affairs, former Ambassador to the United States, former President of the International Court of Justice (from 1964 to 1967). At a Reef symposium held in Sydney on 3 May 1969, in a paper called "The Great Barrier Reef: Legal Aspects", Sir Percy had laid down the law of the sea with special reference to that section of it bordering the coast of Queensland. It was a paper which, among other things, seemed to offer a way of realizing the promise which the dead Prime Minister, Harold Holt, had made to John Busst – that if necessary the Commonwealth would take over the Reef from Queensland. Sir Percy, a lightly built, well tailored man with smoothed-down greying hair, delivered in an even voice an opinion which seemed likely to make the Queensland Premier feel that perhaps he ought to secede and take the Reef with him. Queensland, said Sir Percy, had no rights at all in the sea off its coast. The seas bordering Australia, and the seabed thereof, with all its natural resources, were those of the Commonwealth. "There is no doubt," said the former President of the International Court of Justice, "that the right to explore and exploit the resources of the Australian continental shelf is, under international law, recognized as vested exclusively in the Commonwealth of Australia". The continental shelf (on which the Great Barrier Reef was located) was an underwater extension of the coast. "The most fundamental of all the rules of law relating to the continental shelf," Sir Percy said, "is that the rights of the coastal State in respect of the area of the continental shelf, constituting as it does a natural prolongation of its land territory under the sea, exist by virtue of its sovereignty over the land. . . ." But, he emphasized, the coastal State referred to in the foregoing was not

Queensland. The reference was not to a province or State within a federation "but to a sovereign State recognized in international law as an International Person. In our case that state is the Commonwealth of Australia". (The state of Queensland, of course, could not accept that it was not an International Person. Later, the Queensland Minister for Justice was to express Queensland's case in this way: "The State claims and has always claimed that its right to explore and exploit the natural resources of the seabed of the continental shelf and its subsoil arises out of an inchoate right which vested in it before federation and that it is the coastal State in which the right vests. . . .") Sir Percy had an ingenious suggestion for settling the argument of Commonwealth versus State. Why shouldn't the Commonwealth sue Queensland? Before the High Court of Australia? In a perfectly friendly way? "There is, in my view," he explained, "no difficulty in having these issues determined with despatch. . . ."

The discussion which followed Sir Percy's address at the symposium revealed some of the unresolved complexities of the new laws governing the conduct of nations as they moved out into the sea to exploit its resources. On some questions it might not be just a matter of the Commonwealth versus Queensland, but of Australia versus other nations. Professor D. P. O'Connell (Professor of International Law at the University of Adelaide) said that among other things there was the problem of how viable the Geneva Convention would prove to be. "Whereas the International Court's decision two months ago has greatly reinforced the Australian position," he said, "by establishing that the continental shelf exists as a matter of customary international law, independent of the treaty, it still has not gone so far as to establish that the natural resources of the continental shelf which can be exploited include certain types of marine organisms which we all want to protect. Therefore, it is still open for a country not a party to the treaty to argue that it is not bound by Australian legislation with respect to particular marine organisms. This would be unfortunate, but it may be the situation."

A question put to Professor O'Connell from the auditorium on national claims to the sea was phrased in this way: "Precedent set by international law is based on strength. Iceland expanded her limit to twelve miles. Chile has claimed, I think, two hundred miles – yet

Chile is unable to enforce this rule. Now we take Australia, which has granted leases outside the continental shelf on Elizabeth Reefs. What rights had she to grant these except those based on strength? Australia can claim the Barrier Reef on the same basis. Who is going to challenge this?"

To which question Professor O'Connell gave an interesting reply: "I would agree that delimitation of the maritime boundaries of states at the present time certainly takes on the aspect of a trial of strength, but one must remember that Australia could find itself in the International Court having to defend its position.... Therefore, it is not only a question of a trial of strength, but one of a very judicious appreciation of what I might describe as the state of play among the international law community, and the practice of states internationally."

Immediately, though, control of the Reef depended on the state of play between Australia's federal government and the government of Queensland, and this was affected by the outcome of the federal elections of October, 1969. In those elections, the federal coalition politicians came so close to defeat, for reasons which did not exclude the battering they'd had to take on Reef issues, that afterwards they were a little off their game. It was no time for a legal test over ownership of the Reef. And of course it was uncertain if it would ever really be time for such a test, which might unite all the states behind Queensland and raise the panic cry of centralism against the central government. Legal rights were one thing, but state rights were sacred, even when they weren't exactly rights. Besides, it was not too clear what the advantages for the Reef would really be from federal rather than state control. There were among the federal politicians men who would do their best to protect the Reef, but nobody could be sure what their best could amount to at the level of practical politics and enthusiasm for Australia's mining boom. John Busst had come to think that the best thing might be to place the Reef in the care of an international commission under the chairmanship of Australia. The commission would have power to second scientists and advisers. Busst had been corresponding on this matter with such bodies as I.U.C.N. (the International Union for the Conservation of Nature) whose headquarters were at Morges, Switzerland. Judith Wright McKinney, president of the Wildlife Preservation Society of Queensland, had also called in at Morges during a visit to Europe. Still, in late 1969 the reality was that power over the Reef resided with the Queensland government. And the Queensland government had announced that there was to be more drilling for oil in Reef waters. Japex (Australia) Pty. Ltd., a Japanese subsidiary, had an arrangement with the Australian company, Ampol Exploration, whereby it was to drill in an area for which Ampol held Authority to Prospect 103P. In return, Ampol was to receive a share in any oil which might be found. Now Japex was preparing to bring the oil rig *Navigator* from the United States to drill in Repulse Bay, just south of the magnificent islands around the Reef's Whitsunday Passage.

CHAPTER 15

A Cruise around Whitsunday

✳

To explore this area of the Reef threatened by the search for oil – and for other minerals – I joined *Esmeralda*, a long, white motor-yacht which took parties of tourists cruising through the islands along the Whitsunday Passage. Sailing the waterways between Whitsunday's high, green, coral-fringed mountain-islands – so unlike the flat cay-landscapes of Green or Heron Island – *Esmeralda* travelled a route which would be described in different ways by different people. To the tourist promoter, *Esmeralda* was exploring one of the loveliest (and, for tourism, one of the most profitable) sections of the Reef. To the oil man, on the other hand, she was sailing through a map of Petroleum titles, her location seldom very far from the well which Japex intended to drill.

A feature of her cruise was a visit to the Outer Barrier, the last rampart of coral between the islands and the open sea. On the day *Esmeralda* sailed towards this rampart with me among her passengers, the sky ahead looked dark. Tom Evetts, the skipper, remarked that this was the tricky part of the cruise – you had to be sure you could make the distance, get the boat through the coral-strewn approaches and away again, before bad weather caught up with you. In the wheelhouse, scanning the grey seaways between the towering green islands, he reckoned that today we would be all right. The weather would hold. We would make it to the outer reefs while the tide was still low enough for the passengers to explore the corals, and then we would sail back to Hook Island and anchor for the night.

Esmeralda rounded an island into a wide bay. Behind us now was a crescent of white sand. Ahead of us – was, suddenly, a dolphin, upright on the air, twelve foot or more of shining body standing on nothing, bottle nose to the sky, smiling. Then it dropped back through the water, smoothly, making no splash, and was gone. "Get down forward," Evetts called to me. "It'll be swimming with us." I scrambled down the white iron steps and out on to the plunging bow. I looked down at the dolphin, swimming with a young one about half its size. Together they were racing the boat, their action so smooth it seemed they were not moving, that it was the sea which was flowing backwards over them. The big dolphin, close to the boat, rolled on its side and looked up, so that you saw that constant smile. Now it was gone – and now it was twenty yards ahead, standing on air, disappearing, coming up again instantaneously, it seemed, beside the boat. Eventually the two dolphins swam away, lazing and rolling, towards a line of pale green water. That greenness, Tom Evetts said when I climbed back into the wheelhouse again, was the sign of a silica bank underneath. There was a tremendous amount of high-grade silica around here. Back further was the beach they'd been talking about mining. There was talk, too, of dredging the sea bottom. People would protest, he said, but you never seemed to be able to find out exactly what was being planned. Far off, over a fortune in silica, the big dolphin surfaced, wheeling in a silver arc. Watching it, Evetts said, "We used to get a lot of whales around here, too. But I haven't seen any of those in ages."

This skipper of *Esmeralda* was a lean man with auburn hair and eyes set deep under tan eyebrows. From now on the eyes were fixed searchingly on the water ahead, where the outer reefs lay. *Esmeralda* began to go up and down like a lift, and kept on like that for long enough to suggest to me that for the first time in my life I might be seasick. She stopped in time. Our final advance on the outer reefs was a fairly steady one. The sky cleared, and *Esmeralda* sailed down a sunlit channel among ribbons of green water and ribbons of stone-coloured reef formations. Far out there was a line of foam, beyond that the Coral Sea, and beyond that the horizon. This was a world of water, and when *Esmeralda* anchored all you heard was the water slapping coolly at the hull. A glass-bottomed boat was lowered to take us over to a reef. It floated above a coral landscape of great beauty – chasms and cliffs and valleys of coral, with round coral tables where bright fish gathered. The crown-of-thorns had not infested Whitsunday nor these outer reefs. On the reef crest, on which the boat set us down, the display was less spectacular. Under about six inches of water it had rather the look of a submerged rock garden. Small clams, embedded on their hinges, showed brilliant mantles of blue, green, tan, yellow. There were clumps of coral resembling bunches of lavender. There were cone shells. A woman holding a bouquet of corals she had gathered pondered the information that the cones might injure her if touched, and then complained that they ought to provide you with tongs, then, to pick things up. Since the tide was racing in, the boat came back after about twenty minutes and took us off the reef.

By late afternoon *Esmeralda* was anchored on a polished green bay among the steep hills of Hook Island. Some of the passengers began to fish. Others of us just sat around, listening to the forest cries coming over the water. In the hills, raucous kookaburras laughed and laughed. White cockatoos wheeled through the green, screeching from throats in need of oiling. There was a great deal of soft, exotic whistling. When one of the men fishing called, "Look – here's a devil ray," we all got up and rushed to the side. Just under the surface a five-foot width of darkness, with horns, was passing the boat in a slow, flying movement. It looked rather like an underwater flying carpet. "Harmless," said Tom Evetts. We went back to sitting around, and the fishermen went back to fishing.

Early in the morning, under a pale gold sky, *Esmeralda* sailed from Hook to visit other islands in the chain rising like water-girt hills around the Whitsunday Passage. The first call was at Hayman. The Royal Hayman Hotel accommodated its guests in individual white lodges set in tropical gardens suggesting landscaped jungle, and entertained them in a hotel block with an attractive air of light-hearted luxury. It all looked as if it might be just the place for the Reef visitor who thought of himself as a nature-lover, but within civilized limits. There was a lagoon, and swimming, and sailing, but there were as well the glass-walled lounges where guests could drink to the tropic palms and all the energetic people out there enjoying them. In the evening there were meals in the Gold Room, with chandeliers and gold wallpaper and an opportunity for the women who hadn't looked their best in bikinis to dress.

Daydream Island was more theatrical, or rather, cinematic. In fact Daydream was a fief of Hollywood, one of its traditional south seas possessions. Hostesses served luncheon in grass skirts and plastic leis. For dinner they would change into long sarongs and plastic leis. In the middle of the huge swimming pool, reached by a rustic bridge, was a grass-hut bar for dry swimmers. Daydream, the manageress said, was mainly selling nightlife, and the people who wanted nightlife and could pay for it fell into the thirty-five to fifty age group. Daydream's fantasies by night included Hawaiian feasts around the great pool, with gas flares for torches and girls in sarongs serving the food. One of the girls was Dorothy Lamour. Had to be. And somewhere, probably marooned on that lake in the grass-hut bar, were Bing Crosby and Bob Hope. Because this was really their film set, the one they used in – what *was* that picture called? "Road to the Isles"?

Happy Bay, on Long Island, was on the next day's itinerary of the *Esmeralda* cruise. Again there were green hills, and reef, and blue water, and palm trees, and again there was an atmosphere different from that of other islands of the group. The old-fashioned directness of the name turned out to suit this place, which felt rather like a big tropical farm turned loose on the sea. White fowls scratched in a yard shaded by poplar gums with silvery trunks. In the gums and in the bare china-apple trees sat wild scrub turkeys, dark birds with scarlet heads. Their life was all privilege and no responsibility to the guesthouse table. While the fowls were being fed they flew down and ate, too, and then they made off again to freedom. Happy Bay had cabins with flowering vines climbing over the roofs. The beer garden was a collection of tables under one massive tree, a poinciana making a low roof of feathery green fifty feet wide. Its lights were electric globes inside big glass spheres – the marker buoys which all down the Reef drifted in from Japanese fishing gear – and it had the look of a corner of the garden decorated for a family party.

Out in the Whitsunday Passage again, *Esmeralda* continued its cruise through the mountains of the sea. It was warm and still. On the water, a yellowish sea snake lazed in a wide, loose curve. Sometimes, little islands far off seemed to be floating in the air. You stared, but still there was nothingness between the base of the island and the surface of the water. An illusion of the calm, Tom Evetts said. Later we rounded Pentecost Island, rising in brown-gold stone like a massive natural sphinx. "They wanted to mine Pentecost," Evetts said. "For copper. And for some other thing, I've forgotten what. There was a row about it, and they didn't go ahead." They might yet, though. There had been much talk of utilizing Pentecost. And also about exploiting the sea bottom. "In the next few years, you'll find a lot of dredges being built to mine the continental shelf," said the young dredge engineer I had interviewed shortly after his return from a world trip checking on such matters. They would scoop stuff off the bottom, or maybe pump it up, he said. He had the sort of enthusiasm for his subject you sometimes saw in the offshore oil men. Like them, he was speaking of marvels, triumphs of the technological imagination beside which such ancient wonders as the pyramids subsided into the commonplace. "There's so *much* wealth under the sea," he said. "Besides, there's a tremendous investment required these days to work the lowgrade deposits on the continents. There are very few high-grade deposits of anything left now on land. *Known* deposits, that is – there may be a lot of unknown stuff. But take copper. In 1900 they were working two percent copper ore bodies. Today they work ground as low as half a percent copper. They know the seabed is rich in minerals – with the advantage that if you're in the middle of the ocean somewhere you've got no political interference. As they develop their techniques, they'll be able to move further and further out into the sea. But they'll start with the continental shelf."

The continental shelf lay deep under *Esmeralda*, sailing through Whitsunday. The water around us was still, satiny. The mountains were not green now, but blue, darker than the water they were rising from as smoothly as the dolphin. Gold rocks floated in the sun, with nothing but illusion between them and the water. Dredges here? Polluting, destroying feeding areas, cutting the ground from under the grazing dugong, the bottom-dwelling shell, the fish, the dolphin? Within five years, the engineer had said.

And so we came to our last island, Lindeman. This island, with the inference that royalty would choose the best, billed itself as "the island a princess chose". Princess Alexandra had stayed here. Only six hundred yards away, the Queen and the Duke of Edinburgh had set foot on the Reef. Lindeman had one other distinction: it was about twenty miles from the risk of disaster posed by the Japex oil well. The island's director was Tom Evetts' brother-in-law, Lachlan Nicolson, a man with grey wavy hair, glasses, a soft voice. It was Nicolson's interest in birds which gave Lindeman an atmosphere especially attractive to naturalists. It had the standard endowment of Whitsunday beauty – green hills, blue water, coral, beaches. It had palms, hibiscus, a swimming pool, Hawaiian smorgasbords. But it also had birds, Lach Nicholson made you realize, as he charmed them out of the trees. I watched as he brought down a cloud of lorikeets, small parrot-like birds with mauve-blue heads and green wings and bodies coloured in yellow-gold, red and purple-blue. He fed them on water-soaked bread and sugar. When they had eaten they ascended again seemingly by an act of levitation, a rush of gold and blue and red straight up the green hill. Later, he began to talk about the local eagles, especially the white-breasted sea eagle, which he called the most majestic of birds. I could agree. I had seen one of them out over the ocean, very high, wings outspread, drifting back and forth across perhaps a hundred yards of sky, swinging as in a great tide of air, as the fish had been swinging in the sea around Green Island. "A very good soaring bird," Nicolson said. And with an interesting method of fishing. "He comes down and takes fish from the surface. Doesn't dive – grabs backwards with his talons, on the surface. Garfish, say, will begin to skip, and you'll see him come in behind them and grab." All the birds of the area were protected, he said, and a lot of people who came here were interested in them. Later, a man who had been visiting Lindeman for years talked to me enthusiastically about the birds which were so easily observed here, and then went on to speak of the whales he had seen off the island. Sometimes these whales would just be lying around with their calves, he said, as if they were half asleep – although on occasions they would leap. What a sight that was. It was somehow marvellous, really marvellous, looking out and seeing these tremendous animals, leaping.

How long was it, I asked, since he'd seen this? He was bereft-looking, suddenly. "My God," he said. "You know, it must be years, now."

CHAPTER 16

Remembering a Whale Hunt

✳

WHAT had happened to the Reef's whales? Why had they disappeared? Hadn't there been hunting quotas, agreements to protect them? Yes, there had been, said Professor James Thomson, but the arrangements hadn't worked out. Thomson, who was now Professor of Zoology at the University of Queensland, had been from 1948 until 1952 Officer in Charge of the Fisheries Division Research Station at Dunwich, Queensland, run by Australia's Commonwealth Scientific and Industrial Research Organization. He had been a member of the research staff of the C.S.I.R.O.'s Division of Fisheries and Oceanography until 1963. Now he was one of the few people on the Australian east coast with any detailed knowledge of the last years of the whales' migrations between Antarctica and the tropics. Tangalooma, Queensland's old whaling station, had closed, and its site was a holiday resort. The whaling inspectors who, I had heard, had been threatened with violence for trying to enforce agreed-upon protection for the whales, had scattered to other parts of Australia to take up new work. Thomson, although he had not visited the Antarctic on the whaling vessels, had worked with men who had, and as a marine scientist he had been generally concerned with the whale hunt which opened after the end of World War II. At that time, the main whale off Australia's eastern coast and in Reef waters had been the humpback, other species having been largely eliminated by earlier whalers. The humpbacks, less valuable than the species previously attacked, containing less oil, were still valuable enough to interest Australia and to draw northern nations down to the bottom of the world to hunt them in the Antarctic. In the beginning, there was no wish to eliminate these whales. The nations which gathered for the hunt, having been concerned in the extermination of other whale species, knew by now that it was silly to wipe out the animals completely, instead of leaving sufficient numbers of them to breed and keep the industry supplied.

It was known that the humpback female did not breed until she was five years old, and then produced only one calf every second year. This time, it was agreed, the hunters would work to sensible rules. There would be a quota of whales to be taken each year. Whales below a minimum length would not be taken. There would be inspectors on the whaling ships to enforce these rules. And there would be scientists to observe and advise.

Excellent. How was it, though, that a few years later this hunt, too, had to end for lack of prey?

As he remembered it, said Professor Thomson, this was the story. In the summer in the Antarctic there was abundant food. The humpbacks down there fed heavily, built up their blubber, and then headed north before winter. A proportion of them came up Australia's east coast. Some travelled outside the Reef, and some inside. They mated in the tropics, and produced their young in the tropics. The calves, from the mating of the previous season, were born after a gestation period of eleven months. They spent their first weeks of life in a warm and pleasant sea, building up protective blubber. Then all the whales turned back towards the Antarctic. And there the hunters were, waiting to collect them for industrial lubricants, oil for margarine, and sometimes for meat.

In this whaling league of nations there were Norwegians, Russians, Japanese, Americans, Dutchmen, Greeks and perhaps a few others Thomson couldn't remember offhand. Australia sent inspectors to the Antarctic but did its own killing as the humpbacks passed along its coast. The organization designed to control the hunt was an international whaling commission of the various countries involved in it. Countries consented by international agreement that there would be an international whaling commission and that they would follow what it recommended. There was also a sub-committee formed of fishery research scientists. This sub-committee made recommendations to the international body, but the international body was not bound to accept their recommendations. The scientists' reasoning was that if only to keep the industry working it was necessary to set quotas low enough to allow the slow-breeding whales to reproduce themselves. But the national representatives on the whaling commission were often fisheries administrators, each under pressure from his own industry at home to obtain as high a quota as he could. "There was always pressure from industry for a higher quota and a strong recommendation from the scientists for a lower quota," Thomson recalled, "and they had to reach some compromise."

Australia had no Antarctic whaling fleet, but it had a Department of Primary Industries setting whaling quotas. "There were three firms on the east coast," Thomson said, "and two or three on the west coast, plus Norfolk Island, all trying to get as high a quota as they could. Scientists here, too, were advising on the numbers they felt could be safely taken." But again, he said, the scientists were ignored. This pressure for high quotas, Thomson considered, was the main cause of the collapse of the humpback whaling. The old attitudes which had wiped out so many whales in the past hadn't changed after all. "There was a purely business attitude," he said, "of 'let's get what we can while we can'." Even when it became apparent that if the quotas were not lowered the humpbacks, too, would disappear, there was resistance to lowering the quotas.

As the whales duly began to disappear, the chase became even more ruthless. It was felt that an inspector ought not to notice when desperate hunters took a whale protected by the rules. If he did notice he might have to discuss the matter with men working with knives which by accident slipped rather close to him. Thomson considered that Australia had strictly policed the regulations on its own stations. Inspectors there were within reach of police help, and in a better position to resist threats than men on the ships. "But it is almost certain," he said, "that offences were overlooked on the Antarctic whaling ships, because – well, if you've got a threat, for instance, that you'll be tossed over the side in the Antarctic Ocean, you've got to take it rather seriously."

The end came as forecast. The scientists continued to point out that if the whales were killed at a rate which did not allow them to reproduce, the industry would be finished, but the warnings were treated as being of academic interest. "With the combined whaling in the Antarctic and off Australia," Thomson said, "the result was that suddenly the industry just collapsed."

Another result was, of course, that whales were no longer being sighted in the waters of the Great Barrier Reef. Those leaping, singing creators of the gay white foam were gone. They had been destroyed by hunters promising rational exploitation, collaboration with scientists, obedience to regulations as reasonable-sounding as those which these days were being proposed for the exploitation of the Reef itself.

CHAPTER 17

Anticipating an Oil Hunt

✳

THERE would be no need to worry about the safety of the Reef, the Queensland government assured its public, when the offshore oil rig *Navigator* began drilling for the Japanese subsidiary, Japex (Australia) Pty. Ltd. Not only had stringent regulations been formulated to prevent accidents, but to make sure that the regulations were obeyed *Navigator* would have a government inspector on board.

The rig, it was expected, would begin drilling early in 1970. In about February, in fact. In the cyclone season.

And so it appeared that the protests, the petitions, and the conservationists' poll of more than four thousand Queenslanders showing that ninety percent of them were against drilling, were to be ignored.

On New Year's Day, 1970, Australians learned that in about a week's time *Navigator* would set out for the Reef from the United States port of Orange, Texas.

On 6 January they learned that Labor Senator Georges had sent a cable to the owners of *Navigator* in Texas. The cable said, "Public opinion in Australia is strongly against drilling in the Barrier Reef areas. Failure of State and federal governments to take action to ban drilling without thorough surveys necessitates direct action". The direct action Senator Georges felt the situation necessitated was a trade-union black ban on *Navigator*. If it attempted to drill in Reef waters, unions would stop all deliveries to the rig. There would be no food, fuel or water from the Australian coast. There would be no labour for hire, no equipment, no help with repairs. And in case the oil explorers thought they could get around these difficulties through a long-distance liaison with New Guinea, or the United States, or Japan, there would be a request to the international union movement for a world-wide black ban.

As well as cabling the owners of *Navigator*, Senator Georges addressed a telegram to the Japanese Ambassador in Canberra. He referred in it to his understanding that in Japex (Australia) Pty. Ltd., the company about to drill the Reef, the Japanese Petroleum Development Corporation, set up by the Japanese government, owned six hundred and sixty thousand shares, Mitsui owned sixty-four thousand shares and the general manager of Japex one share. "Is your government aware," he asked the Ambassador, "that Japex (Australia) is about to commence drilling in the vicinity of the Great Barrier Reef which the Australian people treasure as a heritage and which is regarded as one of the great natural wonders of the world? The Australian people fear for the safety of the Reef which is threatened by the proposed drilling and the likelihood of its extension. Therefore I ask you to make known to your government the position which has arisen so that it may discourage Japex (Australia) from proceeding with the drilling." Senator Georges felt that Japex might also be discouraged from drilling by Ampol, the holder of Authority to Prospect 103P, which it had farmed out to Japex for a share in any oil which might be found. Ampol spent a great deal of money on advertising campaigns keyed to the suggestion that Australians should fuel their cars with petrol sold by their friendly Australian oil company. Senator Georges informed Ampol that there were circumstances in which he would launch a campaign questioning whether Ampol was really an Australian company, as it advertised, and whether its products were worthy of support. A union spokesman in agreement with Senator Georges explained, "We are lending industrial backing to public opinion. A vast majority of Australians are opposed to drilling on the Reef".

Nevertheless this was government by trade union, and on past attitudes large numbers of citizens should have been opposed to it. Instead, everybody seemed to be delighted. "For once," said a columnist of the Sydney *Sun-Herald*, "I find myself in sympathy with a trade-unions' plan to invoke industrial action against government policy...." An editorial in *The Australian* declared, "The black ban proposed by Senator Georges to abort drilling plans will have an unprecedented measure of public support and will probably succeed. It deserves to." As people of all political opinions came together to cheer, there seemed to be only one question: Why hadn't somebody thought of this sooner? All kinds of ideas for direct action were cropping up. On 12 January *The Australian* printed a spare little letter from Clive Sansom, of Hobart, Tasmania. "Those who object to Barrier Reef drilling,"

Sansom wrote, "should immediately stop buying petrol from the oil company concerned."

On 14 January Australia learned that Ampol had recommended that its Japanese partner suspend drilling. Further, Ampol had sent telegrams to the Queensland Premier and Prime Minister Gorton suggesting a Commonwealth-State inquiry into the likelihood of damage from oil drilling. It had offered five thousand dollars towards the cost of the inquiry.

The Prime Minister's reply to Ampol praised its "nationally responsible attitude", declined the five thousand dollars, and indicated his agreement to an investigation should the state government agree. His telegram, which was released to the public, underlined the point that "the commonwealth government was bound to confirm the oil leases issued by the state on and near the Reef and is virtually unable to prevent drilling on these leases if the state agrees to drilling".

As it happened, the State still agreed to drilling. The Queensland Premier's reaction to the moves to suspend the operation was to indicate that he wanted it to proceed immediately. And Japex might try to proceed, people suddenly realized. The company had not yet indicated its intentions and was awaiting instructions from its head office in Japan. Meanwhile, the oil rig *Navigator* was ready to leave Texas.

Something else which was realized around this time, because of Ampol's reference to it, was that while agitation against oil drilling had been centred on the plans for the Japex-Ampol well, to be located near the coast, drilling was actually going on in a lonelier part of the Reef. On 26 February 1969, Tenneco Aust. Inc., an American subsidiary, had drilled in area Q1P, in the far north-east of the Reef region, about twenty-two miles north-east of Darnley Island. The well had been unsuccessful and had been abandoned on 4 May 1969. The conservationists had not agitated against the drilling, a circumstance into which some people were attempting to read significance. Why were there these protests against the Japanese when there had been none against the Americans? There was a suggestion that the campaign against Japex was actually inspired by the American oil companies trying to rid themselves of competitors. But as this theory made the conservationists the tool of the U.S. oil interests, it did seem more likely that the reason there had been no conservationist campaign against the Tenneco drilling was the same as the reason there had been none against the Gulf Oil drillings – people hadn't realized what was going on in an isolated section of the Reef. Japex, though, was in a different position, with its plan to drill in one of the more accessible areas, and now it was the subject of exchanges between the Australian Prime Minister and the Queensland Premier.

Countering the Prime Minister's moves to obtain a suspension of the Japex drilling, the Premier attacked his willingness to hold an inquiry now, although two years ago the Queensland government had vainly asked that the Commonwealth take part in just such an inquiry, except that the terms were to have been wider. The Prime Minister replied that what he now had in mind was "a truly joint Commonwealth-State inquiry", something which should not be confused with an inquiry suggested by Queensland in 1968. That suggestion had been for an eleven-man committee, with the Commonwealth appointing only one of the eleven men.

Another point the Queensland Premier made was that an inquiry into oil drilling on the Reef could not include the Japex operation, since it was not *on* the Reef. Japex planned to drill in Repulse Bay, and that, said the Premier, was sixty miles from the Barrier Reef. This seemed to mean that Repulse Bay was sixty miles from the outermost line of reefs which ran down the continental shelf at a varying distance from the Australian coast, and that these largely inaccessible outer reefs were all that counted in the definition, Great Barrier Reef. Repulse Bay was only about twenty miles from Lindeman Island and the Whitsunday Passage, but apparently these did not qualify for inclusion in the Reef nor for any protection which might be agreed upon for areas which did qualify. Yet the inner reefs and islands were inseparable from the Reef system and a map issued by the Division of National Mapping showed them that way, with the Great Barrier Reef Region extending from just beyond the outer reefs all the way in to the coast, and from Papua in the north to Fraser Island in the south. Repulse Bay was a part of those inshore waters which belonged with the whole Reef system of life. If there were to be an oil leak in Repulse Bay, it was the opinion of E. C. Fison, retired engineering consultant to the Queensland Department of Harbours and Marine, that winds could sweep the oil up past the green mountains of Whitsunday to the shores of Townsville and Magnetic Island. But then, would that matter? Was Magnetic Island a part of the Reef? It was distinctly an inner island, only five miles out from Townsville. It was one of the finest islands of the region. Like Green Island, off Cairns, it was accessible to crowds of tourists, but unlike that small cay, so easily overrun, it was big and rocky and difficult to penetrate. Towering Magnetic rolled boulders in the way of its invaders, brought them up short at breath-stopping drops of cliff, smothered their motels amongst its trees and their roads in its gorges and mountains. On Magnetic you were hardly conscious of anything but Magnetic, the wild mound of rock and forest rising out of glittering blue sea. Under the glitter were the reefs where Ian Croll found the exquisite corals and fish he put on show in Magnetic's Marine Gardens. He gathered corals like red rosettes in the undersea grottoes in the island's cliffs. Nearby, he collected gorgonians resembling large red and orange ferns. Anemones like giant chrysanthemums he found only seventy-five yards from the island's shore. All these specimens were so good and so easily collected around Magnetic that he scarcely bothered to visit the deep water further out. "We do very little Outer Barrier Reef work for coral now," he said. "We've cut it down practically to nil. We're working here." And "here" meant an area only five miles from the coast. Still, the Premier believed that the Great Barrier Reef was sixty miles away from the Japex well, which should thus be excluded from any inquiry into Reef drilling. Those who nevertheless worried about the Repulse Bay area had his government's assurance that it would not be endangered by the Japex operation.

And now, as if in contradiction, one of the worst cyclones in the Reef's history swept down on Whitsunday. And as if to emphasize the hazards of drilling in these waters, the cyclone swept across Repulse Bay, where Japex was scheduled to begin operations. On its way through Whitsunday, the cyclone razed Daydream's south-seas film set, which, as it turned out, had been extremely solid. "I believed the buildings which have been destroyed were built to withstand anything," the owner said. The cyclone reminded those who already feared an oil spill that the Reef had a record of shattering storms. To the north, near Bathurst Bay, a cyclone in 1899 had trapped a pearling fleet, smashing fifty-five boats and drowning about three hundred men. In 1918 two cyclones had struck the Reef coast within a few days of each other, and a tidal wave had smashed through Mackay, the port now nearest the Japex site. In 1934, more luggers were lost, and seventy-five men with them. In 1938, Mackay Harbour suffered again. What would happen if a cyclone trapped an oil rig? What if there were a blowout in a storm? The answer seemed to be that even in favourable weather the job of controlling a blowout was immensely difficult and dangerous, and that in bad weather it was impossible. When the Santa Barbara offshore well blew out early in 1969, capping efforts were defeated for days by stormy seas. When the Marlin gas well blew out in waters off the southern Australian coast on 2 December 1968, it took just on a month to stop it. The oil company involved flew in Red Adair, the Texan who combined unique skill with willingness to risk his life controlling oil disasters (it was said that seven men understudying his job had been killed). Even so, in unfavourable weather it was 31 December before Adair, backed by a team hundreds strong, managed to subdue Marlin. In the sort of storm which in January of 1970 devastated Whitsunday and the coast, it was hard to see how anything effective could be done to counter an oil mishap before immense damage had been done to Reef life. It was a point people brooded on as they listened to the Japex debate.

Another matter they pondered was whether, if the Queensland Premier continued to refuse co-operation in an inquiry into Reef drilling, the Prime Minister would take Queensland to court for control of the Reef. Fairly clearly, Prime Minister Gorton had wanted to protect the Reef and had been hampered by pressures within the coalition. With the threat that the nation would unite behind Senator Georges and the Labor Party – which had nearly won the last election anyway – the Prime Minister appeared to have been able to get his head. Ever since, he had been moving vigorously for an inquiry. If the Premier continued to resist, mightn't the Reef become a court issue? It was a fascinating question, but the need to answer it receded as the State Premier indicated that after all he would discuss an inquiry into drilling in Barrier Reef waters, the definition to include Repulse Bay.

During the debate on the Japex drilling, there were signs that a minority of Queenslanders may have come to feel that their State was positively unlucky to have the Reef off its coast. If a ban were put on drilling in Reef waters, then Queensland would be the only Australian state without an offshore oil industry. Was that fair? Well, no, perhaps it wasn't. But the question fast coming up was not simply whether Queensland was entitled to an offshore oil industry but whether any state, and for that matter any continent, was entitled to an offshore oil industry. The Great Barrier Reef was a special area, but the rest of the ocean was not less than marvellous. Besides, it was not less than indispensable to life on earth, since the masses of small plants floating in its plankton produced much of the world's oxygen. Yet the sea was being poisoned, and oil was one of the chief agents of pollution. In addition to offshore oil blowouts, and pipe breakages, and wrecked tankers, there were miscellaneous oil spills – from tankers cleaning out at sea, for example – which deposited an estimated two hundred and eighty-four million gallons of oil into the ocean every year. The old idea was finished that any amount of pollution was no more than a drop in the ocean. The ocean's balances were as delicate as those of the land, with all life depending on the plankton, the drifting masses of plants and eggs and larvae so easily affected by pollutants. Lakes had died, and so had rivers. Now some of the scientists were actually talking of the death of the sea. And as they talked the offshore wells with their threat of escaping oil were multiplying. It seemed that the ocean was being treated in the same way as its whales had been treated before they vanished: as the need for protection increased, the hunt for raw materials accelerated. And so the sea might die. This was the new science non-fiction, and it had a trick ending in which the impossible horror turned out to be the reality.

But there was just one encouraging sign – reader reaction. All over the world, at the beginning of the nineteen-seventies, there was a realization among ordinary people that what was now at stake was their own survival, and that survival was indivisible. Either the earth was saved, and the ocean, and the air, or the whole of earthly creation perished, including the agent of its destruction, technological man. Encouraged by concerned scientists, people were realizing that they had to set a watch on technology and on the scientists who served it. Lord Ritchie-Calder had warned that the planet was in hazard, that the earth, air and sea were being used as an experimental laboratory. The scientists who were experimenting were concerned only with their own work, not with its ultimate results for the world. "Because of over-specialization," Lord Ritchie-Calder said, "most scientists are disabled from exercising judgments beyond their own sphere." All this was not to say that the unspecialized multitude had no responsibility. It was true, as Heron Island's scientific director had suggested, that people had to ask themselves where the petrol was coming from that they were using in those cars decorated with conservation slogans. Encouragingly, though, people were beginning to ask such questions, and were pondering the answer that was coming back so clearly: what the consumer society was consuming was its own environment. With the planet already overtaxed to provide food and shelter for the human population explosion, hunks of the habitat were being fed to a sub-explosion of machines, and weapons, and objects destined for a non-disposable scrapheap. Obviously it had to stop. The only question was, would it stop while there was still life on Earth? In what were quite possibly the living planet's last days, people were beginning to divide not between the capitalist technocrat and the communist technocrat, but between those determined to go on destroying the environment and those who wished to stop now. At the beginning of 1970, the Australian Prime Minister seemed to speak on the side of those who wished to stop now. "In my view," John Gorton said, stating his attitude on whether the Great Barrier Reef should be drilled for oil, "the slightest danger is too much danger."

Every conservationist rejoiced. If this was to be the guiding consideration in the inquiry into oil drilling, then the verdict was assured. After all, not even the oil companies had denied that there must be *some* danger in drilling.

When the Commonwealth and State representatives met to negotiate the terms of the inquiry it was in an atmosphere of some strain. Even as the meeting was being arranged, the oil rig *Navigator* had sailed from Texas. Now it was somewhere at sea – its Australian agents refused to say where – a one-ship oil armada which might yet invade the Reef. Japex was reputed to be asking for about a million dollars to cover its costs in hiring *Navigator* and in making general preparations to drill. Other oil companies holding permits were thought to be planning big claims for compensation if there was interference with their drilling programmes. The conference on the conditions of the inquiry was a long one. When the negotiators at last emerged it was with terms which expressed, not the Prime Minister's aversion to the slightest danger for the Reef, but the Queensland Premier's feeling that the inquiry should be as wide as possible. Now the inquiry (which, it was to be announced later, would take the form of a royal commission) was to seek answers not only in the fields of biology and oil engineering but of the nation's economy. It was to investigate the probable benefits which would accrue to Queensland and Australia from oil exploration and drilling in Reef waters. It was also to apply itself to a question involving the whole range of Reef life: "What will be the likely effect of an oil or gas leak and subsequent remedial measures on the coral reefs, the coastline, the ecological and biological aspects of life in the area?" And it was to investigate "whether there are areas, and if so, which, where an oil leak, if it occurred, would cause no damage to the reefs, or their ecological or biological aspects."

After the announcement of these terms, the Reef issue subsided. Japex announced it would not drill pending the outcome of the inquiry, but thought it fair that it should be compensated for its expenditures. The conservationists, after their first shock at realizing the range of the questions to be asked, applied themselves to preparing answers. Some were unhappy. A preliminary survey period of at least two years mentioned in the Ladd report had appeared inadequate enough, considering the number of species and the complexities of the area which would be affected by exploitation. Now it seemed that the result of the royal commission might be that there would be no preliminary research at all, that a decision to exploit could be arrived at on the basis of opinions and estimates. Rather grimly, conservationists settled down to marshal conservationist opinions and estimates.

CHAPTER 18

Offshore Rights: Whose?

✳

A MONTH after the inquiry terms had been agreed on between the federal and state governments, the federal government led by John Gorton moved to establish its sovereignty over Australia's continental shelf, and thus over the Reef.

At the opening of the federal parliament on 3 March, the Governor-General, Sir Paul Hasluck, said, "My government has examined the presently unresolved legal question as to which government is entitled to exercise sovereign control over the resources of the seabed off the Australian coast to the outer limits of the continental shelf.... It is the view of my government that it would serve Australia's national and international interests to have the legal position resolved.

"My government will ask the parliament to pass legislation to assert and establish what the commonwealth conceives to be its legal rights."

There was a rider that the legislation would not affect the existing agreement between the Commonwealth and the States concerning offshore petroleum, but observers wondered how that could be. No doubt a State would keep its royalty payments from the oil companies, but how much power over policy would it retain after the offshore concerns of its minister for mines had been transferred to the federal sphere? It was pointed out that in any case the Commonwealth-State arrangement over petroleum was basically a gentleman's agreement. In such a matter, was the Prime Minister – well, a gentleman? The Queensland Premier interpreted the new legislation as meaning that the commonwealth would acquire "a dominant role over oil and minerals found off the coast of the State." He said he was astounded by the move, and opposed it. But what could an objecting State do? It could go to court. Discouragingly, though, this was just what the Commonwealth wanted it to do. Surely there was some other way of defeating the offshore legislation? It seemed there was. Many states-rights men in Prime Minister Gorton's own Liberal Party were interpreting the legislation as added evidence that their party, pledged to oppose centralism, was being led by a centralist. It could be, then, that the Prime Minister did not have a particularly high political life expectancy. That impression was to strengthen as the opposition within the government parties grew, and the Prime Minister was forced to delay the offshore legislation for further consultation with the states. And yet even at that moment of near-defeat it appeared likely that in one way or another, through this Prime Minister or a successor, the Commonwealth would move to assert its offshore rights. In the coming era of contest between nations for the riches of the sea, it seemed that that International Person based on the federal capital must search for ways to strengthen his powers offshore, and thus over the Great Barrier Reef. And if he managed to acquire those powers, the conservationist wondered, what would it mean for the safety of the Reef? The implication of the promise which the dead Prime Minister, Harold Holt, had made to Busst – that in an emergency the federal government would take over the Reef – was that the Reef could in this way be made safer from exploitation.

And yet, in the event, could it? In the face of all the pressures, could the Reef's friends in federal politics really take effective steps to protect it? The Commonwealth might be persuaded to delegate some of its powers over the Reef to an international commission advised by scientists, and that might be a very good thing. But then again, it might not. After all, it was an international commission advised by scientists which had been entrusted with the fate of the whales. And in the future, pressures for exploitation of the Reef would be very strong, coming not only from interests in Australia but from some of the world's most powerful industrial nations. All in all, as the State and the Commonwealth battled for control offshore, only one thing appeared clear, and that was that for a long time to come there would be a need for the conservationists and the trade unions to be vigilant in their watch on the Reef.

CHAPTER 19

A Tanker Pours Oil on Reef Waters

❋

THE Australian Governor-General's announcement of the offshore legislation happened to coincide with another important event in the Reef's life – an event long prophesied and long feared. On Tuesday, 3 March 1970, the Liberian tanker *Oceanic Grandeur*, bringing oil from Sumatra to Australia's east coast, was wrecked. It ran on submerged rock near Wednesday Island in the Torres Strait area – that area which, it had been suggested, might be made safe for tankers and other big ships by nuclear blasting. Its cargo of oil could have been brought around the western and southern coast of Australia, but the longer journey would have meant higher costs. And so, since even at this late hour in the pollution crisis costs were of more interest than the life of the sea, here was a tanker loaded with fifty-five thousand tons of black crude oil trying to make its way through the Great Barrier Reef – through that passage which is possibly the most dangerous in the world – and failing. Ironically, the *Oceanic Grandeur*, with its draft of thirty-eight feet, had been specifically mentioned in a letter of warning which Lieutenant-Commander T. F. Roberts (Royal Australian Navy, retired) had written in 1967 to the Great Barrier Reef Committee, of which he was a member. His letter had pointed out that the latest sailing directions by the authority of the Marine Board of Queensland stated that "considerable ingenuity would be needed to navigate a deep-draught vessel of thirty-eight feet draught with safety in the Prince of Wales channel" – the channel in which, as it turned out, *Oceanic Grandeur* was to be wrecked – and also that "this route cannot be considered a safe route for a vessel of thirty-eight feet draught". The Great Barrier Reef Committee had forwarded Commander Roberts' observations to the Portmaster of Queensland and had received a reply which read, in part,

"Regarding the element of risk by deeply laden tankers grounding in the Torres Strait and Great Barrier Reef areas thereby causing widespread pollution I feel that the danger whilst present is remote."

And now *Oceanic Grandeur*, ripped open in the Torres Strait, was spilling out black oil in a slick about six miles long. To the south, conservationists dug into their funds to send two observers to the wreck. The observers were Edward Hegerl, who had given evidence in the Ellison Reef case, and D. R. Robertson, both of the Queensland Littoral Society. The frustrations they met with in trying to track down just what harm the oil was doing as it floated away from the wreck was summed up later in Robertson's report: "The slick released when the tanker originally grounded appears to have moved in a south-easterly direction towards reefs of the northern Great Barrier Reef. What happened to it, where it eventually ended up, and what damage it did could not be determined by either Mr Hegerl or myself. Transport to these remote areas was simply not available". Nevertheless Robertson and Hegerl were able to make a number of valuable observations. Hegerl, for instance, found that in samples of water taken in the vicinity of the tanker the plankton, basis of life in the sea, was dead.

Immediately after the wreck there was caution about attacking the escaped oil with detergents in case they inflicted extra damage on marine life. Later, as oil escapes continued, detergents were used. It turned out to be a long job, off-loading *Oceanic Grandeur's* oil into other tankers. Owned by Oceanic Petroleum Carriers of Taiwan, and registered in Liberia, *Oceanic Grandeur* was under charter to Ampol of Australia. Ampol happened to have a tanker in ballast in the vicinity of the wreck, but this tanker did not proceed to off-load oil from *Oceanic Grandeur* for some days. By good luck, the cyclone weather which was a feature of this season did not arrive in the area of the wreck. It could have arrived, though, at any time, and smashing down on the damaged tanker could have turned an intermittent escape of oil into a flood. More than two weeks after the disaster of 3 March, and despite some off-loading, *Oceanic Grandeur* still lay crippled with a huge quantity of oil in its tanks. In Australia's federal capital there was anger at the delay in removing a massive pollution threat to the Reef. On 19 March the Brisbane *Courier-Mail* reported: "The federal government last night rushed stringent emergency legislation through parliament to give it power to remove the remaining 30,000 tons of crude oil from the tanker *Oceanic Grandeur*. . . ." The bill was put through, the newspaper said, against a background of some confusion, "in which Oceanic Petroleum Carriers was arguing about salvage rights and Ampol was reported as having told the government it did not have a relief tanker available to keep off-loading the oil from the stranded vessel". Under the new legislation the Federal Shipping and Transport Minister was given wide powers. He could, for example, order a shipowner to take effective action to remove a threat of oil pollution; he could impose a fine of two thousand dollars a day for failure to comply with his order; and he could take action himself, by hiring a relief tanker and charging the cost to the offending shipowner. Not long after these measures were introduced *Oceanic Grandeur* was removed from Reef waters and eventually taken for drydocking to Singapore.

There could scarcely have been a less appropriate time for such an incident. The year 1970 was a period of festivity, the bicentenary of the discovery of Australia's east coast by the British. As the black mats of oil floated through the lonely northern islands, the Reef coast to the south was preparing to celebrate. Captain Cook was rehearsing to land again near the Endeavour River, where once before he had put in to repair his reef-torn ship. The Queen and the Duke of Edinburgh and Princess Anne were on their way to watch. It was, in short, an important occasion that was being prepared for as the tanks of *Oceanic Grandeur* began to pour out blackness on the Reef's blue waters. As the oil and the detergents spread from the wrecked tanker, it seemed, suddenly, that it was late indeed in the life of the Great Barrier Reef. And yet, in terms of the time it had existed for civilized man, the Reef was only two centuries old. It was two hundred years, that was all, since the great navigator from the north had entered these waters – a mere two hundred years since James Cook had come sailing into the sea of flowers, the summertimes of the shearwater, the nursery of the whales, and laid them open to all of us.

Proposals Relating to the Conservation and Controlled Exploitation of the Great Barrier Reefs

❊

I. PREAMBLE

The Great Barrier Reefs occupy an area of 80,000 square miles off the north-eastern coast of Australia between latitudes 10°S. and 24°S. They form an almost continuous rampart over 1,200 miles in length, varying in distance from the Queensland coast from about eight miles at Cape Melville (near Cooktown) in the north to over 150 miles at the Swain Reefs (east of Rockhampton) in the south.

The area embraced by the Great Barrier Reefs is of major scientific importance for it contains the densest assemblage of marine organisms to be found in any region of comparable size in the world. Moreover, the Great Barrier Reefs comprise the largest assemblage of coral reefs the world has known. The fauna and flora of the Reefs and the Reefs themselves will occupy the attention of scientists in many disciplines for an indefinitely long period.

As well as being one of Australia's major scientific assets and attracting scientists from all parts of the world, the Reefs are Australia's principal tourist attraction. Indeed, their value in this regard to Queensland alone currently runs into millions of dollars per annum. For example, it was stated in a recent issue of the *Courier-Mail* that 250,000 tourists visited tourist resorts on the Great Barrier Reefs last year and that each visitor spent an average amount of $200 at the resort visited. Also, it should be remembered that the full potential of the Reefs as a tourist attraction has not been realized. Ultimately, Barrier Reef tourism could well become Queensland's greatest dollar earner.

Exploitation of the mineral resources of the area has scarcely begun but exploitation on a large scale is imminent. At present, several oil companies are amassing geophysical data in the region and at least two companies are currently preparing their drilling rigs for an

* See page 84, above.

intensive search for oil believed to lie in the sedimentary rocks beneath the platform on which the Reefs stand. High grade lime for building, manufacturing and agriculture is present in enormous quantities. High grade silica for glass manufacture is present in quantity in some areas. The nature and extent of submerged mineral deposits are not known.

The potential of the area embraced by the Reefs to provide food has not been explored. Even the exploitation of obvious food sources, such as fish and crustaceans, is in its early stages. In view of the phenomenal increase in the world's human population which is now occurring, the time is fast approaching when all available protein resources must be exploited. This fact is appreciated by the U.S. Government which has initiated an "intensified, long-range programme to exploit the oceans as a source of food to help feed the undernourished people of the world." The old concept of the ocean as a source of food in the direct form of fish (fresh, frozen, dried and canned) has expanded to include fish protein concentrates. In addition, other forms of marine life, e.g. invertebrates and marine plants are also being contemplated as potential sources of marine protein concentrates. Pilot plants for the production of marine protein concentrates are already in operation in the U.S.A. and in Japan. The flora and fauna of the Reefs are diverse and abundant. It seems inevitable that, in the future, some elements of the flora and fauna will be cropped to provide food.

Then, too, the Reefs provide a recreation area for the inhabitants of a coastal strip of Queensland over 1,000 miles in length. As Queensland's population grows, increasing numbers of Queenslanders will seek recreation on the Reefs. The advent of economical, high speed outboard motors in recent years has resulted in a marked increase in the number of Queenslanders who spend a day or a week-end in Barrier Reef waters. Ten years ago the islands of the Bunker Group, for example, were visited only sporadically. Today, when one visits the islands of the Group it is usual to see fishing parties, boating parties, parties fossicking on the reefs surrounding the islands and parties picnicking on the islands themselves.

The recent destruction of several reefs in the Cairns-Innisfail district by the "crown-of-thorns" starfish (*Acanthaster planci*) has highlighted the urgent need for the adoption of effective conservation measures in the area embraced by the reefs. Research carried out to date on the reasons for the starfish plague has indicated strongly that human interference with the marine life of the Reefs is responsible for the starfish plague. It is believed that intensive collecting by shell collectors of the trumpet shell (*Charonia tritonis*) – the only known predator of the starfish – has permitted *A. planci* to attain plague proportions. The idea that human interference with only one element in the fauna of the Reefs can lead to destruction of coral reefs has come as an unpleasant surprise to most people.

Economic pressures will inevitably result in exploitation of the mineral and food resources of the Reefs. New tourist resorts will be required on Barrier Reef islands to cope with increasing numbers of tourists. There will be increasing pressure from conservation and allied societies and from the Queensland public generally for the establishment of large marine national parks and for the setting aside of islands for recreational purposes. Scientists and scientific organizations will request that certain key areas be reserved for scientific study. *Unless a plan for the controlled exploitation and conservation of the Great Barrier Reefs is formulated in the near future major clashes of interests among the various parties who wish to exploit the Reefs will occur. Also, major clashes of interests will occur between the exploiters on one hand and conservationists and scientific organizations on the other. Moreover, unless exploitation of the Reefs is rigidly controlled and policed the fauna and flora of many of the islands and coral reefs in the area, particularly the fauna and flora of the more accessible islands and reefs will be adversely affected. Action is required now.*

II. MINERAL EXPLOITATION

It is essential that an overall plan for the controlled exploitation of mineral resources on the Great Barrier Reefs be formulated. Uncontrolled exploitation of minerals in the area could result in incalculable harm being done to the fauna and flora of the Reefs and would arouse massive opposition from conservation bodies, scientific organizations and institutions throughout the world as well as from the Australian public generally and Queenslanders in particular. Even limited mining activities in certain areas could lead to a clash of interests among mining companies, people engaged in the tourist industry, scientists, fishermen (professional and amateur) etc. Of course, it is to the advantage of the Government of the day, and of the mining companies involved, to foster good public relations and to prevent a situation from arising where massive public opposition to mining activities is aroused. Further, it is to their advantage to ensure that major clashes of interests among groups interested in exploiting the Reefs for economic or scientific reasons do not occur.

Unfortunately, there is a dearth of information on the effects which mining activities could have on the fauna and flora of any area within the Great Barrier Reefs. Obviously, the effects would be determined largely by the nature and location of the mining operations. Large quantities of oil coming into contact with coral polyps and other sedentary organisms on a reef exposed at low tide would certainly cause massive destruction to the fauna of the reef and to the intertidal fauna of mainland islands and the mainland coast itself (c.f. the effects on the fauna and flora of the coastline of Cornwall and Devon of oil pollution from the unfortunate *Torrey Canyon* disaster). Also, a constant rain of detritus stemming from dredging activities associated with the removal of coral debris for lime manufacture would certainly kill a large part of the fauna on any reef exposed to this rain of sediment. However, it would be necessary to take into account factors such as the strength and direction of local ocean currents, the amplitude of local tides, the nature of the fauna and flora directly affected, the proximity of adjacent reefs and islands, the water depths in the area, etc. when attempting to assess the overall effects of mining operations on the fauna and flora and topography of a particular area.

The location of sites for drilling operations in the search for oil is nowadays determined largely by geophysical information obtained about the probable nature of rock strata and the probable existence of suitable geological structures in sedimentary basins. The pinpointing of suitable sites for drilling operations must be left to oil exploration companies and government geological surveys. However, the co-operation of oil exploration companies should be sought to ensure that, where several alternative and equally promising sites for drilling operations are available, the sites selected are those which would result in the least damage occurring to the fauna and flora of the region involved and those which would obviate the necessity for radical changes in any overall plan drawn up for the conservation and controlled exploitation of Reef resources.

With respect to the exploitation of coral reef debris as a source of lime for industrial and agricultural purposes, here it would seem necessary (*a*) to obtain an overall assessment of the location and extent of reserves of coral reef debris, and (*b*) to study the effects of dredging operations associated with the removal of reef debris on the fauna and flora of the region involved. Initially, the number of mining leases which involve the removal of coral reef debris should be severely restricted, should be sited in areas which are not key areas as far as scientists are concerned and should be regarded as test cases rather than as setting precedents for the indiscriminate granting of further mining leases involving the removing of coral reef debris.

It would be necessary to make a rapid survey of the fauna and flora and to examine the physiography of an area selected for dredging operations before these operations began. Further surveys should then be made at regular intervals over an extended period whilst mining operations are in progress. Such investigations would provide scientific data for the assessment of the likely effects of similar mining operations in other areas of the Great Barrier Reefs. In the interim, the location and extent of reserves of coral reef debris in readily accessible parts of the Reefs could be mapped. At this stage, and before any additional mining leases are granted, the necessity to possess an overall plan for the controlled exploitation and conservation of the Reefs becomes of vital importance. A start should therefore be made as soon as possible with the formulation of this plan.

III. STAFF REQUIRED FOR THE INVESTIGATION OF THE EFFECTS OF MINING OPERATIONS INVOLVING THE REMOVAL OF CORAL REEF DEBRIS AND FOR ASSESSING THE LOCATION AND EXTENT OF RESERVES OF CORAL REEF DEBRIS IN ACCESSIBLE PARTS OF THE GREAT BARRIER REEFS

It is assumed that, initially at any rate, only small areas of coral reef will be involved in the mining operations. Financial considerations must necessarily impose restrictions on the number of staff employed and the extent to which they could move from one locality to another. Assuming that mining companies directly concerned would co-operate by providing, where practicable, boat facilities and accommodation at the site of mining operations, it is estimated that the following staff and finance would be required:

(*a*) A science graduate with experience in
marine biology.   Salary $3,500 (approx) per annum
(*b*) An assistant with experience in
underwater work.   Salary $2,000 (approx) per annum

(c) Recurrent expenditure (travel allowances,
   boat hire, compressed air for
   SCUBA bottles, etc.) $2,000 per annum
(d) Non-recurrent expenditure (Purchase of
   SCUBA gear, instruments such as current
   velocity meter, automatic tide gauge,
   drift bottles, collecting gear, etc.) $2,000
(e) Contingency fund $500

Cost Summary:
   1. First Year – $10,000
   2. Subsequent years $8,000 p.a.

IV. CONSERVATION AND CONTROLLED EXPLOITATION

In the preceding section the immediate problem of assessing the effects of current and projected mining operations on the fauna and flora of the Reefs is tackled. There are, however, wider and longer ranging issues involved. It is vital that an overall plan be formulated which will permit the controlled exploitation of areas of the Reefs in a way which will ensure that damage to the fauna and flora of the Reefs is kept to a minimum, that tourists and the Queensland public will have access to areas of the Reefs, that certain large areas will be reserved as marine national parks for conservation purposes and that certain key areas are reserved for scientific study.

The task of formulating an overall plan will not be an easy one as the Reefs cover a very large area and some reefs (e.g. those in the Swain Group) are virtually unexplored. Any plan must be based on broad scientific principles and must take cognisance of the legitimate interests of Government departments, commercial undertakings, scientific groups, conservation bodies and the Australian public generally.

A good deal of well oriented scientific research will be required and an analysis of possible ways in which Barrier Reef resources could and would be exploited in the future will be required before a plan for the conservation and controlled exploitation of the Reefs can be formulated. A start should be made now to obtain the necessary background information and an experienced scientist should be appointed as soon as possible to obtain and collate the required data.

There is also a need for the establishment of a planning, co-ordinating and advisory

body consisting of people with specialized knowledge of the Reefs and their resources.
This body would have the task of formulating an overall plan and would make
recommendations based on this plan to relevant government departments.

This body could, for example, using the data obtained by the
scientist mentioned above and information received from interested
government departments, mining companies, conservation groups,
etc. recommend that certain areas of the Reefs be reserved as marine
national parks, that certain islands be reserved for future tourist
resorts, that certain reefs be opened for mining, etc.

The Great Barrier Reef Committee is a body consisting of

(*a*) scientists chosen for their specialized knowledge of the Reefs
and contributions made to scientific knowledge of the Reefs, and

(*b*) representatives (many of whom are scientists) of government
departments, conservation bodies, tourist resort proprietors, the
R.A.N. etc.

The prime aims of this Committee as set out in its Memorandum of
Association are "to conduct stimulate encourage and assist research
into all aspects and attributes of the Great Barrier Reef of Australia of
scientific significance or interest including the nature, origin and
potentialities of the Great Barrier Reef and all forms of life to be found
thereon or in the surrounding waters and to carry on marine,
biological and other scientific research generally and to protect and
conserve the said Reef and to determine and report upon and advise
on the proper utilization of the said Reef". The Committee has no
political affiliations and has a world-wide scientific reputation. Hence
it would be an ideal body to handle the formulation of an overall plan
for the conservation and controlled exploitation of Barrier Reef
resources. Moreover, it could act as an advisory or referee body in
contentious matters relating to the Reefs (e.g. applications for mining
leases contested in Mining Wardens' Courts, applications for new
tourist resorts, etc.) and as a buffer between the government of the
day and vocal parties affected by legislation dealing with Great Barrier
Reef matters.

The Great Barrier Reef Committee owns and operates the only
scientific research centre on the Great Barrier Reefs (Heron Island)
and is currently planning the establishment of a field station in the
northern portion of the Reefs. It has access to records of all the
scientific work carried out on the Reefs to date and can, e.g., provide
lists of the fauna and flora of the Reefs to be used as a basis for surveys.

It is the logical body to employ and direct the activities of scientists engaged in projects relating to the exploitation and conservation of the resources of the Reefs. Moreover, it could provide accommodation, laboratory and boat facilities at the Heron Island Research Station for a scientist charged with the task of obtaining and collating the scientific data required for the formulation of an overall plan for conservation and controlled exploitation of Reef resources. However, the Committee would require financial assistance to meet the increased costs involved in providing accommodation and facilities at the Heron Island Station and elsewhere which would be used in the projects discussed above. Also, in order that the Committee could play its full role in the projects discussed it should be provided with some financial assistance to help it overcome a major problem with which it is faced at the moment. This problem is the provision of adequate finance for maintenance of the Heron Island Station. In particular, it requires an additional $2,200 per annum to cover the salary of a second maintenance officer at the Station. This second maintenance officer is required to cope with the maintenance of the boats associated with the Station and with the maintenance of sea water supplies and aquarium facilities. Other maintenance tasks at the Station could then be handled comfortably by the present maintenance office.

V. STAFF AND FINANCES REQUIRED FOR PROJECT INVOLVING THE OBTAINING AND COLLATING OF SCIENTIFIC DATA AND OTHER RELEVANT INFORMATION REQUIRED FOR THE FORMULATION OF AN OVERALL PLAN FOR THE CONSERVATION AND CONTROLLED EXPLOITATION OF THE GREAT BARRIER REEFS

    (*a*) A science graduate in zoology and/
        or geology and with considerable
        research experience $6,000 per annum
    (*b*) A technician to assist the above scientist $2,000 per annum
    (*c*) Recurrent expenses for travel to various
        parts of the Great Barrier Reefs $2,000 per annum

These personnel would be based at the Heron Island Research Station and would use facilities at the Station (including laboratory, boat and secretarial facilities).

The senior scientist would be responsible for directing the activities of the scientist and technician engaged in the mining study and for obtaining and collating the scientific data and other relevant information required for the formulation of an overall plan for the conservation and controlled exploitation of Great Barrier Reef resources. His services would also be available for work on minor research projects compatible with the overall scheme of investigation.

Staff and Finances Required for Heron Island Station so that Facilities and Accommodation for Personnel Associated with the Project can be Provided

(*a*) A maintenance officer whose prime task would
be to attend to maintenance of boats, sea
water supplies and aquarium facilities
at the Heron Island Station.   Salary $2,200 per annum

(*b*) A sum to cover the use of accommodation
facilities, laboratory facilities, boat facilities,
etc. required for the scientist and his
assistant $4,000 per annum

(*c*) A sum to cover the cost of specialized
scientific apparatus which would be used
by the scientist and his assistant $3,800 per annum

Cost Summary:
First Year $20,000
Subsequent Years $16,200

VI. DURATION OF PROJECTS

It is suggested that three years should be allowed for carrying out of the work involved in the projects discussed. It is evident that the task of surveying the reefs of the Great Barrier Reefs could not possibly be accomplished within this period. However, surveys could be made of the reefs in accessible areas most likely to be affected by proposed mining operations or by the establishment of new tourist resorts and a tentative plan could be formulated for the conservation and controlled exploitation of Barrier Reef resources. Undoubtedly, modification to this overall plan will be required in the future as new information becomes available and new problems occur. Possibly, it might be found desirable to continue these projects indefinitely. At any rate, a period of three years should be allowed for the projects initially. At the end of this period the value of the projects could be assessed and recommendations made for their continuance or discontinuance.

Total Cost Summary of the two projects

First Year	$30,000
Second Year	$24,200
Third Year	$24,200
	$78,400

VII. FINANCING OF PROJECTS

In the first instance it is intended to place these proposals before the Ministers in charge of relevant Queensland Government departments, the Managers of mining and exploration companies, the Managers of tourist resorts and the Director of the Australian Conservation Foundation. Comments on the proposals themselves and on ways of financing the proposals are sought.

1. *The Premier's Department*. This department handles public relations and could benefit from having access to the advice of a body established for the purpose of planning, co-ordinating and advising on matters relating to the conservation and controlled exploitations of the Reefs. Contentious issues could be referred to this body which, since it has a world-wide scientific reputation and is non-political could act as a buffer between the government of the day and vocal parties affected by current or proposed legislation dealing with the Reefs.

2. *The Department of Mines*. This department would benefit directly from the carrying out of the projects envisaged. It would benefit as a result of the obtaining of scientific data on the effects on the fauna and flora of coral reefs of dredging activities associated with the removal of coral rubble in mining operations. It would benefit from having at its disposal an assessment of reserves of coral reef detritus on accessible reefs. It would also benefit greatly as a result of the formulation of an overall plan for the conservation and controlled exploitation of the Reefs, the same way as the Premier's Department would benefit.

3. *The Department of Harbours and Marine*. This department is already providing the services of a scientist and a technician for a study of the reasons for the outbreak of the "crown-of-thorns" (*Acanthaster planci*) plague and for a study of methods of controlling the plague. The activities of the scientist are currently being directed by the Chairman of the G.B.R.C. in association with Officers of the Department of

Harbours and Marine. Probably this Department would make available the results of the *Acanthaster planci* study to the body charged with formulating an overall plan for the conservation and controlled exploitation of the Reefs. Certainly the co-operation of the Department of Harbours & Marine would be essential for the success of the projects envisaged. In turn, the department would benefit greatly from the carrying out of the projects as envisaged.

4. *The Department of Labour and Tourism.* This department would benefit greatly if an overall plan for the conservation and controlled exploitation of the Reefs were formulated. Tourists are attracted to the Reefs primarily because of the rich and varied fauna and flora of the reefs. The conservation of this fauna and flora is vital if tourism is to increase in importance in Queensland.

5. *The Australian Conservation Foundation.* The Director of the A.C.F. (Dr D. McMichael) has already discussed with the Chairman of the G.B.R.C. matters connected with the formulation of an overall plan for conservation and controlled exploitation of the resources of the Reefs. The A.C.F. will co-operate with the G.B.R.C. in initiating a survey of the Reefs, will add its expertise in the general field of conservation to the specialized knowledge of the Reefs possessed by the G.B.R.C. and will help in seeking financial support for the project involving conservation and controlled exploitation of Reef resources.

6. *The Barrier Reef Tourist Proprietors' Association.* This Association could benefit greatly as a result of the carrying out of the projects mentioned. It would also benefit from having access to the specialized advice on Barrier Reef matters which would be obtained from scientists associated with the co-ordinating body (the G.B.R.C.). For example, it could receive specialized advice on venomous and dangerous marine animals, or the setting up of marine aquaria, or submersibles, etc.

7. *Oil Companies.* From the viewpoint of fostering good public relations oil companies holding prospecting rights over areas of the Reefs or carrying out exploratory work in the area of the Reefs would benefit greatly if they contributed towards the cost of obtaining the scientific data necessary to formulate a plan for the conservation and controlled exploitation of Reef resources. There is undoubtedly opposition from several quarters to the activities of oil companies in Australia's major

tourist area and it will help their cause considerably if their support for conservation of the fauna and flora of the Reefs were announced to the general public, particularly if this support took the form of assistance for the carrying out of the projects outlined above. Also, oil companies would benefit from having access to data on water currents, tidal amplitudes, etc. in Barrier Reef waters obtained by scientists working on the projects outlined earlier.

8. *Companies interested in exploiting coral debris as a source of lime for agricultural and industrial use.* Obviously, such companies would benefit greatly if a survey of reserves of coral reef debris in accessible areas were made and if a plan for conservation and controlled exploitation of Reef resources were formulated. From the viewpoint of fostering good public relations it would seem to be in the interests of these companies to provide financial support for at least the project involving the effects of dredging activities associated with exploitation of coral reef debris and the flora and fauna of areas affected.

9. *Others.* It is possible that these proposals should be brought to the attention of government departments, companies, societies and organizations other than those mentioned above. Any suggestions regarding bodies, other than those mentioned, who might be interested in these proposals, are welcomed.

H. ENDEAN
Chairman, Great Barrier Reef Committee

Statement issued by the
Australian Academy of Science

✳

GREAT BARRIER REEF

The President of the Australian Academy of Science, Dr D. F. Martyn, today announced the conclusions and recommendations of the Academy's Committee to consider the reported destruction of coral on the Great Barrier Reef. He stated that the Committee would prepare an extensive report which would be available early next year for release. The Committee consulted with biological scientists and with geologists who have expert knowledge of the Great Barrier Reef and also obtained statements from a number of others who were not able to attend its meetings.

The Committee found that in some parts of the Great Barrier Reef the population of the Crown of Thorns starfish (*Acanthaster planci*) has shown a considerable increase during recent years and this has been associated with more destruction of coral than is normal in these areas. Only a small part of the Reef has been surveyed and the Committee was unable to ascertain the extent of destruction. It was stressed, however, that the geological structure known as the Great Barrier Reef is not in danger and that the coast of Queensland will not suffer adverse effects as a result of the coral destruction.

The Committee feels that there is a surprising lack of knowledge of the biology generally of the Great Barrier Reef and particularly of the biology of coral and of the Crown of Thorns starfish and its predators. The Committee emphasizes that the increased population of *Acanthaster* causing coral destruction has been and is currently being reported on reefs in many parts of the Pacific and Indian Oceans and that the phenomenon is not confined to the Great Barrier Reef. The Committee considered several hypotheses that have been advanced to explain the increased numbers of *Acanthaster* on the Reef. However, it was not able to obtain evidence to support any particular one. The

* See page 154, above.

Committee feels that in the future special attention should be paid to the possibility that destruction of coral by *Acanthaster* is a cyclical phenomenon which has occurred on previous occasions and been followed by regeneration and recolonization with coral polyps. The Committee also believes that research should be undertaken to ascertain the factors which permit survival of eggs and larvae of *Acanthaster*. A minor disturbance of these factors could explain the increased populations currently being reported.

The Committee considered that it is not possible at the present time to attempt long term or widespread control because practical methods are not available. Interim control measures should be confined to the established tourist sites and the Committee suggested that these should not extend beyond a 50-mile radius of Heron Island, Green Island, the Whitsunday Group and Dunk Island. This short term control consists of the removal of Crown of Thorns starfish by hand or of measures designed to destroy the starfish *in situ*. The latter will require further experimentation but hopeful results have apparently been achieved with a recently manufactured electric gun and with the injection of formalin from a syringe into the starfish.

The Committee also recommended that an advisory committee should be set up to recommend, co-ordinate and seek financial support for basic long term research on the biology and physical environment of the Great Barrier Reef. The Academy will shortly consider the appointment of such a committee to co-operate with all interested bodies including the Commonwealth Department of Education and Science, the Great Barrier Reef Committee, the Queensland Government and its interested departments, the C.S.I.R.O., the University of Queensland and the Townsville University College. The Committee would also seek the co-operation of scientists from other countries.